Money Map

A Professional's Guide to Investing

BY JOHN P. NICHOLAS

Sara,

Best Wishes

John

Money Map contains my views and opinions. The recommendations in this book should be considered for informational purposes only and not investment advice for your specific situation. No investment result should be expected from following any of the approaches outlined in this book. As is often said, past performance is no guarantee of future results. See the Disclaimer at the end of this book.

John Nicholas' career has spanned politics, law and money management. John graduated as an undergrad from Harvard University and then worked as a foreign policy analyst for Senator Joseph R. Biden, Jr. After finishing law school at Northwestern University, he practiced corporate law for a major US law firm before transitioning into investment management. Over the past twenty-five years John has managed money for some of the largest investment firms and private investors in the world. He has invested across all asset classes, from traditional equities and bonds, to private equity and venture capital, to hedge funds and derivatives.

In this book, John shares his experience and expertise with the layperson investor who is trying to make sense of the overwhelming amount of information in the financial marketplace. John helps the investor sort the wheat from the chaff and develop a coherent picture of how to manage their money.

For Sonja, John, Alexandra and Michael

INTRODUCTION   **13**

CHAPTER 1   **Your Life Investment Plan**   **15**

Lifemap   15

     Ant Priorities and Grasshopper Desires   16

     Make a Lifemap   18

Summary   23

CHAPTER 2   **Expected Returns on Your Investments**   **25**

The Base Case: Expected Long-Term Returns of Investing   25

How Long Might It Take to Earn the Base Case?   32

Will I Earn the Base Case in the Future?   34

Summary   37

CHAPTER 3   **How to Invest Your Money**   **39**

The Path to Prosperity: Martia Maps the Way   39

     How an Alien from Outer Space Sees the World   40

Global Citizen   41

     Home Country Bias   44

     Company-Specific Risk   47

Expand Your Time Horizon   48

How to Efficiently Invest   50

     Index Funds   50

     Sustainability of Indexing   52

Focus on What You Can Control   52

Summary   53

CHAPTER 4   **Core Asset Classes: The Primary Colors of Investing**   **55**

Cash, Bonds and Stocks   56

Cash   56

Bonds   57

Stocks   59

Asset Classes Have Similar Risk-Adjusted Returns   61

Summary   62

CHAPTER 5   **Building Your Investment Portfolio**   **63**

Asset Allocation   63

Diversification   67

Sample Asset Allocation with Core Asset Classes   69

Rebalancing   70

The Endowment Portfolio Model   71

Summary   74

CHAPTER 6   **Non-Core Asset Classes**   **75**

High Yield Bonds   77

Tax-Exempt Bonds   79

Asset-Backed Securities   80

Foreign Bonds   81

Hybrids and Derivatives   81

Real Estate   83

Alternative Investments: The Emperor's New Clothes   85

IPOs   88

Private Equity   88

Venture Capital   92

Hedge Funds   93

    Hedge Fund Fees   93

    Hedge Fund Returns   95

    Reporting Bias, Stale Pricing and Fat Tails   96

    Inadequate Data   100

    Fiduciaries Kicking the Performance Can Down the Road   101

    Protection on the Downside   101

    Best of the Bunch   102

Annuities   102

Life Insurance   104

Risk Parity   105

Environmental, Social, and Governance (ESG)   106

Currencies   108

Cryptocurrencies   108

Summary   110

CHAPTER 7   **Active vs. Passive Investing**   **111**

The Illusion of Skill   111

Beating the Base Case   116

Fees   117

The Cost of Active Management   118

Odds of Beating the Market   121

Beating the Spread   126

Value Is in the Eye of the Beholder   128

Luck or Skill   128

A Handful of Stocks Drive Returns   130

Picking a Manager that Outperforms the Market   132

No Persistent Skill   134

Chasing the Past   137

Magnitude of Underperformance   138

Institutional Investors Do No Better than Anyone Else   140

Timing Markets: You Need to Get At Least Two   141
Decisions Right

Taxable Investors   144

ETFs, Mutual Funds and Direct Indexing   146

Hidden Risks of Active Investing   147

Modeling Risk   147

Concentration Risk   148

High Correlation   148

Your Savings as a Form of Entertainment   151

Summary   153

CHAPTER 8   **Factor-Based Investing**   **155**

Can We Go Any Faster?   155

Why Factors?   156

Market Beta   158

Size   159

Value   162

Value Stocks Are Riskier   162

Stocks as Lottery Tickets   163

Critics of the Value Premium   164

Momentum   165

Profitability & Quality   166

CHAPTER 8   (Continued)

Term Premium and Default Premium   167

Carry Factor   169

Trend Following   171

Deterioration of Factor Premiums   171

Summary   172

CHAPTER 9   **Risks**   **175**

Investment Volatility   175

Inflation   176

Longevity Risk   177

Shortfall Risk   179

Regret   180

Cognitive Decline   180

    Team of Advisors   182

    Consolidate Assets & Financial Information   183

    Durable Power of Attorney   183

Summary   184

CHAPTER 10   **Using an Investment Advisor**   **185**

To Manage or Not to Manage Your Money Yourself   185

Your Investment Personality   187

What Advisors Cannot Do for You   189

What Advisors Can Do for You   190

The Ulysses Factor   191

The .7 Percent Solution   192

    Younger Person Example   194

    Older Person Example   195

    Lower-Cost Providers   195

Advisor Hack: Splitting Your Assets Between Fee and Non-Fee Accounts   196

Who Should I Use?   197

Advice Is Never Entirely Objective   198

    Fiduciary Standard   198

Don't Hassle Your Advisor   200

Summary   202

CHAPTER 11   **Guideposts for Managing Your Wealth**   **203**

Brain Bounds   203

Less Is More   206

Mr. Vinegar: A Wealth Management Bedtime Story   209

You Are Likely an Average Investor   211

    Long-Term Capital Management   215

    Paul Allen   216

    2007-2008 Crash of Asset-Backed Securities   218

Baking the Cake: Investment, Tax and Estate Planning   219

On Your Own   220

The Energy of Money   221

Conclusion   225

BOOKS FOR FURTHER READING   227

NOTES   228

BIBLIOGRAPHY   238

INDEX   242

ACKNOWLEDGMENTS   251

DISCLAIMER   253

Introduction

This book covers what I think is important for you to know to be a successful investor. **It is written for a person who has some experience with investing, but who feels overwhelmed by the amount of information in the financial marketplace, and is looking for a frame to make sense of it.**

The first five chapters of the book provide the fundamentals of investing, including developing your investment plan, what returns to expect from your investments, how to build your portfolio and the optimal way to execute your plan and achieve your financial goals.

The remaining chapters discuss issues such as alternative investments, 'active' vs. 'passive' investing, and how to use an investment advisor.

My perspective on investing comes from twenty-five years of managing money for several of the world's largest investment firms and wealthiest people. In addition, included in this book are insights from the world's most prominent investment sages: David Swensen, chief investment officer of Yale University; Warren Buffett, Berkshire Hathaway CEO and investor extraordinaire; Jack Bogle, leader of the index approach to investing, and Nobel laureate Daniel Kahneman, a pioneer in behavioral finance.

I do not traverse the entire landscape of investing here. Nuances have been trimmed so as to better see the forest for the trees. To the generalizations I make about markets and human behavior there are of course exceptions, and there are subtleties of investment practice that are beyond the scope of this book.

Sometime during your life, when you are facing an investment decision, I hope you will remember something from this book and it will help you think things through.

CHAPTER 1

Your Life Investment Plan

Your goals and dreams for your life guide how you earn, spend and invest money. Do you know exactly what you want from your money? You might say, "My goal is financial security," or "I'm saving for retirement," or "I want to be rich." Go further.

How much money will it take for you to feel financially secure? What kind of retirement exactly do you envision? How rich is rich for you? And if you get rich, what then?

Make your life goals vivid and concrete. Well-defined goals make for a well-defined lifetime plan for earning, spending and investing your money.

LIFEMAP

At wakes, there are often pictures posted showing some of the deceased's better moments in life—playing trumpet in the grade school band, Thanksgiving dinner with grandma and grandpa, high school and college friends, marriage, children, vacations—happy times. They encapsulate the person's life and how they chose to spend their money and their time.

What pictures do you want in those frames? Is it a picture of retirement in a beautiful condo on Miami Beach? You digging wells to provide clean drinking water for villagers in Africa? Shaking hands with the English professor whose university chair you endowed? Traveling to far-off lands?

Your grandchild, smiling as they receive their diploma from the ivy-covered college whose tuition you paid for?

In framing your life story, your "lifemap," be a reporter covering yourself. Ask the tough questions—the 5Ws—who, what, when, where, and why.

WHO am I, and how does consuming and sharing my wealth fit with my beliefs?

WHAT are my life objectives—what am I working for and toward?

WHEN and how will I use my wealth—do I hope to consume it all by the time I die, or give away much of it to other people during my lifetime or after?

WHERE am I spending my time and money, and does this reflect who I am?

WHY am I investing my wealth rather than consuming it today or giving it away to others? [1]

ANT PRIORITIES AND GRASSHOPPER DESIRES

The most important lessons in life I think are learned by the age of five. Everything after that are variations on the early lessons. When I was five, one story that intrigued me was Aesop's fable, *The Ant and the Grasshopper*. The grasshopper chose to fiddle away the summer days, while the ants chose to gather grain for the winter. Like the grasshopper, I, too, enjoyed playing outside on summer days. But I felt the ants were acting more responsibly and that work comes before play. Or at least I had been told that. Back and forth I went. It was a conundrum for a young boy.

How about you? As a kid, did you identify more with the ants or the grasshopper?

How about today?

Everyone balances *ant priorities*—"must haves" you feel are essential, and *grasshopper desires*—"wants and wishes" you aspire to.

Define yours.

Saving for your children's college education may be a must-have
ant priority. Buying a château in France for your retirement may be a
grasshopper desire.

Ant and grasshopper goals can be complementary, of course. You may
feel that achieving success in your career or business is a must-have. Doing
so may give you a sense of accomplishment, as well as the means to pay for
your children's college education, and the ability to enjoy time with family
and friends at your French estate.

Laying out your ant priorities and grasshopper desires helps shape your
investment approach. For example, assume you are forty years old and have
the following life goals:

> **1)** Having enough money to pay all of your ten-year-old
> daughter's college tuition, and

> **2)** Retiring to a wine estate in the Burgundy region of
> France at fifty-five.

If having money for your daughter's college education is a must-have
priority, and owning a winery is more of a wish, then this will guide you as
to how to spend and invest today. You'll probably spend, save and invest
more conservatively to maximize the chance that you will have the college
money in hand when needed in eight years.

Alternatively, if you feel that your child should pay their own way
through college, and for you it's château-or-bust, then you may invest more
aggressively to achieve the high investment returns needed to pay for the
pricey French *château de rêve*.

But when you do that, you should understand that you are taking more
risk with your wealth. Not only may you not achieve your dream, but you
may suffer a significant financial loss, which could affect the timing and
quality of your retirement.

If, in reaching for your château dream, you invest aggressively and lose
a chunk of your wealth, you may still be comfortable with your decision.
For you, it was a 'must-have.' You would feel regret if you didn't go for it.

If the joy of owning a château outweighs the despair of having
a reduced standard of living if things don't go well, you will at least
understand, if not like, the consequences of your decision.

Of course, you will never hear the end of it from your daughter.

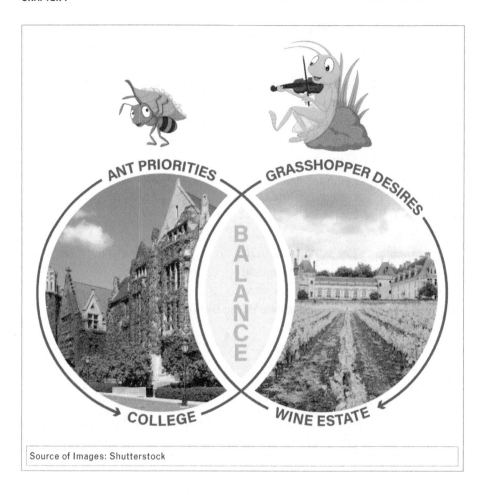

Source of Images: Shutterstock

MAKE A LIFEMAP

A *lifemap* serves as both a list of goals and a timeline for achieving them. It's a map of where you want to go and how to get there.

What is your lifemap? As a start, make a list of five to ten life goals, ordered by priority, that are dependent on money. Some life goals, of course, such as spiritual fulfillment, or being close with your children, may not require money. Or much of it. Maybe some, if you need to fly to Nepal and commune with Buddhist monks in order to achieve the frame of mind you desire.

Note whether these goals are ant "must haves" or grasshopper "wants and wishes." Think about the utility to you of achieving or not achieving each of these goals—utility being the joy or personal fulfillment you would feel in achieving a goal—and how bad you would feel if you did not (college for your daughter or the French winery). This helps you put your goals into context and prioritize them.

Additionally, as it relates to investing, your lifemap defines what you are willing to risk, and not risk, to achieve your various goals.

Also note whether your goals are short-term (in the next 5 years), intermediate-term (10-20 years), or long-term (20+ years).

For example, here is a lifemap for a couple, Dan and Kathy, both 34 years old, who live in Chicago. Dan is a salesperson for a medical device manufacturer and Kathy is a hospital administrator. They have three children, Thomas, 6, Claire, 4, and Connor, 2.

SHORT-TERM GOALS

Must Have: Enough money for a down payment to buy a larger house in three years. They are planning on this to be $100,000, and they have $70,000 saved today.

Wish: Enough money to upgrade the kitchen of the new house, expected to be about $30,000.

INTERMEDIATE-TERM GOALS

Must Have: Be able to pay most of Thomas, Claire and Connor's college tuition at either a public or private college. They are targeting about $125,000 in today's dollars for each child.

Wish: To be able to pay all of Thomas, Claire and Connor's college tuition so they can graduate debt free.

LONG-TERM GOALS
Must Haves:

1) Enough savings to retire at age 65 and maintain their current lifestyle.

2) Having a financial cushion when they retire so that if they have an unexpected health event they can manage that and not be a burden to their children.

Wishes:

1) Kathy would like to retire or work part-time after age 50 and focus her efforts on volunteer work related to kids with special medical needs.

2) Keep their home in Chicago, if that is where their kids are as adults, and then have a second home in Fort Myers, Florida, where they will spend the winter months.

3) Buy and maintain a 35' sailboat in retirement.

4) Contribute to their grandchildren's college savings plans.

See **SAMPLE LIFEMAP** »

Go ahead and make a list. Do it now. This book can wait. The words here aren't going anywhere. And, really, defining your life priorities is more important than reading this book.

A lifemap is something you can hold onto in times of doubt, despair or craziness in your life or the world's. When you are considering a significant action related to money, bring out your list. Look at it, and ask yourself, "How does this action further my lifemap?"

For example, when the stock market is roaring ahead in a given year, you may be tempted to put more of your money into stocks. Hard to resist seeing the big gains in the news and hearing friends and relatives going on about how much money they are making in the market. You look at your lifemap. At the top—buying a new house in three years. Do I want to chase a high-flying stock market with my down payment? Probably not, particularly if you understand that the stock market can quickly change, and has "bear market" declines of over 20% every few years.

It is mentally challenging to not chase a bull market when investor sentiment is exuberant or to sell at a market bottom when the economy's prospects appear grim. Even professional money managers find it difficult to exercise self-control in these situations. In times of exhilaration or fear, most people make decisions with the intuitive, emotional part of their brain, rather than the deliberate, more rational part of their brain. [2]

A lifemap will help you during these times. It will serve as a compass pointed toward the true north of your long-term investment goals. It helps

SAMPLE LIFEMAP

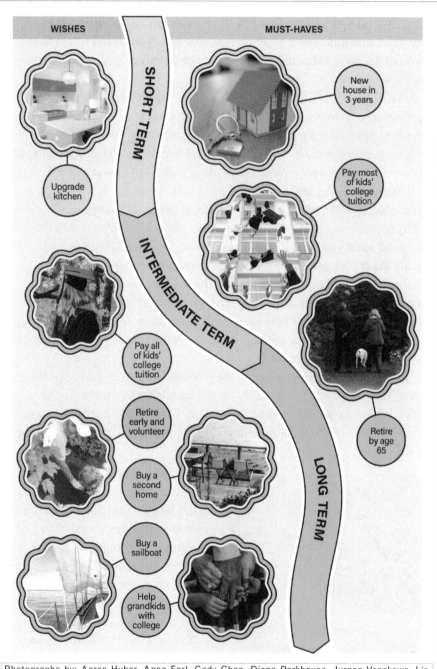

Photographs by: Aaron Huber, Anna Earl, Cody Chan, Diana Parkhouse, Jurgen Venakowa, Liz Brenden, Shayna Douglas, Tierra Mallorca and Vasily Koloda on Unsplash (www.unsplash.com).

shift the frame of your investing focus from a short-term and emotional one—missing out on the market going up—to a longer-term, more deliberative one—buying a home in three years, and other financial goals many years down the road. It reminds you of how you would feel if an impulsive decision today undermined your ability to achieve your longer-term life goals.

Referring to your lifemap will help reduce the chance that you make a significant investment mistake that will take you far off track from your investment plan. As your life twists and turns, viewing your life objectives over a longer time horizon will help you make more reasoned decisions. It's like driving a car. If you stare at the road right in front of you while driving, you'll likely oversteer and be in for a tense ride. Look far down the road, and the ride smooths out. You almost don't notice small bumps and curves.

Laying out your longer-term investment goals also helps you better understand what you need to do in order to achieve them. It helps you estimate the time it may take given your current course of saving and investment, and what the least risky, or volatile, path is to reaching your goals. In addition, if you work with an investment advisor or financial planner, your lifemap will help them build your financial plan. And if your life priorities change, your lifemap will help you understand how a change may affect your other life goals.

Imagine your retirement lasting 30 years or more. It is a difficult thing to know fully in advance, but really think about what you are trying to achieve with your savings and financial plan, particularly later in life when you may be free of the commitment and the cost of raising children and be able to do what you want.

Source of Images: Shutterstock

When I was working as an investment advisor for a bank years ago, I had a client dinner in Florida. I sat next to a former executive of a Fortune 500 company, who was a dinner guest of my client. We got to talking about how he had retired early at age fifty-five to enjoy the carefree life and the exceptional fishing in Florida. I said, "Sounds great. I'd like to retire at 55." He gently grabbed my arm, looked me in the eye and said, "Don't do it." Fishing can become less appealing, almost a chore, when you do it every day and have little else to do. The reality of being retired at the relatively young age of 55 was less attractive than the idea of it. You know the old saying, "be careful what you wish for."

Do your best to have the life that your financial plan is leading to be the one that you really want.

SUMMARY

• Make a lifemap of the money-related goals you hope to achieve in your life.

• Write down your short, intermediate and long-term goals. After each goal, write down whether this is a must-have goal (ant objective) or a hoped-for wish (grasshopper objective). That is, whether it is essential, something you must have, or whether it is something you hope happens if things work out well.

• Look at your lifemap once a year and ask yourself, is this who I am, what I want and where I want to go?

CHAPTER 2

Expected Returns on Your Investments

THE BASE CASE: EXPECTED LONG-TERM RETURNS OF INVESTING

How has saving and investing money, rather than spending it, been rewarded over time? What do you think people have been willing to accept in terms of a greater amount of money tomorrow in order to let other people use their money today? It is important to know the historical returns on investment assets, because it provides a reference point from which to evaluate your own investments and to understand how likely you are over time to achieve your investment goals.

Despite the many economic recessions, political upheavals and wars over the last 100 years, the return on stocks has been impressive. A dollar invested in large US stocks in 1926 was worth $10,826 by the end of 2020 (see **Chart 2.1**). In contrast, a dollar invested in long-term US government bonds would be worth $199. Taking a risk on equities and sticking with them paid off.

Over the last century, the real return on stocks in the United States has averaged about 7% per year. High quality bonds such as US government bonds and top-rated corporate bonds have returned about 2.5%. If you add in the average rate of inflation during this period—about 3%—you get a nominal return (includes inflation) of about 10% for stocks and 5.5% for bonds (see **Chart 2.2**). An equal mix of the two (50% stocks and 50% bonds) provided a return of 7.75%.

I will call these returns for stocks and bonds the **"Base Case"** returns of investing.

"BASE CASE" LONG-TERM MARKET RETURNS

Asset Class	Nominal Returns (annualized)	Real Returns (annualized)
US Stocks	10%	7%
US Bond Market	5.5%	2.5%
50% - 50% Mixed Portfolio	7.75%	4.75%

Based on the approximate historical returns of the S&P 500 Index and Long-Term Government Bonds (20-year US government bonds), 1/1/26-7/31/21, and inflation of 3%.

CHART 2.1 MONTHLY GROWTH OF WEALTH ($1) 1926-2021

Source: Data is from January 1926 through March 2021. In US Dollars. US Small Cap Index is the CRSP 6-10 Index; US Large Cap is the S&P 500 Index; Long-Term Government Bonds Index is the 20-year US government bonds. Treasury Bills are One-Month US Treasury Bills; 1-Month Treasury Bills Index is the IA SBBI US 30 Day TBill TR USD. Treasury Index data sourced from Ibbotson Associates, via Morningstar. Inflation is the Consumer Price Index. CRSP data provided by the Center for Research in Security Prices. S&P data © 2020 S&P Dow Jones Indices LLC, a division of S&P Global. All rights reserved. Bonds, T-bills and inflation data provided by Morningstar. Past performance is no guarantee of future results. Indices are not available for direct investment. Their performance does not reflect the expenses associated with the management of an actual portfolio.

Why do you earn the Base Case returns? With stocks, you are giving your money to others to use in an economic endeavor typically carried out through a legal entity called a company. Hopefully the company will produce more money than what was put into it. The timing of when you get your money back and any profit is uncertain. You might not get any money back. That's the risk you take and why you are paid a higher return on equities than bonds.

In **Chart 2.2**, you can see that historically stocks have had higher and more volatile returns than bonds. The volatility of stocks around their average return, shown in the chart as standard deviation, is two to three times that of 20-year US Treasury bonds. Stocks are more volatile than bonds largely because stockholders profit after everyone else, such as employees, suppliers and creditors, has been paid. As a bondholder, you usually have some collateral backing your loan to a company. This collateral, such as inventory, equipment, land or intellectual property, can be sold if the company fails, helping ensure that you will receive back at least part of your investment. With stock, if a company fails, your investment can go to zero. The good part of being a stockholder, though, is that you have unlimited upside if the company is successful.

For example, a $1,000 investment in Microsoft at its IPO in March of 1986 was as of 2020 worth around $2,500,000. Also, the dividend on Microsoft stock as of 2020 was $0.51 per share, so you were earning $7,000 every quarter and $28,000 every year.

The 4.5% difference between the 10% historical return of stocks and the 5.5% return of bonds is called the *risk premium* of stocks. The volatility and uncertainty of stock returns relative to bond returns is what drives this risk premium. In contrast, the risk of US government bonds is much lower than that of stocks, because the government can forcibly tax everyone in the US to get the money to pay you your principal and interest. Or, the government can just print more dollars. So that's the tradeoff—higher, more volatile returns for stocks, and lower, but steadier returns for bonds. Despite their higher volatility and uncertainty, however, stock returns have historically been positive about 73% of the time (see **Chart 2.3**).

CHART 2.2   ANNUAL RETURNS OF STOCKS, BONDS, BILLS AND INFLATION

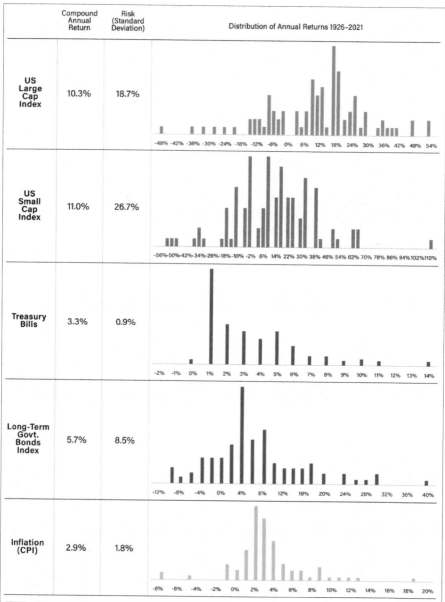

Source: Data is from January 1926 through March 2021. In US Dollars. US Small Cap Index is the CRSP 6-10 Index; US Large Cap is the S&P 500 Index; Long-Term Government Bonds Index is the 20-year US government bonds. Treasury Bills are One-Month US Treasury Bills; 1-Month Treasury Bills Index is the IA SBBI US 30 Day TBill TR USD. Treasury Index data sourced from Ibbotson Associates, via Morningstar. Inflation is the Consumer Price Index. CRSP data provided by the Center for Research in Security Prices. S&P data © 2020 S&P Dow Jones Indices LLC, a division of S&P Global. All rights reserved. Bonds, T-bills and inflation data provided by Morningstar. Past performance is no guarantee of future results. Indices are not available for direct investment. Their performance does not reflect the expenses associated with the management of an actual portfolio.

CHART 2.3 DISTRIBUTION OF US LARGE CAP INDEX ANNUAL RETURNS (1926-2021)

Positive Years	69	73%
Negative Years	26	27%

Distribution of annual returns by range:

-50% to -40%: 1931 -46.1

-40% to -30%: 1937 -37.5; 2008 -33

-30% to -20%: 1930 -29.4; 1974 -25.8; 2002 -20.9

-20% to -10%: 2001 -14.9; 1946 -14.2; 1929 -13.5; 1973 -13.3; 1934 -11; 1966 -10.6

-10% to -0%: 2018 -9.6; 1989 -7.9; 1941 -7.3; 1987 -7.2; 1957 -7.1; 1940 -6.6; 1932 -5.6; 1962 -5.3; 2000 -4.3; 1977 -2.4; 1994 -2; 1981 -0.6; 1953 -0.5; 2011 -0.3

0% to 10%: 1947 3.1; 1990 3.9; 2007 3.9; 2015 4.5; 1939 6.8; 1984 7; 2005 7.5; 1960 8; 1965 8.7; 2004 8.9; 1993 9.2; 1948 9.7; 1992 9.7; 1971 9.7

10% to 20%: 1956 10.4; 1976 10.6; 2012 11; 1959 11.4; 1926 11.6; 1988 12; 1970 12.4; 2006 12.8; 1964 13.3; 1978 13.3; 1979 13.6; 1967 14.8; 1968 16; 1999 16.2; 1952 16.2; 1951 16.6; 1972 16.7; 1963 16.9; 1943 17.3; 1944 17.7; 2014 17.8; 2016 17.8; 1986 18; 1949 18.3; 1983 18.4; 1942 18.4; 2020 18.4; 1996 18.9; 1961 19.2; 2010 19.4; 2017 19.6

20% to 30%: 2019 21.7; 1975 22; 1989 22.6; 1985 22.7; 1982 23.4; 1980 24.8; 1991 25; 1936 25.5; 1997 25.5; 2013 25.9; 1998 27.2; 1955 29; 1938 29.2; 1950 29.2

30% to 40%: 2013 32.2; 1995 34.1; 1945 34.3; 1958 37.3; 2009 38.1

40% to 50%: 1927 40.2; 1928 44.2; 1954 44.9

50% to 60%: 1933 52.6; 1935 54

Annual Returns Range

Source: Data is from January 1926 through March 2021. In US Dollars. US Large Cap is the S&P 500 Index. S&P data © 2020 S&P Dow Jones Indices LLC, a division of S&P Global. All rights reserved. Past performance is no guarantee of future results. Indices are not available for direct investment. Their performance does not reflect the expenses associated with the management of an actual portfolio.

The return you earn on a share of stock consists of corporate earnings (E) plus the dividend paid by the company (Y) plus the change in its price-earnings ratio (P/E ratio). The P/E ratio is the price of a stock divided by its earnings (such as 12-month forward expected company operating earnings).

For example, if a stock is selling for $100 per share, and expected earnings are $5 per share, then the P/E is 20 (100/5 = 20).

$$\text{Market Return } (R_M) = E + Y + \Delta \text{ P/E}$$

If a company earns 8% on its equity capital, pays a dividend of 2%, and the P/E remains unchanged, your total return will be 10%, (8% + 2% + 0% = 10%). If the P/E changes from 20 to 21, a 5% increase, your total return will be 15%, (8% + 2% + 5% = 15%). Alternatively, in a recession, for example, where earnings fall to 3% and the P/E changes from 20 to 15, a 25% decrease, your total return will be -20% (3% + 2% + -25% = -20%).

Benjamin Graham, often referred to as the "father of value investing," and mentor of Warren Buffett, is attributed the maxim that "In the short-run, the market is a voting machine . . . but in the long-run, the market is a weighing machine." [3] The voting machine aspect of investor behavior is based on emotion and expectations and tends to affect the P/E ratio of stocks. The more confident people are about the economy and the growth of corporate earnings, the more likely they are to bid up the price of stocks relative to their earnings. The weighing machine aspect of the market centers on the actual earnings and dividends received.

In **Chart 2.4** you can see that the proportion of stock returns attributable to dividends, earnings growth and P/E change has varied by decade. Over long periods of time, almost all the return comes from dividends and earnings growth—the weighing machine. As the economy grows, so do corporate earnings, and the growth in earnings over time supports higher dividends and higher stock prices. As Buffett says, "the most that owners in aggregate can earn between now and Judgment Day is what their businesses in aggregate earn...there is simply no magic—no shower of money from outer space—that will enable them to extract wealth from their companies beyond that created by the companies themselves." [4] So what counts over time is the growth in dividends and earnings. The fluctuations in the P/E ratio, reflecting what investors are paying at the time for earnings, is, to borrow from Shakespeare, "full of sound and fury, signifying nothing."

Economic growth, both in the US and the world, has been punctuated by recessions, depressions, market euphorias and panics, wars and political upheavals. But despite the many setbacks, economic growth, corporate earnings and stock market returns have moved upward (see **Chart 2.5** and **Chart 2.6**).

CHART 2.4 TOTAL STOCK RETURN BY THE DECADE (PERCENTAGE/YEAR)

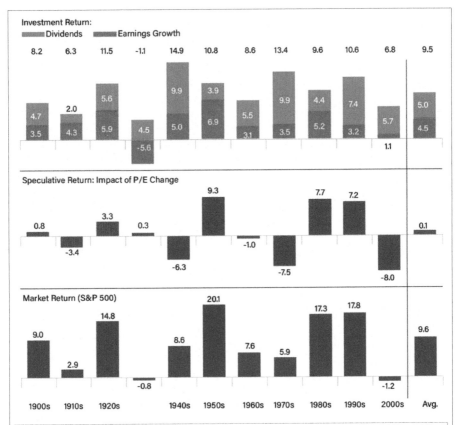

Source: John C. Bogle, *The Little Book of Common Sense Investing: the Only Way to Guarantee Your Fair Share of Stock Market Returns* (John Wiley and Sons, 2007), 17, Exhibit 2.4.

CHART 2.5   S&P 500 EARNINGS & US GDP BILLIONS (1929-2020)

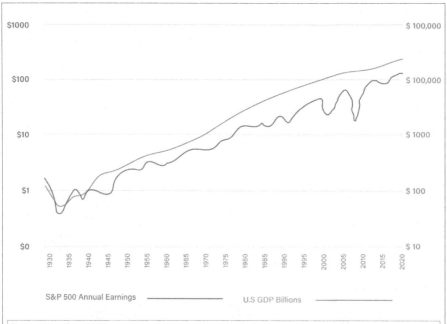

HOW LONG MIGHT IT TAKE TO EARN THE BASE CASE?

It is useful to know that the average long-term return for stocks is 10% and for bonds is 5.5%, but do you get that every year? No. As noted, stock returns are more volatile than bonds. **Chart 2.7** shows that over a one-year time frame the high for equities was +54% and the low was -46%, compared to a high of +40% and low of -11% for bonds. You can see that over longer time frames, the returns for equities and bonds begin to coalesce around their long-term averages. Over 20-year rolling time periods, for example, based on the time period 1926-2021, equities range from +18% to +2% (averaging 10.3% annually), and bond returns range from +13% to +0% (averaging 5.7% annually).

CHART 2.6   DESPITE WARS AND ECONOMIC CRISES THE STOCK MARKET HAS MOVED UPWARD
US Large Cap Stocks 1926-2021

Source: Data is from January 1926 through March 2021. In US Dollars. US Large Cap is the S&P 500 Index. S&P data © 2020 S&P Dow Jones Indices LLC, a division of S&P Global. All rights reserved. Past performance is no guarantee of future results. Indices are not available for direct investment. Their performance does not reflect the expenses associated with the management of an actual portfolio.

CHART 2.7   RANGE OF STOCK, BOND AND BLENDED TOTAL RETURNS
Annual total returns, 1926-2021

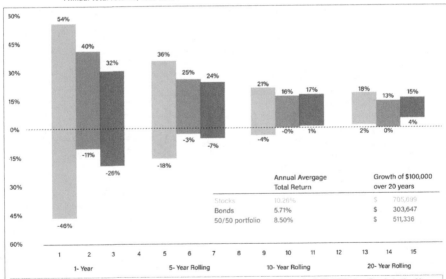

	Annual Avergage Total Return	Growth of $100,000 over 20 years
Stocks	10.26%	$ 705,699
Bonds	5.71%	$ 303,647
50/50 portfolio	8.50%	$ 511,336

Source: Data is from January 1926 through March 2021. In US Dollars. Stocks is the S&P 500 Index. Bonds is the 20-year US government bonds. Treasury Index data sourced from Ibbotson Associates, via Morningstar. S&P data © 2020 S&P Dow Jones Indices LLC, a division of S&P Global. All rights reserved. Past performance is no guarantee of future results. Indices are not available for direct investment. Their performance does not reflect the expenses associated with the management of an actual portfolio.

WILL I EARN THE BASE CASE IN THE FUTURE?

It's hard to say if the past returns of the Base Case will be repeated in the future. Much of the investment industry assumes this, but there is no certainty. The US was favorably positioned over the last century given its economy being the largest in the world, positive demographics and having won two world wars and one cold war. **Chart 2.8** summarizes the past returns of stocks and bonds of different countries. You can see there is significant variation. The differences are largely due to political upheavals and war, and economic events around these, such as hyperinflation and wholesale destruction of the productive capacity of entire countries during and after war. Germany and Japan are examples of this with regard to World Wars I and II. Not even shown in the chart are countries such as China and Russia, where private investments were wiped out following communist government takeovers during the first half of the 20th century. Note in **Chart 2.9** that for many countries and the world, cumulative negative equity returns ran for decades. You can understand why investors in some European countries have been less enthusiastic about equities than investors in the US and UK.

CHART 2.8   REAL ANNUALIZED RETURNS (%) ON EQUITIES, BONDS AND BILLS, 1900-2017

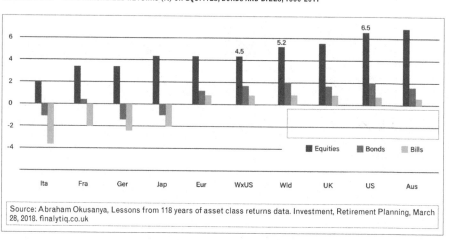

Source: Abraham Okusanya, Lessons from 118 years of asset class returns data. Investment, Retirement Planning, March 28, 2018. finalytiq.co.uk

CHART 2.9   REAL EQUITY RETURNS DURING MAJOR MARKET EVENTS AND SELECT TIME PERIODS

Period (calendar years)		USA	UK	France	Germany	Japan	World	World ex-US
Real rate of return (%) over the period								
Six Worst episodes								
1914–18:	World War I	-18	-36	-50	-66	66	-31	-35
1929–31:	Wall Street Crash	-61	-31	-44	-59	11	-54	-44
1939–48:	World War II	22	34	-41	-88	-96	-12	-41
1973–74:	Oil shock/recession	-52	-71	-40	-26	-49	-47	-39
2000–02:	Internet 'bust'	-42	-38	-45	-58	-49	-44	-46
2008:	Credit/banking crash	-38	-33	-41	-43	-41	-41	-44
Four best episodes								
1919–28:	Post-WWI recovery	376	234	171	18	30	168	82
1949–59:	Post-WWII recovery	430	212	269	4373	1565	395	345
1980–89:	Expansionary 80s	176	337	297	220	431	257	327
1990–99:	Nineties/tech boom	276	198	218	154	-42	111	42
Longest runs of cumulative negative real returns								
Return (%) over stated period		-8	-4	-19	-3	-1	-8	-2
	Period	1905–20	1900–21	1929–82	1900–54	1900–50	1910–31	1905–31
	Number of years	16	22	53	55	51	22	27

Source: Abraham Okusanya, *Lessons from 118 years of asset class returns data.* Investment, Retirement Planning, March 28, 2018. finalytiq.co.uk

Equities have remained a good investment compared to other investments such as collectibles and houses. **Chart 2.10** shows that collectibles appreciated 2.9% annually over the time period 1900-2017. Over the same period, a global equity portfolio, including reinvested dividends, appreciated 5.2% annually (real return). You can also see from **Chart 2.11** that annual returns on houses have been in the low single digits, with US houses rising 1.39 times over the last 100 plus years, an annualized return of just 0.3%. Of note, it's "unfair to compare house prices with total equity return because that comparison ignores rental yield for property investors or imputed rent for owner-occupiers." [5]

CHART 2.10 PRICE INDEXES FOR COLLECTIBLES IN REAL USD, 1900-2017

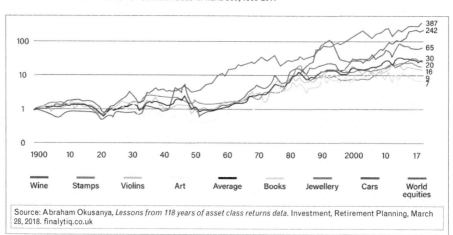

Source: Abraham Okusanya, *Lessons from 118 years of asset class returns data*. Investment, Retirement Planning, March 28, 2018. finalytiq.co.uk

CHART 2.11 REAL PRICE OF DOMESTIC HOUSING IN 11 COUNTRIES, 1900-2017

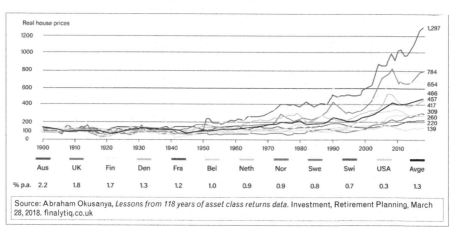

Source: Abraham Okusanya, *Lessons from 118 years of asset class returns data*. Investment, Retirement Planning, March 28, 2018. finalytiq.co.uk

SUMMARY

• The long-term return for stocks has been about 10% per year, and for bonds about 5.5%.

• Stocks are more volatile than bonds, and the premium you earn for accepting this volatility has been about 4.5% annually.

• The long upward trend of global economic growth, corporate earnings and dividends has supported the long-term return of stocks.

• Stock and bond returns can vary considerably over short time periods, and converge around their average returns over longer time periods.

• Stocks can go many years with little or no real return.

• No one knows what stock and bond returns will be in the future.

CHAPTER 3

How to
Invest Your Money

 $\mathbf{Y}$ ou are reading this book in part because you want a recommendation as to what you should invest in. Although you may have good intentions to read this book cover to cover, your brain is distracted with thoughts such as, "What should I do so that I and my family will financially be OK?" or "When is this getting to how I can achieve my financial goals?" or "If I have to plow through all this turgid prose, I sure hope there's a secret to investment success in here somewhere."

So, I will tell you now, rather than later. But I encourage you to read the rest of the book. You may find some useful things in it.

An investor whom I admire and suggest you emulate is Martia. Martia is from the planet Martian in outer space, and my imaginary friend. She is serene and spectacularly intelligent. She literally has the knowledge of the cosmos at the tips of her tentacles.

Martia is also navigationally challenged. She missed a turn at an intergalactic vortex and crash-landed on Earth. Her spaceship needs repairs.

Martia scans Earth to see if there is material on our planet to fix her ship. In doing so, she finds that human creatures dominate the planet. These humans, middling in terms of ability and intelligence as far as the universe goes, produce different things for their survival and amusement, roughly as follows:

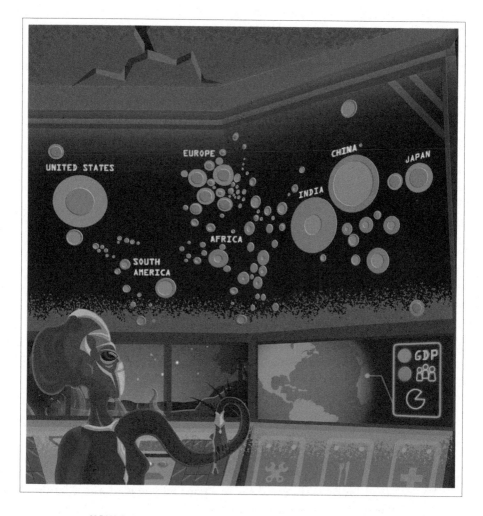

HOW AN ALIEN FROM OUTER SPACE SEES THE WORLD

Of course, quicker than you can say "Milky Way," the humans are falling all over themselves to meet and greet Martia. These charitable Earthlings give her $1 billion toward repairs. She finds out these dollars can be exchanged for things. But after some calculations as to how much material $1 billion can buy on Earth, Martia concludes that $2 billion is required for what she needs to get her ship shipshape and zip back to her galaxy. Several tons of rare earth elements aren't cheap.

Martia wants to return home as soon as possible, but doesn't want to impose on her human hosts for another $1 billion. She also does not want to risk losing her $1 billion grubstake, because then she may never go home.

So what to do with the $1 billion to turn it into $2 billion as quickly and as safely as possible?

Martia runs some more scans of Earth to assess how she can maximize the chance of doubling her money, while minimizing the chance of losing it. She sees that humans invest their wealth in various endeavors of their fellow humans. She searches for the most productive and least volatile places on Earth to do this. Among the 7.9 billion Earthlings, there are groupings of people who are more productive than others.

In an area called the United States, humans are very productive relative to their number. They are 5% of Earth's human population, but produce over 15% of its goods and services (approximated by Gross Domestic Product, or GDP). The United States also has had less war, famine, and political upheaval than any other part of Earth over the last 100 years (Martia scanned Earth's history in a minute).

Martia also sees that humans are quite productive in an area called Europe, and in another place called Asia, namely Japan and South Korea. She notices that China and India, in particular, have very large human populations, and that their economies and wealth are growing quickly.

Additionally, Martia observes that politically stable countries where the rule of law is strong are where your wealth is best protected from the capricious actions of other humans, particularly those who wield the coercive power of government.

Martia spreads her $1 billion investment around the most productive and stable places on Earth. These countries and regions are where the most excess wealth is created, that is, wealth beyond what is necessary to support a basic standard of living. For Martia, who does not fully understand human behavior, allocating to the most productive and stable places on Earth seems reasonable.

It's a reasonable approach for you, too.

GLOBAL CITIZEN

Like Martia, take a global view. Invest in the most productive and stable regions of the world via a mix of publicly available investments, such as stocks and bonds. Of course, assets that are publicly traded are only a subset of the world's productive capacity, much of which is privately owned. You cannot, for example, invest in the açai berry trade among indigenous

Amazonian tribes. But there are plenty of public investments available for you to have a globally diversified portfolio to tap into the world's productivity.

Summaries of global stock and bond markets are shown in **Charts 3.1, 3.2** and **3.3**. You can see that the area Martia identified as being the most productive and stable on Earth, the United States, also happens to have the largest stock and bond markets. Millions of humans looking for the best place on Earth to invest their money and earn a good return came to the same conclusion as Martia.

Although Martia's global investment allocation would have a large percentage in the US, it would also include a meaningful allocation to other economic regions of the world, such as Europe and Asia. From a risk standpoint, and a consistency of return standpoint, a globally diversified portfolio is a better allocation than one overly concentrated in any one country, including the US.

Martia knows that the returns of stock markets in different countries can vary substantially from year to year, and even from decade to decade. Sometimes the US stock market outperforms Asian and European markets, and sometimes Asian and European markets outperform the US.

Martia also knows that humans are unpredictable and that there have

CHART 3.1 WORLD MARKET CAPITALIZATION AS OF DECEMBER 31, 2019

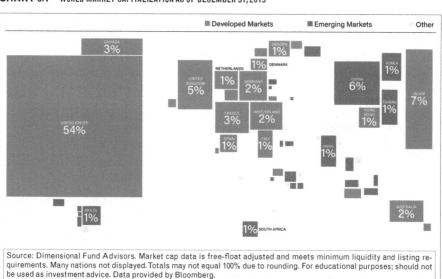

Source: Dimensional Fund Advisors. Market cap data is free-float adjusted and meets minimum liquidity and listing requirements. Many nations not displayed. Totals may not equal 100% due to rounding. For educational purposes; should not be used as investment advice. Data provided by Bloomberg.

been many upheavals of established orders on Earth over the millennia, so she is not going to put all her pods in one basket. (Martians gestate in pods, which are similar to eggs.)

CHART 3.2 GLOBAL INVESTMENT GRADE BOND MARKET AS OF DECEMBER 31, 2019

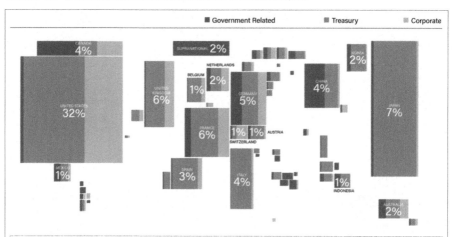

Source: Dimensional Fund Advisors. Data is from Bloomberg Barclays Global Aggregate Ex-Securitized Bond Index. Index excludes non-investment-grade securities, bonds with less than one year to maturity, tax-exempt municipal securities, inflation-linked bonds, floating rate issues, and securitized bonds. Many nations not displayed. Totals may not equal 100% due to rounding. For educational purposes; should not be used as investment advice. Bloomberg Barclays data provided by Bloomberg.

CHART 3.3 MARKET CAPITALIZATIONS OF GLOBAL STOCK MARKETS
January 1990-December 2019

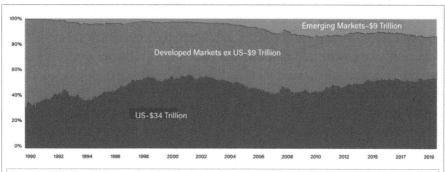

Source: In US Dollars. Market cap data is free-float adjusted and meets minimum liquidity and listing requirements. Data provided by Bloomberg.

HOME COUNTRY BIAS

You might be tempted to just invest in your own country. Many investors around the world do this. It's called *home country bias*. They favor companies that are within the economic and political sphere with which they are most familiar. Japanese people overweight Japanese companies in their investment portfolios, and Germans overweight German companies.

CHART 3.4 HOME COUNTRY BIAS
Percent of Equity Market Owned by Domestic Investors & Weight in MSCI All Country World Index

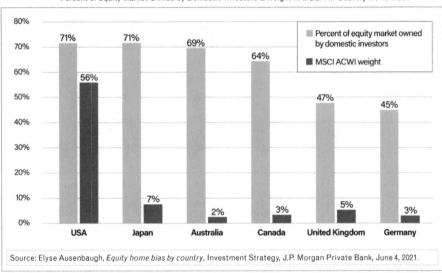

Source: Elyse Ausenbaugh, *Equity home bias by country*, Investment Strategy, J.P. Morgan Private Bank, June 4, 2021.

One argument for just investing in US-based companies is that US companies are global, and that much of their earnings comes from outside the US. You will still benefit, however, from owning companies based in other countries. China is a good example. Chinese companies dominate the opportunities in China, and provide a diversified source of earnings and growth relative to US-based companies.

See **CHART 3.5** »

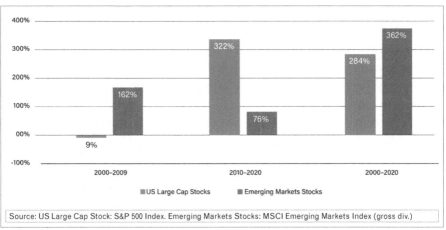

CHART 3.5 DIVERSIFICATION OF EQUITY INVESTMENTS
US Large Cap and Emerging Markets Stocks
Cumulative Returns (%)

Source: US Large Cap Stock: S&P 500 Index. Emerging Markets Stocks: MSCI Emerging Markets Index (gross div.)

Some investment advisors in the US stick with US-centric investment allocations for their clients despite the US becoming a smaller percentage of Global GDP over time. This is due in part to *client reference risk*. That is, clients tend to look at US-based stock indexes such as the S&P 500 Index or the Dow Jones Industrial Average when assessing their advisor's investment performance. It is difficult for a client to hear about how well the S&P 500 is doing, and then see their international and emerging market equities lagging far behind over a 10-year period, as they did from 2010-2020.

As behavioral finance studies indicate, people's herd instinct, or their desire to feel part of the group, makes them more comfortable with investments that perform similarly to those of people around them. People like to do well when others they know are doing well, and feel losses less painfully when those they know are losing, too. People are inclined to follow the crowd even if an allocation different from that of the crowd would produce greater real growth of their wealth over time. It's just too painful to see others doing well when you are doing less well.

FOMO (fear of missing out) will often guide suboptimal investment decision-making. For example, a client may tell their investment advisor that they are unhappy that they are in emerging market stocks when the recent returns of S&P 500 stocks have been much higher. The investment advisor does not want to lose their client, which of course is the advisor's source of income. So what is the advisor tempted to do? The advisor may allocate more of the client's portfolio to US stocks so that the client feels heard and sees their advisor "taking action." This shift toward what has done well recently, however, is often poorly timed. It comes just before a period of what has not done well recently, emerging market stocks, begins to outperform US stocks.

It is true that US markets have produced about the best investment returns over the last 100 years. The average annual real return of US equities over that time has been about 6.5%, whereas a global basket of equities produced a return of 5.2% (see **Chart 2.8**). It is not surprising, though, that US stocks outperformed those of other countries. The US was the preeminent economic and political power of the 20th and early 21st centuries.

The US market, of course, does not always outperform other markets. The COVID-contagion stock sell-off of 2020, the global market breakdown related to the subprime mortgage crisis of 2007-2009, the bankruptcies of Lehman Brothers, Washington Mutual, and General Motors in 2008-2009, and the collapse of Enron and WorldCom in 2001-2002, remind us that the US can be a volatile place to invest. The peak-to-trough drawdown of US equities during the period 2007-2009 was over 50%. In addition, from 2000-2009, the cumulative return of the S&P 500 was negative, while the returns of international and emerging market stocks were positive.

Unless you have an overwhelmingly positive conviction that the US market will outperform those of other countries over the next 50 years, prudence would suggest that, just like Martia, you diversify your investment assets broadly across the world, particularly to those countries whose economies are growing faster than the developed economies of the US, Europe and Japan.

This would be tempered by considerations such as political risk and currency risk in these developing countries. Investments around the world may be priced in currencies which move up and down in value relative to the US dollar. And of course, if a country is a poorly run, failed state, where respect for law and private property is low, then you would avoid investing there unless the potential returns were so high as to justify the risk.

If you believe that people around the world will eventually have similar access to education, capital, and political stability, that their capabilities are similar, and that they have a common desire to improve their standard of living, then a rational expectation would be that there will be a leveling of wealth among countries. This is what you have seen historically, from Japan to Korea to China, and it is likely to continue (see **Chart 3.6**). GDP growth does not always directly translate into stock market gains, but as noted in Chapter 2, the appreciation of the stock market generally follows corporate earnings and dividend growth over long periods of time.

CHART 3.6

	GDP Per Capita	Projected Growth Rate
US	$ 52,000	2.5%
Europe	$ 39,000	2.0%
Japan	$ 47,600	1.2%
South Korea	$ 25,458	3.0%
China	$ 6,894	6.4%
India	$ 1,861	7.4%

Source: GDP data as of 2019: http://data.worldbank.org/data-catalog/world-development-indicators; http://data.world-bank.org/data-catalog/global-economic-prospects.

COMPANY-SPECIFIC RISK

Investing globally in a diversified basket of stocks also negates a key investment portfolio risk—*company-specific risk*. By investing in a number of companies, you avoid the risk that the failure of any one company will severely negatively affect your portfolio. By diversifying away company-specific risk, you are left with the risk of the overall market. And getting this diversification is inexpensive and easy to do via index funds. As Nobel laureate and financial theorist Harry Markowitz said, diversification is the only "free lunch" in investing.

Additionally, if you own stock or stock options in the company you work at, and your pension is dependent on the health of your company, a good part of your earnings and wealth is closely linked to the well-being of one company. If your company is an economic mainstay in the town you live in, the value of your house may also be linked to the fate of the company. As the bankruptcies of Enron, WorldCom, Lehman Brothers and Washington Mutual attest, even major companies can fail. It's good to be loyal to the company you work for, but you don't want your retirement to be dependent on the health of one company.

EXPAND YOUR TIME HORIZON

Just as you expand your investment horizon to include the world, expand the time frame with which you view your investments from days and months to years and decades. It is fairly easy for Martia to be patient with her investments, because Martian years are equal to seven human years. (Yes, in this regard, Martia does look on us humans as we do our dogs.) She has analyzed historical equity and bond returns on Earth and understands the benefit of being patient.

In **Chart 3.7**, you can see that for 17 years, from 1965-1981, cash, as represented by one-month US Treasury bills, outperformed US equities, as represented by the S&P 500 Index. By year fifteen, in 1979, you may have been ready to throw in the towel on equities. It certainly was the sentiment of many investors. There were seven million fewer individual shareholders in 1979 than there were in 1970. [6] Many people had given up on the stock market. The August 13, 1979, *BusinessWeek* cover story titled "The Death of Equities: How Inflation Is Destroying the Stock Market," [7] encapsulated the investment zeitgeist:

> . . . this 'death of equity' can no longer be seen as something a stock market rally—however strong—will check. It has persisted for more than 10 years through market rallies, business cycles, recession, recoveries, and booms. . . . For better or worse, then, the U.S. economy probably has to regard the death of equities as a near-permanent condition—reversible some day, but not soon. [8]

Time frames of 10 years, and even 17 years, are too short to conclude anything about long-term stock market returns. From its bottom in 1982 through 2020, the S&P 500 far outperformed one-month Treasury bills. The compounded total return of the S&P 500 during this time was about 7,400%. If only the people writing the *BusinessWeek* article, and many investors at the time, could have been like Martia and expanded their time frame from an intermediate one of a dozen or so years to a decades-long one, closer to an average person's lifetime.

CHART 3.7 THE IMPORTANCE OF LONG-TERM DISCIPLINE
Annualized Compound Returns (%)

	1926–2020	1965–1981	1982–2020
Large Cap US Index	10.3%	6.1%	12.0%
Treasury Bills	3.3%	6.6%	3.7%

Source: In US Dollars. US Large Cap is the S&P 500 Index; Treasury Bills are One-Month US Treasury Bills; 1-Month Treasury Bills Index is the IA SBBI US 30 Day T Bill TR USD. Treasury Index data sourced from Ibbotson Associates, via Morningstar. S&P data © 2020 S&P Dow Jones Indices LLC, a division of S&P Global. All rights reserved. T-bills data provided by Morningstar. Past performance is no guarantee of future results. Indices are not available for direct investment. Their performance does not reflect the expenses associated with the management of an actual portfolio.

Broaden your time frame, then, and be patient. Don't look at your stocks every hour or every day or every month. Or even every year. All the countless hours spent monitoring stock prices does not add up to anything, really. It's too much stress and work for too little or no reward. At a weak moment, when you are tired or scared, you could make an investment decision that negatively affects your long-term goals. So, don't tempt yourself by looking at your stock portfolio all the time.

Think of Martia, calmly waiting for the billions of Earthlings to do the work that will turn her $1 billion into $2 billion. Let your fellow humans go about building their companies and building your wealth. You go about your life doing things that you enjoy and can have a significant impact on—your family, your career and your community.

HOW TO EFFICIENTLY INVEST

What is the best way to follow Martia's approach and invest globally to achieve the Base Case? Invest in global equity and bond index funds. Index funds provide you a low-cost way to invest in a diversified basket of stocks and bonds.

INDEX FUNDS

You will outperform the great majority of investors by investing in index funds. You will likely do better than those who speculate on actively managed funds which have expenses of 0.5%-2% or more per year. With index funds, you can access global equity and bond returns for an annual cost of around .05% (1/20 of 1%). Some funds don't even charge a management fee. Therefore, with a few funds, at little to no cost, you can achieve the Base Case return. Investment allocations using index funds will be covered in more detail in the next two chapters.

Also, since index funds hold a large number of stocks representing the market, they trade less frequently and have less turnover than most active funds, which select a narrower and more frequently changing group of stocks. Index funds, therefore, are more tax efficient than most actively managed funds.

Save yourself time and money and avoid the active management game. Says David Swensen, who was the chief investment officer at Yale University, "I concluded that individuals fare best by constructing equity-oriented, broadly diversified portfolios without the active management component." [9] Efficient investing applies to bonds as well as equities. Says Burton Malkiel, professor of economics at Princeton University and author of the classic book on investing, *A Random Walk Down Wall Street*: "Because bond markets tend to be at least as efficient as stock markets, I recommend low-expense bond index funds. Bond index funds and ETFs, which just buy and hold a broad variety of bonds, generally outperform actively managed bond funds." [10]

...a low-cost, highly tax effective all-market index fund, is the ultimate winning strategy for the long-term.

JOHN BOGLE

A useful rule of thumb for earning the best return on your capital is to keep your money as close as possible to the people actually doing the work in the world. Have as few layers of fees between you and the companies trying to earn a return on the capital you are giving them. Own the stocks of every US public company, weighted by their market capitalizations, and hold them forever, recommends Warren Buffett. John Bogle, who was the founder and chief executive of The Vanguard Group, and helped create the first index fund, concurs: "I firmly believe that such a strategy, when administered with effectiveness through a low-cost, highly tax effective all-market index fund, is the ultimate winning strategy for the long-term." [11] Bogle continues,

> One wonderful aspect of this all-market strategy is that it eliminates three of the four great risks of investing: (1) the risk of individual stock selection; (2) the risk of picking the wrong investment style, or even the right style (if there is one) at the wrong time; and (3) the risk of selecting the wrong manager to implement whatever style you choose. . . . both the history of our financial markets and the future growth and productivity of American business suggest that owning the US stock market for a lifetime should pose extremely limited risk for those who have the courage to stay the course. There are, indeed, few better alternatives to long-run capital appreciation. [12]

CHART 3.8 LET THE MARKET WORK FOR YOU

When you try to outwit the market, you compete with the collective knowledge of all investors.

By harnessing the market's power, you put their knowledge to work in your portfolio.

Source: Dimensional Fund Advisors

SUSTAINABILITY OF INDEXING

Some investors worry that as indexing becomes a bigger part of the market the approach will underperform active management strategies. Indexing has become a greater proportion of the market as investors withdraw funds from active managers and allocate toward passive strategies. Index funds reached 48.1% of total US stock-fund assets as of November 30, 2018. [13]

The best estimates, though, are that we are a long way from index funds being too large a proportion of the market. Active managers still make up a significant percentage of overall assets under management. More importantly, they make up a majority of trading on global securities exchanges. Burton Malkiel observes, "And even if the proportion of active managers shrinks to as little as 10 or 5 percent of the total, there would still be more than enough of them to make prices reflect information. We have far too much active management today, not too little.[14]" Let active investors spend their time and money keeping stock prices rational. Being in an index fund, you benefit from their activity without incurring the cost.

FOCUS ON WHAT YOU CAN CONTROL

In closing this chapter, when reflecting on your investment approach, remember The Serenity Prayer [15]:

> *God, grant me the serenity to accept the things I cannot change,*
> *Courage to change the things I can,*
> *And wisdom to know the difference.*

Focus on things you can control, such as diversifying your investments globally, expanding your time horizon and indexing your investments. Other things you can control include:

- Maintaining a disciplined investment approach over time and across different market environments,

- Reducing your investment expenses,

• Minimizing taxes related to your investments, and

• Limiting the time you spend on superfluous monitoring of your investments.

Accept those things you cannot control, such as the direction of the stock market in any given year.

My hope is that this book gives you some wisdom about what will help you achieve your wealth goals, and what will not. You will have to come up with the courage to act.

SUMMARY

• Approach investing with a global perspective.

• Invest across the world, emphasizing the most productive and stable regions.

• Expand your time horizon from days and months to years and decades.

• Access the productivity of the world via low-cost global equity and bond index funds.

• Improve your investment returns by focusing on things you can control: diversification, investment self-discipline, costs and taxes.

CHAPTER 4

Core Asset Classes: The Primary Colors of Investing

So far on our money journey, you saw in Chapter 1 the benefits of creating a lifemap laying out your financial goals. In Chapter 2, what to reasonably expect as Base Case returns on your invested money. And in Chapter 3 how, like Martia, to invest globally in index funds to benefit from the wealth creation of humans around the world.

But how should you invest given your objectives, age, circumstances and personality? That's the realm of *asset allocation*. Asset allocation involves how you split your money among different asset classes such as stocks, bonds and cash based on your investment goals, time frame and tolerance for volatility.

Of the three main contributors to an investment portfolio's return—asset allocation, security selection and market timing—asset allocation is by far the most important. It drives 90 percent, and some say 100 percent, of investment returns.[16]

This chapter and the next provide an overview of the core asset classes of cash, bonds, and stocks, and how to use them in combination to build investment portfolios with different risk/return expectations.

Chapter 6 provides an overview of non-core asset classes, including hedge funds, private equity and venture capital. If you would like to dive into more detail on asset classes and asset allocation, there are reference sources at the end of this book.

CASH, BONDS AND STOCKS

As a kid, I learned that by squishing together red, yellow and blue Play-Doh you could make a rainbow of other colors. Do you remember what mixing together the primary colors of yellow and blue makes? Red and yellow? Blue and red? Yes, green, orange and purple. To make a menagerie of colorful creatures with Play-Doh, all you needed was the three primary colors. If you had white Play-Doh, you could make even more color shades (and white helped in making the eyes of the Play-Doh creatures).

The primary colors of investing are cash, bonds, and stocks. They are the core asset classes. Core asset classes meet three criteria. [17] They

1) are based on a central function in a capitalist economy and rely on markets, not active management, to generate returns;

2) represent a broad and deep investable market; and

3) add a fundamentally useful, differentiable characteristic to a portfolio.

To create a portfolio suited to your objectives, age, circumstances and personality, all you need are the core asset classes of cash, bonds and stocks. There isn't any fund or investment strategy that provides a better return, or really a much different return, than cash, bonds and stocks used in some combination.

In addition, you can access cash, bonds and stocks at very low cost. Therefore, you might as well use these three and avoid everything else. You will have a better chance of achieving your investment goals than someone who speculates in more esoteric, higher-cost active investments, as discussed in more detail in Chapter 7.

Let's review each of these three core asset classes.

CASH

Cash, the first primary color of investing, is an easily exchanged form of stored wealth. Cash is the conservative anchor in an investment portfolio. Its return has little volatility. Ideally, cash is a stable form of wealth, and retains its value after inflation. This is not always the case. Harrowing examples of how much the value of money can depreciate due to bad economic circumstances and poor government policy include the hyperinflation of 1920s Weimar Germany, and more recently, the economic devastation in Zimbabwe and Venezuela coinciding with rampant inflation. Cash is also very liquid, although there have been times when certain cash vehicles have not been readily accessible due to mismanagement or extreme market environments.

Cash includes hard currency such as the US dollar, Treasury bills and checking and savings accounts at banks insured through the Federal Deposit Insurance Corporation (FDIC). Cash broadly defined also includes a number of short-term investments or obligations, including banker's acceptances, repurchase agreements, and short-term corporate paper. Most instruments deemed cash have maturities of less than a year. A money market fund may hold several different types of these short-term cash instruments.

For cash, there is no expectation for meaningful returns after inflation (see **Chart 2.1**). Therefore, cash is usually held in a portfolio for near-term expenditures. Cash is king when paying living expenses and tiding over family budgets in times of stress, such as a stock market panic, job loss or health emergency.

BONDS

High quality government and corporate bonds are ballast for a portfolio, providing more consistent, less volatile returns than stocks. The tradeoff, as noted in Chapter 2, is that stocks have meaningfully outperformed bonds over longer time periods (10% annualized return for stocks vs. 5.5% for bonds). High quality bonds are those issued by governments of countries that are fiscally stable and able to pay their debts, or bonds of companies that have consistent revenue and manageable levels of debt.

With bonds, you lend your money to people doing something, typically a business or government entity, with an upfront understanding of the return you will receive and the date you will be repaid your principal. The return often comes as a fixed coupon rate, or yield. For example, if you buy a 10-year bond for $1,000 with a 5% coupon, your expectation would be that you would get $50 in interest each year for ten years, and then your $1,000 back at the end of the 10-year period.

Furthermore, for high quality investment-grade corporate bonds, the money you have lent typically is backed by the assets of a company—things of value such as equipment, inventory, receivables, land or intellectual property. So even if the company fails, as a bondholder you usually will get all or at least some of your money back upon liquidation of the company.

In the case of US Treasury bonds, where the "full faith and credit" of the United States backs the bonds, you are about 100% certain of receiving interest and your money back on time. Bonds range in reliability, from certainty of getting paid in the case of US Treasury bonds, to near certainty in the case of high quality corporate bonds, to uncertainty in the case of high yield bonds issued by companies on shaky financial footings.

Bonds are sensitive to rising interest rates (term risk) and default risk (the company can't pay its debts). When interest rates rise, bond prices fall, as existing bonds adjust to the pricing of new bonds being issued at the now higher interest rate. Alternatively, when interest rates fall, and new bonds are issued at lower interest rates, existing bonds with higher interest rates appreciate in value. A financial measure called duration reflects the sensitivity of a bond to interest rates. [18] So the price of a bond with long duration moves more when interest rates go up or down compared to a bond with shorter duration.

CHART 4.1   BONDS AS BUFFER IN BAD MARKETS
Cumulative Performance (%)

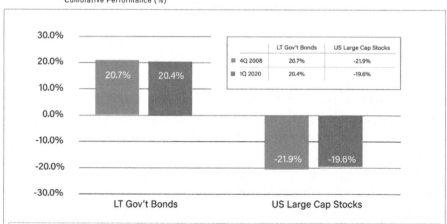

	LT Gov't Bonds	US Large Cap Stocks
■ 4Q 2008	20.7%	-21.9%
■ 1Q 2020	20.4%	-19.6%

Source: In US Dollars. US Large Cap is the S&P 500 Index; Treasury Bills are One-Month US Treasury Bills; 1-Month Treasury Bills Index is the IA SBBI US 30 Day TBill TR USD. Treasury Index data sourced from Ibbotson Associates, via Morningstar. S&P data © 2020 S&P Dow Jones Indices LLC, a division of S&P Global. All rights reserved. T-bills data provided by Morningstar. Past performance is no guarantee of future results. Indices are not available for direct investment. Their performance does not reflect the expenses associated with the management of an actual portfolio.

High quality bonds, particularly US Treasury bonds, provide a distinct form of diversification, and tend to have positive returns in "flight to quality" situations. These are times of economic, political and financial distress when investors sell equities and seek the most secure place for their money.

In the fourth quarter of 2008 during the subprime mortgage crisis, when large cap US stock sold off about 22%, long-term US Treasury bonds gained about 20%. Similarly, in the first quarter of 2020 during the covid crisis, when US stocks declined about 20%, long-term US Treasury bonds gained about 20%.

Non-governmental bonds, such as corporate bonds, have higher yields than US Treasury bonds and perform less well in times of market distress, because they have additional risks, including default, illiquidity and early call provisions (the issuing company can redeem the bond earlier than its stated term).

Given that Treasuries are the highest rated credit, the yield on Treasuries is typically lower than that of other bonds. In addition, given their fixed interest rates, Treasuries perform poorly in times of unanticipated inflation and rising interest rates. Alternatively, Treasury Inflation-Protected Securities (TIPS), which include a base return plus inflation, do better in an environment of rising and unanticipated inflation.

STOCKS

Stocks (equities) are the real generator of wealth for long-term investors. Stocks are the greatest source of return in your overall asset allocation and the greatest source of volatility. For example, in a portfolio split equally between stocks and bonds, stocks drive over three-quarters of the portfolio's volatility.

Equities are the best hand in the investing deck, and one you should play as much as your financial plan and risk tolerance allows. By owning stock, you share in a company's profits after all costs and expenses have been paid. Other contributors of capital to the company, such as bondholders, get paid before you do. However, you have unlimited upside to profit if the business is successful. As discussed previously, the equity risk premium, or the return to equity holders for taking risk above that of bonds, historically has been around 4.5%. Bond returns of 5.5% plus the equity risk premium of 4.5% equals the 10% long-term return of equities. (See **Charts 2.1** and **2.2** comparing the long-term returns of stocks to bonds.)

As a stockholder, your interests are closely aligned with the corporate executives running the company. Executive compensation almost always includes incentives to increase the company's stock price. Examples would be stock options and similar performance-based stock bonuses. An executive's personal wealth, therefore, is much more dependent on the price of the company's stock than its bonds. When companies borrow money via bonds, they want to borrow at the lowest cost possible and pay back as little as possible. If they can, they often will call in existing bonds and issue new bonds when interest rates are low, just the time when an investor does not want to get money back and have to reinvest it at the now lower interest rates.

Stocks provide reasonable protection against long-term inflation. Inflation is built into the labor and material used by companies, and is reflected in the products and services companies sell and the profits they earn. Earnings and dividends rise along with the rate of inflation. Stocks as an inflation hedge may not work so well in the short run, however. Notes David Swensen, "In 1973 and 1974, inflation eroded purchasing power by 37 percent and stock prices decreased by a total of 22 percent, hitting equity investors with a double whammy that caused losses of 51 percent in inflation-adjusted terms." [19]

Over longer periods, equity investment in different countries and regions should have similar returns adjusted for risk factors such as government control and intervention in the private sector, corporate governance issues (majority shareholders discriminating against minority shareholders), and company management favoring non-shareholder stakeholders, such as workers and the broader community over stockholders. In addition, investors in foreign equities assume foreign exchange exposure, which may provide some return variability in a portfolio, but no expected excess return over time.

Stocks, therefore, are where you receive the greatest long-term appreciation of your capital. In exchange for accepting the volatility of stock returns and the possibility of low-to-negative performance over long periods, you receive a return (equity risk premium) significantly above that of bonds, cash and inflation.

ASSET CLASSES HAVE SIMILAR RISK-ADJUSTED RETURNS

Stocks, bonds, and other asset classes have similar returns over time adjusted for risk. An investment which is producing above-average returns compared to others quickly attracts attention. There are too many experienced, knowledgeable, and hungry investors looking for market inefficiencies and outsized returns for opportunities to remain hidden for long. Investors pour money into the opportunity, which drives the excess return down to a rate of return commensurate with its risk (and sometimes below its risk, as momentum from stampeding investors causes the investment to be overbought).

Due to competition in capital markets, therefore, over long periods of time investments tend to have similar risk-adjusted returns. See **Chart 4.2** for a comparison of the risk-adjusted returns of asset classes as measured by the Sharpe ratio, which calculates return relative to its volatility. (For a definition of the Sharpe ratio see **Chart 6.8**).

CHART 4.2   SHARPE RATIOS OF DIFFERENT ASSET CLASSES

1926–2020	Sharpe Ratio
US Large Cap Stocks	0.37%
US Small Cap Stocks	0.32%
Long-Term Corp Bonds	0.39%
Long-Term Gov't Bonds	0.29%

Source: In US Dollars. US Large Cap Stocks is the S&P 500 Index; US Small Cap Stocks is the CRSP 6-10 Index; Long-Term Corp Bonds is the DFA Long-Term Government Bond Index; Long-Term Government Bonds Index is the 20-year US government bonds. Treasury Index data sourced from Ibbotson Associates, via Morningstar. CRSP data provided by the Center for Research in Security Prices. S&P data © 2020 S&P Dow Jones Indices LLC, a division of S&P Global. All rights reserved. Bonds data provided by Morningstar. Past performance is no guarantee of future results. Indices are not available for direct investment. Their performance does not reflect the expenses associated with the management of an actual portfolio.

SUMMARY

You can successfully reach your investment goals by sticking to the primary colors of investing—cash, bonds and stocks.

• Cash provides liquidity for near-term living expenses. Cash has little expectation of return above the rate of inflation.

• Bonds provide a more consistent, less volatile return than stocks. Bonds typically have a regular yield and the expectation of a return of principal.

• Stocks have a higher but more volatile return than bonds, with the expectation of a return significantly above the rate of inflation.

CHAPTER 5

Building Your Investment Portfolio

ASSET ALLOCATION

So, how to mix cash, bonds and stocks into a portfolio? Even for a Nobel Prize winner, asset allocation is not an exact science. When asked how he would allocate his retirement fund, Professor Harry Markowitz, father of modern portfolio theory and recipient of the 1990 Nobel Memorial Prize in Economic Sciences, said:

> I should have computed the historical co-variances of the asset classes and drawn an efficient frontier. Instead, I visualized my grief if the stock market went way up and I wasn't in it—or if it went way down and I was completely in it. My intention was to minimize my future regret. So I split my contributions 50/50 between bonds and equities.

Many people share Harry's view on asset allocation. In my experience, most people, when you take into account all of their assets, have around a 50/50 allocation between stocks and bonds/cash. This would include treating equity value in a home as a cash or bond-like investment. People tend to gravitate toward a balanced allocation, likely because, like Harry, they do not want the regret of seeing their investment portfolio decline drastically during stock market sell-offs, and they value the feeling of safety that bonds and cash give them.

In addition, since people's investment objectives have varying time frames, they sensibly keep some money in cash and bonds for nearer-term expenditures, and invest in stocks for longer-term growth. Young people may be saving to pay off student loans (shorter-term), for a down payment on a house (intermediate-term), and for their retirement (longer-term). Middle aged people may be saving for home improvements (shorter term), for their children's college education (intermediate-term), and for their retirement (longer-term). Older people who are retired need to pay their current living expenses (shorter-term), save some money to pay for their daughter's wedding (intermediate-term), and invest longer-term so that the after-inflation purchasing power of their wealth is maintained through what could be a thirty-plus year retirement.

Even older people tend to have more in stocks than suggested by rules of thumb such as "the proportion of bonds in your portfolio should equal your age." If you are 90, you might live to be 95 or 100, and having more than 10% in stocks may make sense, especially if you are mentally bucketing some of your wealth for your children and grandchildren. You therefore would be investing more aggressively in equities based on their life expectancies rather than your own. Additionally, you would be planning that when you die they would receive a step-up in basis on your appreciated stocks (they would not owe tax upon sale of the stocks for any gains accrued during your lifetime).

People do vary by how tolerant they are of volatility. In general, though, most people feel the pain of losses about twice as much as they feel the joy of gains, so they have a natural inclination to be more conservative than they probably should be with regard to the investments in their long-term investment portfolio. [20]

In addition, many people's tolerance for risk is situational—they are bold with their equity allocation when the market is soaring, and meek when it is collapsing. Investment advisory firms often have forms with questions that try to determine your tolerance for risk. But your risk tolerance may change over time, and you may find that how you think about risk today is different from how you act in the midst of a financial meltdown or melt up. If you need help, you can work with an investment advisor or financial planner to fine tune your mix of investments based on your life objectives and your sensitivity to volatility. More discussion on this in Chapter 10.

Investment allocations should also take into account unexpected life events and market environments. Since one does not know when the stock market will crash or negative life events will occur, it is sensible to model investment portfolios with these uncertainties in mind.

Almost everyone should have a cash reserve for unanticipated events such as job loss or a medical crisis. It may be unlikely that in a short time period you will lose your job, suffer a divorce, have a serious medical problem, and need to pay college tuition, all in the midst of a large market contraction, but it has happened before, and should be taken into consideration when determining your investment allocation.

What portfolio allocation is best for you? One you are comfortable with and can stay with in good markets and bad. Asked about how much an investor should have in equities, the great financier J.P. Morgan said they should "sell down to the sleeping point." [21] Your investments should not keep you up at night. Ideally, you will be comfortable with the amount of risk necessary to achieve your desired investment objectives. If you are not, then you may want to lower the bar for your investment objectives. Benefiting from long-term investing requires long-term commitment. You will maximize the chances of reaching your goals by staying the course with your portfolio allocation. As will be discussed in Chapter 7, being out of the market for even a handful of days can make a significant difference in the growth of your wealth.

To determine what level of volatility in your investment portfolio is right for you, imagine how you would feel if your portfolio had a negative "three-standard deviation event," such as in the 2007-2008 period, when the equity market was down 50%. As a rough calculation, assume your investment-grade bonds and cash will have a flat to slightly positive return in such a scenario. Then, multiply the percentage you have in equities by the percentage of the market decline. This will be the approximate amount your total portfolio would decline in the downturn.

For example, if you have a $1,000,000 portfolio that is invested 50% in equities and 50% in bonds, and the stock market goes down 50%, your rough approximation is that your portfolio will go down half of 50%, or 25%.

That's $250,000 of your $1,000,000 savings.

Are you comfortable with that? How do you think you would feel, and how do you think you would react?

Imagining these scenarios is a way to inoculate yourself against making emotional, reactive moves in the moment, such as liquidating your stock portfolio and going to cash. If such a down market does occur, you can remember that you previously thought through how you would react. Even if you are feeling nauseous and tempted to sell all your equities, the mere act of remembering that you already thought about this and promised yourself you would act in a disciplined manner will help push your thinking from the emotional, amygdala "fight or flight" part of your brain to the contemplative, prefrontal cortex "long-term planning" part of it.

It is worth noting that recovery times from these types of market drawdowns can be several years or more. You have to determine what tolerance you have for drawdowns and whether you have the ability to weather through them.

CHART 5.1 AVERAGE ANNUALIZED RETURNS AFTER MARKET DECLINE OF MORE THAN 10%
S&P 500, 1/1926–12/2020

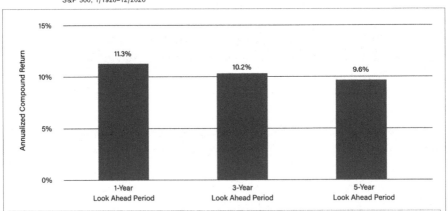

Source: Dimensional Fund Advisors. In US Dollars. Past performance is no guarantee of future results. Declines are defined as months ending with the market below the previous market high by at least 10%. Annualized compound returns are computed for the relevant time periods after each decline observed and averaged across all declines for the cutoff. There were 1,127 observations in the sample. January 1990-present: S&P 500 Total Returns Index. S&P data © 2020 S&P Dow Jones Indices LLC, a division of S&P Global. All rights reserved. January 1926-December 1989: S&P 500 Total Return Index, Stocks, Bonds, Bills and Inflation Yearbook™, Ibbotson Associates, Chicago. For illustrative purpose only. Index is not available for direct investment; therefore, its performance does not reflect the expenses associated with the management of an actual portfolio. There is always a risk that an investor may lose money.

DIVERSIFICATION

Combining different asset classes such as stocks and bonds increases the efficiency of your investment portfolio. That is, it helps you achieve a higher level of return for the same level of risk. This is because each asset class performs differently in different market environments, and in combination provide a more consistent return.

For example, US Treasury bonds tend to have positive returns in recessionary periods when interest rates and stocks decline. The defensive nature of Treasuries, therefore, offsets some of the negative returns of stocks during these periods. An example of this would be for the first quarter of 2020 during the coronavirus crisis, when the US equity market was down about 20% and Long-Term Government bonds were up about 20%.

CHART 5.2   DIVERSIFICATION SMOOTHS OUT RETURNS

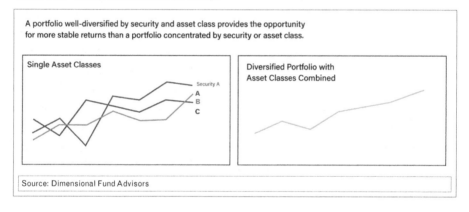

A portfolio well-diversified by security and asset class provides the opportunity for more stable returns than a portfolio concentrated by security or asset class.

Single Asset Classes

Security A
A
B
C

Diversified Portfolio with Asset Classes Combined

Source: Dimensional Fund Advisors

The benefit of diversification also applies at the security level. By investing in a large number of stocks, such as via an S&P 500 Index fund, you avoid the risk that the failure of any one company will have a significant negative effect on your portfolio. As noted earlier, Nobel laureate Professor Harry Markowitz called diversification "the only free lunch in finance." For almost no cost you can obtain the benefits of portfolio diversification by investing across a broad number of stocks and avoid the risk of having your investments concentrated in a few stocks.

Wall Street firms do not like investment-related benefits that are free. They like to charge investors for investment-related benefits, real or perceived. So they try to convince investors that their firm's investment fund or strategy adds beneficial diversification, diversification which will help an investor achieve superior risk-equivalent returns compared to a basic portfolio of stocks, bonds and cash. Phrases like "getting closer to the efficient frontier" are used quite often, the "efficient frontier" being a series of hypothetical portfolios that will give you the maximum return for a given level of risk.

A portfolio of indexed stocks and bonds, however, makes for a fairly diversified and efficient portfolio. For example, the S&P 500 Index has 505 stocks in it and covers about 80% of the US equity market by market capitalization. The Barclays Aggregate Bond Index includes most investment-grade bonds traded in the US. That is plenty of security diversification. And via index funds it costs very little to access this diversification.

CHART 5.3 PERFORMANCE FOR STOCK/BOND PORTFOLIO VS HEDGE FUNDS

	2008
US Stocks Market	-36.7%
US Bonds	5.2%
50/50 US Stocks & Bonds	-15.7%
Hedge Funds	-18.0%

A basic portfolio of stocks and bonds holds up well across a range of economic environments. A good example of this is in the period 2007-2008, when a 50/50 equity/bond portfolio did better than portfolios using alternative strategies such as hedge funds, private equity and real estate. A 50/50 stock/bond portfolio was down about 16% in 2008. Hedge funds as a group were down 18% on a reported basis in 2008,[22] and more likely down over 20% given that many managers stopped reporting their performance (see **Chart 5.3**).

Even the best of the best in using portfolios heavily weighted toward alternative investments, such as the Yale and Harvard endowments, were down about 30% for their fiscal years following the 2008 crisis, a combined loss of $17.8 billion.[23] And the equity/bond portfolio did far better in the 10-year period following the 2007-2008 crisis than much more complicated portfolios using alternative asset classes and strategies (see **Chart 5.5**). In addition, for a taxable investor, a simple stock and bond portfolio has an even more attractive after-tax risk/return profile than one using tax-inefficient alternative strategies such as hedge funds.

Therefore, when Wall Street comes a-knocking with pitches on strategies providing superior investment diversification, you can take a pass. Over-complexity and numerous non-core investments is a recipe for "deworsification," a term connoting an investment portfolio where additional investments no longer provide a benefit by diversifying away individual security risk or moderating broad macro factor risks. Instead, they add cost and unproductive complexity which erodes long-term investment returns.

SAMPLE ASSET ALLOCATION WITH CORE ASSET CLASSES

Below is a sample asset allocation to give you a flavor for a basic, low-cost global portfolio using core asset classes. **Chart 5.4** is a sample portfolio balanced 70/30 between stocks and bonds. There is a range of portfolios you can create by varying the mix of asset classes. As with Play-Doh, by mixing cash, bonds and stocks in different proportions you can create a portfolio suited to your return goals and risk tolerance.

The more desirous you are for higher returns and the more tolerant you are for volatility, the higher the equity allocation. A more conservative portfolio will have a higher weight in investment-grade bonds, which, as noted in Chapter 4, are on the more conservative end of the risk spectrum and have lower volatility and return expectations.

Other factors affecting your allocation include your current assets, foreseeable expenditures, life expectancy and your ability to generate new wealth, such as through your job or business. The more years you have ahead of you to earn wealth through your job or business, the more aggressive you can be in your allocation. If you are in retirement and what you have now is what you will live on for the rest of your life, the more thoughtful you have to be about your allocation.

A simple asset allocation such as that shown in **Chart 5.4** is a reasonable course for achieving your investment goals. As indicated in the chart, you can invest in a portfolio like this using a handful of low-cost mutual funds or ETFs or an indexed separate account. You do not need to add active managers to the mix. As will be discussed more in Chapter 7, there is a strong correlation between high fee funds and underperformance, since most managers underperform the market by about the amount of their fees.

Please keep in mind that the portfolio shown is not a recommendation for your particular situation, just an example of a simple, low-cost portfolio. In addition, whether a portfolio is in a taxable or tax-exempt/tax-deferred account, such as an IRA or 401(k), will also affect its composition. For example, in an IRA account you would have taxable bonds, as you are not taxed on the interest, whereas in a taxable account you might invest in tax-exempt bonds if you are in a high tax bracket.

CHART 5.4 SAMPLE 70/30 PORTFOLIO ALLOCATION

Asset Class	Target %	Fund	Mutual Fund/ ETF Ticker Symbol	Fund Expense Ratio % (as of 2021)
U.S. Equity	40	Vandguard Total Stock Market Index	VTSAX/VTI	0.04/0.03
Non-US Developed Equity	20	Vandguard Developed Markets Index	VTMGX/VEA	0.07/0.05
Emerging Market Equity	10	Vandguard Emerging Markets Index	VEMAX/VWO	0.14/0.10
Investment Grade Bonds	30	Vandguard Intermediate-Term Bond	VBILX/BIV	0.07/0.05
	100			

REBALANCING

Given market movements, your long-term allocation may stray from its initial percentages. For example, if your stock/bond allocation is 50/50, in a bull market where stocks are appreciating more than bonds it might move closer to 60/40.

You can rebalance your investment portfolio back to your preferred 50/50 allocation by reducing stocks and increasing bonds. Rebalancing can be done whenever your portfolio moves meaningfully from your target allocation.

For a taxable investor, there may be some benefit to annual tax-loss harvesting of portfolio positions that have a loss. That is, you sell positions that are below the value you purchased them to recognize or "harvest" a loss. These recognized losses are valuable, because they can be used to offset recognized gains in your portfolio. You thereby eliminate or reduce the money you pay in taxes on the recognized gains.

After a few years of positive markets, however, most of your equity positions will have unrecognized capital gains, and there will be fewer opportunities for tax-loss harvesting unless you are contributing new capital to your equity allocation.

THE ENDOWMENT PORTFOLIO MODEL

A handful of investors, such as the Yale University endowment, have better returns over time compared to the Base Case and the simple allocations discussed above in this chapter. Their superior returns, however, are largely due to special circumstances not replicable by the average investor. These include priority access to top venture capital and private equity managers, top investment research talent and opportunities to invest the endowment's money alongside private equity firm's capital in the most attractive private deals.

And even for Yale, much of its excess return, that is, returns above and beyond the Base Case over time, comes from venture capital funds investing in risky early-stage companies and private equity and real estate funds leveraging their investments. These private allocations are in effect riskier than a stock index fund tracking the S&P 500.

Many people running pension funds and investment advisory firms like to think that by imitating the Yale endowment model and allocating a sizable part of their portfolios to high-cost active alternative managers, they will outperform the Base Case. Studies have found, though, that pension plans do not generate returns better than their benchmarks, and there is no persistent performance, a hallmark of skill.[24]

David Swensen, the poster boy for the endowment model, tells individual investors not to try to ape the Yale endowment. When many in the financial industry are trying to sell investors on complicated portfolios with many different asset classes and alternative strategies similar to Yale's portfolio, David's message to the typical investor is keep it simple and invest in low-cost index funds.[25] You are not missing anything by not trying to replicate the Yale endowment portfolio, because neither you nor your investment advisor will be able to replicate Yale's portfolio or its returns.

A simple portfolio of indexed stock and bonds performs better than most of the elaborate, complex portfolios of institutional investors.[26] One study shows that for the 58-year period ending 2019, the average US endowment's return of 8.1% underperformed a 60/40 equity-bond benchmark return of 9.1%.[27] Another study concluded that endowment funds have underperformed passive investment by a significant margin over the past decade, with only a handful of endowments generating alpha, or returns above their benchmarks.[28] The proof, as it is said, is in the pudding.

You can see from institutional investment returns that few of these institutions' portfolio managers, advisors, consultants and managers are adding any value with regard to higher risk-equivalent investment returns. Even the most sophisticated investors in the US as represented by the top university endowments have underperformed, as shown in **Chart 5.5**. The ones that do show higher returns are often taking on greater risk via leveraged private equity, real estate and hedge funds, and sometimes leveraging their entire portfolio using borrowed funds. Therefore, they have a higher total risk exposure than a 60/40 stock and bond portfolio.[29]

CHART 5.5 ENDOWMENT PERFORMANCE OF ELITE UNIVERSITIES
10-YEAR PERIOD ENDING JUNE 30, 2019

School	10-Year Annialized Return %	Assets (Billions $)
Brown University	10.0	4.2
Dartmouth College	10.7	5.7
Harvard University	8.5	40.9
Yale University	11.1	30.3
Cornell University	8.6	7.3
University of Pennsylvania	10.3	14.7
Colimbia University	10.2	11
Princeton University	11.6	26.1
Stanford University	10.2	27.7
Massachusetts Institue of Technology	11.6	17.4
Duke University	10.4	8.6
Bowdoin College	12.0	1.7
Mean for colleges and universitiests (149 insititutions)	8.6	N/A
S&P 500	14.7	

Source: Cambridge Associates; company reports. Barron's, *Harvard and Yale Missed the Stock Market Rally. Here's Why.* October 12, 2019.

Pension funds and other institutional investors who have upped their allocations to alternative investments over the last 20 years have generally failed their responsibilities as fiduciaries. Underlying all investment decisions of US pension funds is the requirement that the trustees who oversee plan assets make prudent decisions with regard to investments made on behalf of plan beneficiaries. The trustees also have a duty to act loyally to the plan beneficiaries whom they serve.

A pension board may delegate authority to the plan's investment officers and outside investment experts, but the board is still responsible for prudently selecting and responsibly overseeing these agents. This includes only incurring expenses that are reasonable. The whole point of the standard is to protect beneficiaries from incompetence and self-dealing on the part of those managing the beneficiaries' money, and to maximize the chances that the beneficiaries receive their benefits.

Would you consider it prudent to invest plan assets in a portfolio of high cost alternative investments which have a 75% or greater chance of underperforming the Base Case? No. Most people would say that speculating in this manner with taxpayer funded pension plan assets is imprudent. But it's what most pension plans do, like moths to a flame.

Some allocators contend that alternative investments provide beneficial diversification and reduce portfolio volatility. But over the long term, and pension funds are long-term investors, what counts is total return to provide the benefits promised beneficiaries. Modestly moderating the volatility of portfolio returns in certain time frames at the expense of significantly lower growth longer term is an unwise trade.

Adding insult to injury to plan beneficiaries, pension plan managers, on top of their poor risk/reward decision-making in selecting investments, often hire biased advisors. Under a "safe harbor" provision of pension law, a pension fund manager can claim they are fulfilling their fiduciary duty if they hire and rely on the advice of investment consultants or other advisors with specialized investment knowledge in asset allocation, manager selection and portfolio management. Although plan sponsors can hire consultants to advise them on such matters, the pension fund itself must see to it that the hiring of the consultants is done in a responsible manner. And here many fail in their responsibilities.

Pension funds often pay consultants more for research and recommendations on alternative investments such as hedge funds and private equity funds than for recommending simple allocations of index investments. Consultants who are paid higher fees for advising on alternative investments have an inherent conflict of interest in the advice they are providing to pension funds. Any fiduciary who is paying a consultant a higher fee for advice on alternative investments should not be surprised if the recommendation is to invest more in alternative investments. Some consultants also receive payments via "soft dollars" from the fund managers they recommend to their pension fund clients.

These soft dollars are used to pay a host of costs of the consultant and adds to their bottom line. Do you think a pension fund has met its fiduciary standard of care when it hires an investment consultant offering conflicted advice?

By wallowing in a morass of needless complexity, some pension fund investment managers and the consultants they hire provide themselves a form of job security. They create a contraption that only they can operate, and give boards the impression that the wheels will fall off of pension performance if the managers and their consultants are not in the driver's seat. It's an elaborate crock. They do all of this while being wined and dined and taken on excursions by alternative investment managers growing fat on the exorbitant fees the pension funds pay them for mediocre performance. Pension funds should be held accountable for their contemptible decision-making, and the likely subpar investment results their allocations will produce.

SUMMARY

Wall Street manufactures many different products and stories because they are in the business of selling investments. Institutional investors like to fuss over complex asset allocations and investment strategies because it helps justify their jobs and compensation. Odds are, though, that by keeping your asset allocation simple you will do better than people investing in high cost, complex asset classes.

• Define your near-term, intermediate-term and long-term investment objectives. Have your investment portfolio take these various objectives into account.

• Have a cash reserve on hand for unexpected life events such as job loss or a health crisis.

• Determine what level of portfolio volatility will allow you to sleep at night.

• A simple portfolio of cash, bonds and stocks will serve you well.

CHAPTER 6

Non-Core Asset Classes

In this section I touch on a number of non-core, "alternative" asset classes. These include high yield bonds, private equity, venture capital and hedge funds. Some investors use non-core asset classes for investment diversification, and some believe they can add additional return.

You do not need to invest in non-core asset classes to be a successful investor. You are likely to be better off, actually, if you avoid them altogether. Compared to a portfolio using core asset classes, whatever diversification non-core asset classes may provide to a portfolio are usually outweighed by their costs and lower expected risk-adjusted returns.

If you believe in a simple, low-cost investment plan with core asset classes, you can skip this chapter. If you would like to read on, note that my comments on alternative asset classes are general and only touch on key considerations. If intrigued, further exploration may be in store for you.

Non-core asset classes fail to meet at least one of the following three criteria which define core asset classes:

1) are based on a central function in a capitalistic economy and rely on markets, not active management, to generate returns;

2) represent a broad and deep investable market; and

3) add a fundamentally useful, differentiable characteristic to a portfolio.[30]

For example, alternative strategies such as hedge funds may have low correlation (degree to which two securities move in relation to each other) to stocks in ordinary market environments. However, they may become highly correlated to stocks in negative markets when volatility spikes and investors flee riskier assets for the safe havens of US Treasury bonds and cash. Additionally, alternative strategies often rely on active security selection and invest in illiquid securities with thin trading volumes and wide spreads (the difference between the price at which a buyer is willing to buy and a seller is willing to sell).

The market sell-off in 2007-2008 was a good stress test of how well alternative asset classes provide useful diversification and low correlation to equity markets during a time when your portfolio needs it most. They failed. The result was similar in 2020. For example, the flagship hedge fund, Pure Alpha II, of the largest hedge fund manager, Bridgewater, was down 20% in the first quarter of 2020. This performance was slightly worse than the -19.6% performance of the S&P 500 Index. Bridgewater's "all-weather" Pure Alpha II strategy proved to be neither all-weather nor pure alpha, but a collection of market exposures adding no value relative to an allocation using core asset classes.

Sensible investors avoid non-core asset classes.

DAVID SWENSEN

In addition, for an investor to achieve superior performance with alternative investments such as hedge funds, venture capital and private equity, the investor has to either be very lucky or very skilled at manager selection. Few investors are skilled enough to consistently select top-performing managers of any sort. You are therefore better off sticking to the core asset classes of stocks, bonds and cash. Says David Swensen, arguably the most talented alternative investment allocator of our time, "Understanding the difficulty of identifying superior hedge-fund, venture-capital, and leveraged-buyout investments leads to the conclusion that hurdles for casual investors stand insurmountably high. . . . Sensible investors avoid non-core asset classes." [31]

HIGH YIELD BONDS

High yield corporate bonds have a risk and return profile between that of stocks and US Treasury bonds. In contrast to Treasury bonds, which play a valuable role in an investor's portfolio because they are default-free, noncallable, extremely liquid and perform well in times of market stress, investment-grade corporate bonds, high yield bonds, foreign bonds, and asset-backed securities have a higher correlation to the equity market, which undermines their usefulness as diversifying assets in portfolio construction. These include: [32]

Credit Risk: High yield bonds are issued by companies that typically have high levels of debt and uncertain business prospects. Defaults occur regularly, and more often in times of economic stress. Triple-A rated corporate bond ratings have nowhere to go but down.

Illiquidity: Corporate bonds are infrequently traded, and liquidity is even worse in bad markets.

Callability: An issuer can redeem bonds after a certain date at a fixed price, and issuers tend to call in higher-yielding debt when interest rates are low. This leaves an investor having to reinvest the proceeds at lower interest rates. Callability also prevents a bondholder from profiting from an improving credit market as interest rates decline and bonds appreciate in value. Callability benefits equity holders at the expense of bondholders.

Says David Swensen,

Junk-bond investors cannot win. When fundamentals improve, stock returns dominate bond returns. When rates decline, noncallable bonds provide superior risk-adjusted returns. When fundamentals deteriorate, junk-bond investors fall along with equity investors. Well-informed investors avoid the no-win consequences of high-yield fixed income investing.[33]

CHART 6.1 RETURN AND RISK OF BONDS COMPARED TO EQUITIES 1990-2020

1990 to 2020	Annualized Return	Std. Deviation	Sharpe Ratio
US Equities	10.50%	18.36	0.43%
High Yield Bonds	7.09%	7.99	0.66%
Invest. Grade Corp.Bonds	6.87%	6.99	0.61%
US Treasury Bonds	5.64%	5.12	0.59%
Municipal Bonds	5.71%	6.58	0.47%
Treasury Bills	2.64%	0.87	
Source: Dimensional Fund Advisors			

CHART 6.2 HIGH YIELD HAS HIGH CORRELATION TO EQUITIES IN DOWN MARKETS

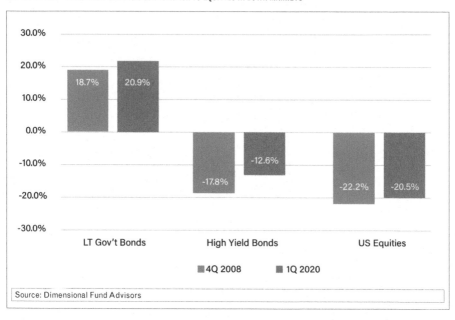

Source: Dimensional Fund Advisors

In addition, shareholders benefit by reducing the value of a company's debt obligations, and corporate management teams are shareholders. Corporations have an incentive to leverage corporate earnings for the benefit of shareholders at the expense of bondholders.

High yield managers, whether they be mutual fund or hedge fund managers, like to promote the idea that they can rummage through the discount rack of high yield bonds and find ones that provide more upside and less downside than the market. This looks not to be the case. S&P Dow

Jones Indices reports that for the 15-year period ending 2020, 98.47% of active high yield funds underperformed their benchmark.[34] For the 15-year period the annualized performance of the Barclays US Corporate High Yield Index was 7.50%, whereas the equal-weighted return of the active managers was 5.15%.[35] For some perspective, $100,000 compounding at 7.50% for 15 years is $295,888, and $100,000 compounding at 5.15% for 15 years is $212,392. That's $83,496, or 28% less.

If you want a return and volatility between that of equities and bonds, rather than investing in high yield bonds, you can take a "barbell" approach and combine equities with high quality bonds such as US Treasuries. You will get a better risk-adjusted return investing in the unlimited upside of stocks combined with the defensive characteristics of US Treasuries than the constrained potential of corporate and high yield bonds. The stock/bond combination is also more tax efficient, because dividends and capital gains from equities are taxed at a lower rate than income received from taxable bonds, which are taxed at the ordinary income rate. Also, US Treasuries are exempt from state and local taxes.

TAX-EXEMPT BONDS

Tax-exempt bonds are typically issued by states and municipalities, and the interest on the bonds is exempt from federal and sometimes state and local income taxes. The tax exemption is the government's incentive for you to support local investment in things such as airports, highways, utilities, public housing, and hospitals.

High quality tax-exempt bonds have a return similar to US Treasuries adjusted for the incremental risk in municipal bonds. The main risk is callability. Municipal debt often is issued with inexpensive call provisions in which borrowers can repurchase and refund debt at lower interest rates. Unsophisticated retail buyers, which constitute a large percentage of the market for municipal bonds, ask too little in terms of yield for giving an issuer the ability to call in the bond. [36]

In addition, the secondary market in municipal bonds is not very transparent or efficient. Bid-ask spreads in buying and selling bonds (that is, the difference between the price you pay for a bond when buying it and the price you receive when selling it) can be high. This means higher costs and lower returns for investors. If you are an individual, it's generally better to access municipal bonds through a large, low-cost, sophisticated buyer who has the expertise and size to purchase bonds more efficiently than individual investors.

Also, there is always the risk that legislators may modify or do away with the tax-exempt status of municipal bonds, such as if Congress were to limit or eliminate the federal tax exemption for municipal debt.

Tax-exempt bonds do, however, give an investor some flexibility as to how to apportion their equity and fixed income investments among their taxable and tax-exempt accounts, and can provide favorable after-tax returns for investors in high tax brackets. Says Swensen, "Money-market instruments carry no call options and trade in relatively efficient transparent markets. Short-term tax-exempt money-market funds deserve serious consideration." [37]

ASSET-BACKED SECURITIES

Asset-backed securities, such as those backed by home mortgages, have prepayment risk. If interest rates decline, homeowners are able to prepay their mortgages and refinance at lower interest rates. This hurts the holders of mortgage-backed securities, who receive capital back at a time when interest rates have fallen. This dynamic also works against investors who purchase bonds as a safe haven against times of financial distress and deflation, when interest rates decline due to slow or declining economic growth. If rates rise, borrowers tend not to repay their mortgages, leaving the asset-backed security buyer with bonds that are earning less than the going rate for bonds with similar maturities.

The payoff waterfalls of certain asset-backed securities can be very complex. For example, for mortgaged backed securities (MBS), senior securities have priority over junior securities with regard to the cash flow from the payments coming from the underlying mortgages. If some borrowers default on their mortgages, the senior MBS receive their interest payments first, and the junior MBS bear the brunt of any shortfall from reduced interest payments resulting from the borrower defaults. As an investor you should be wary of any investment you do not understand well. It takes a very sophisticated investor to parse out the value of various types of asset-backed securities. In addition, the fees active bond managers charge to do this usually outweigh any benefit to investment returns resulting from their analysis.

Even the creators of asset-backed securities did not expect the implosion of mortgage-backed bonds during the financial crisis of 2007 and 2008. Residential mortgage-backed securities (RMBS) and commercial mortgage-backed securities (CMBS), which collapsed in the 2007-2008 subprime crisis, are examples of mismatched risk and investor expectations. Individual and institutional investors around the world thought they were buying safe, highly-rated securities backed by residential and commercial mortgages. Instead, with these derivative products, investors were way overpaying for returns relative to their risks. The overpayment was pocketed upfront by investment banks and other firms in the asset-backed security food chain, the largesse paid out in bonuses and exercised stock options for bank employees. The end investor and the taxpayer via their elected governments were left to clean up the mess. For years to come, everyone will be paying, via higher taxes, the cost of the debt incurred by national governments to bail out their financial systems and economies which were destabilized by these injurious investment products.

FOREIGN BONDS

When owning foreign bonds, you are exposed to the policy decisions of foreign governments, which may not be supportive of foreign bondholders. Also, these bonds are oftentimes priced in currencies other than the US dollar. This currency exposure provides no expected return, and has risks. Non-US dollar currencies often depreciate against the dollar in negative global market environments. The flight to quality to US assets drives up the demand for the US dollar relative to other currencies. Some investors will try to reduce this volatility by hedging their currency exposure, but there is a cost in doing this. Writes Swensen, "Foreign-currency denominated bonds play no role in well-constructed investment portfolios." [38]

HYBRIDS AND DERIVATIVES

There are a host of investment products that are combinations or derivatives of stocks and bonds. Convertible bonds, for example, pay a coupon like a bond, and have the ability to convert into equity at a certain price. With a convertible bond, you typically get a lower coupon but the possibility of participating in the upside should the equity do well.

Wall Street investment banks have earned a good part of their fortunes by packaging risk and return in products and selling them to investors who do not fully understand the true nature of the risks in the products. The investors in effect are overpaying for the return provided by the product relative to its risk. The difference between the return the buyer is overpaying for and the actual risk/return of the product's underlying investments is what the investment bank is arbitraging and pocketing as profit.

Structured products are an example of this. With structured products, banks carve up the return of the equity market and sell you pieces of it in modified risk/return formats. For example, in a structured note based on the S&P 500, the note pays you the S&P's return for any given year up to 10%, and shields you from losses up to 10%. Returns above 10% go to the bank, and any loss more than 10% goes to you. That may sound good to you, because you have been told that the historical return of the S&P 500 is around 10%, and you want to protect yourself in the event of a market decline.

The returns of the S&P 500, however, vary quite a bit from year to year. For example, in 2019, the S&P 500 was up 32%. You would have given up 22% of return with the structured product (32% - 10% = 22%). When returns are negative, they often are very negative. During the financial panic of 2008 the US equity market was down 36%. You would have been stuck holding the bag in a year like 2008, where your return would be -26% (-36% + 10% = -26%).

Another catch is that a structured product may only give you the *price return* of the S&P 500, not the *total return*, which includes dividends. Assume dividends are 2% on US equities. Without the dividend, in a positive return year your return is 2% less, and in a negative return year your return is 2% worse. For example, in a year when the total return of the S&P 500 is 10%, your return would be 8%. And in a year when the S&P is down 10%, your return would be -12%. Over time, with structured products like this you wind up with a low-to-mid-single-digit return. Probably not what you had in mind, and likely worse than what you could achieve with a risk-equivalent mix of stocks and bonds.

You are likely best off just combining the basics—stocks, bonds and cash—in a manner that suits your financial plan and tolerance for volatility, and avoiding the higher fees and costs of hybrid and derivative products.

CHART 6.3   STRUCTURED PRODUCT ON S&P 500

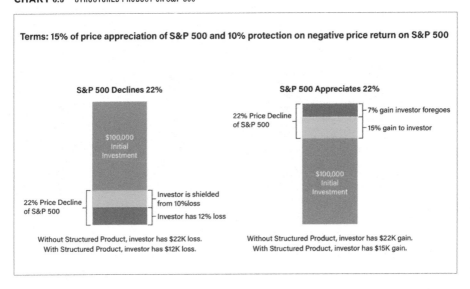

Terms: 15% of price appreciation of S&P 500 and 10% protection on negative price return on S&P 500

S&P 500 Declines 22%

$100,000 Initial Investment

22% Price Decline of S&P 500

Investor is shielded from 10%loss

Investor has 12% loss

Without Structured Product, investor has $22K loss.
With Structured Product, investor has $12K loss.

S&P 500 Appreciates 22%

22% Price Decline of S&P 500

7% gain investor foregoes

15% gain to investor

$100,000 Initial Investment

Without Structured Product, investor has $22K gain.
With Structured Product, investor has $15K gain.

REAL ESTATE

Real estate falls between equities and bonds in terms of risk and return. Some allocators see real estate as a core asset class providing a distinct form of diversification, while others see it as a hybrid with equity and bond-like attributes. Real estate has bond-like attributes due to income from long-term leases, and equity-like attributes due to the residual value of property. Real estate has returned about 8% annualized historically, between the 10% return for equities and the 5.5% return for bonds.

Real estate can provide some portfolio diversification. Although it is highly correlated to equities, real estate has had different returns than equities over certain time periods. Real estate also generally provides a good hedge against inflation. The market value of real estate is closely linked to its replacement cost, that is, what it would cost today to rebuild an existing building. The cost of land, labor and materials used to construct a building rise along with inflation, and leases adjust to inflation over time as well.

One issue for taxable investors, however, is that Real Estate Investment Trusts (REITS) are required to distribute 90% of their earnings to shareholders through dividends. These dividends are taxed as ordinary income, whereas equity dividends are taxed at a lower rate. Given their relative tax inefficiency, REITS are best held in tax-advantaged accounts.

CHART 6.4 PERFORMANCE OF REITS & LARGE CAP US STOCKS
Annualized Return (%)

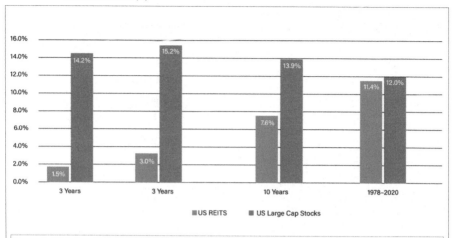

Source: In US Dollars. US Large Cap is the S&P 500 Index; REITS is the Dow Jones US Select REIT Index. S&P data © 2020 S&P Dow Jones Indices LLC, a division of S&P Global. All rights reserved. Past performance is no guarantee of future results. Indices are not available for direct investment. Their performance does not reflect the expenses associated with the management of an actual portfolio.

Publicly traded REITS and private real estate partnerships invest in similar types of properties—commercial office buildings, apartment complexes, industrial warehouses and shopping malls. Their returns, however, have differed widely during some time periods. This is largely due to the private investments being priced infrequently. Some investors find the "stale pricing" of private real estate investments appealing, because it lowers the volatility of return of the investor's real estate portfolio compared to publicly traded REITS.

The long-term return of private real estate investment adjusted for risk, however, is actually lower than that of publicly traded REITS, which have lower management and administrative costs. For the 25-year period ending 2017, publicly traded REITS returned 10.9%, and private real estate funds returned 7.6%. [39]

Says Larry Swedroe,

> For the privilege of investing with the greatest institutional managers, many of whom are not available to the general public, and in return for sacrificing the daily liquidity available with public REITs, the private, illiquid institutional

investments underperformed by 3.3 percentage points a year for 25 years. As bad as that sounds, the reality was actually far worse. The reason is that the private real estate investments used much higher amounts of leverage.[40]

David Swensen agrees that unless an investor can identify unusually attractive private real estate deals, gaining real estate exposure through publicly traded REITS makes the most sense. Private REITS, with their heavy fees and poor investment prospects, should be avoided, says Swensen.

> Although exceptions exist, for individual investors, publicly traded real estate securities generally provide reasonably low-cost exposure to relatively high-quality pools of real estate assets. Unfortunately, with few exceptions, privately offered retail real estate partnerships provide exposure to real estate at such obscenely high cost that the individual investor stands no chance of earning fair returns. [41]

You are not missing anything, then, by not investing in "institutional quality" private real estate funds. All that has really meant historically is getting worse returns than you would have received by buying a low-cost index REIT fund. The greater the simplicity and transparency of an asset class, the more likely it trades on fair terms to the investor.

ALTERNATIVE INVESTMENTS: THE EMPEROR'S NEW CLOTHES

What about private investments that are off the beaten path from stocks and bonds, such as private equity, venture capital and hedge funds? Aren't there opportunities for excess returns in alternative investments?

Based on my 25 years of investing across all asset classes, including alternative investments, my opinion for the individual investor and most institutional investors is this: you don't need to invest in any "alternative investment" to be a successful investor. Actually, you are more likely to underperform the Base Case if you do, because due to their higher fees the average return for alternative investments is below the average return for a risk-equivalent basket of indexed stocks and bonds. David Swensen's comments on private equity apply generally to alternative investments:

"In fact, only top-quartile or top-decile funds produce returns sufficient to compensate for private equity's greater illiquidity and higher risk. In the absence of truly superior fund selection skills (or extraordinary luck), investors should stay far, far away from private equity investments." [42]

In the absence of truly superior fund selection skills (or extraordinary luck), investors should stay far, far away from private equity investments.

DAVID SWENSEN

For alternative investments, you are paying relatively high fees to managers to invest in companies or securities you hope will generate a return that outperforms the market on a risk-equivalent basis. These fees vary, but they range around 2% management fee and 20% performance, or incentive fee. For private equity funds these incentive fees are oftentimes over a hurdle, such as 8%.

So, for example, say an alternative fund manager gets a 10% annual return investing your money, which is the long-term historical return of equities. A 2% management fee would go to the manager, so your return is down to 8%, and then the manager would take a 20% fee on that (.2 x 8 = 1.6), so your return is down to 6.4%. There are also administrative costs of running a fund, and other significant costs for certain strategies, such as trading costs or deal fees. These can range from .25% to several percent or more.

In addition, Fund of Funds (FOFs), which are managers who pool individual private equity funds or hedge funds so that smaller investors can access them, charge their own fees. These can be 1% or more in management fees and around 10% incentive fees.

What you have, then, is one-quarter to one-half of the market return being consumed by manager costs and fees. If the stock market historically returns 10% annually, an alternative manager's underlying investments have to be returning 13% to 20% before fees just to break even with the market return of 10%. They would have to be even higher to provide you a positive return relative to the market, and even higher adjusted for risk, because many private equity and other alternative strategies use leverage, which makes these strategies that much more risky. Writes Swensen:

By paying buyout partnership sponsors 20 percent of all
gains, the fund investors compensate the fund manager
with a significant portion of leveraged market gains over
which the fund manager exercises no control and for which
the fund manager deserves no credit. The large majority
of buyout funds fail to add sufficient value to overcome a
grossly unreasonable fee structure. [43]

After their fees, few alternative managers are able to outperform
the market equivalent. Additionally, chances are very low that you as
an individual investor can access the few managers that do outperform,
and pick these managers consistently over time prior to their periods of
outperformance.

Therefore, leave finding the few alternative managers that outperform to
the handful of endowments and professional investors capable of doing this.
You will almost certainly be better off passing on all of these alternative
investments, in whatever form, and just accessing the Base Case using
stocks, bonds and cash.

Wall Street salespeople and institutional investors who get paid to
research and invest in alternative investments like to talk about how
alternative investments provide diversified sources of non-correlated
returns, which help smooth and improve your compound investment return
over time.

From a portfolio construction standpoint, though, alternative
investments are not a particularly good diversifier of investment return,
because they generally have a high correlation to equity markets in periods
of economic distress and market declines, periods when you most need
diversification and low correlation to equities. The recession of 2007-2008
and the covid crisis of 2020 are good examples of this.

Correlations of private equity (0.71) and hedge funds (0.79) to stocks
have been quite high. Their returns are largely explained by equity market
returns. Private equity and venture capital funds significantly depend upon
robust public equity markets to sell their private investments. Private equity
firms have the best exit opportunities when publicly traded companies are
doing acquisitions, and public companies do more acquisitions when the
economy is strong and they are flush with cash and their stock prices are up.
Venture capital firms, too, need good public markets for exits, and for larger

private companies to be doing well for a healthy market to exist for private acquisitions. REITS and infrastructure investments such as MLPs also have high correlations to equities, particularly in times of strong negative equity market returns.

Concludes Burton Malkiel, "I would also steer clear of hedge-fund and private-equity and venture-capital funds. These can be great money-makers for the fund managers who pocket large management fees and 20 percent of the profits, but individual investors are unlikely to benefit." [44]

IPOs

Initial public offerings (IPOs) have not been a source for investment outperformance. Five years after their initial issuance, IPOs have been found to underperform the stock market by over two percentage points annually.[45] It is generally not a good idea to buy an IPO just after it begins trading at prices higher than the IPO price. Underperformance often kicks in about six months after the IPO. This is when the "lock-up period," the time after the IPO when insiders are prohibited from selling stock to the public, ends. Once the lock-up period ends, insiders sell and the stock price often declines.

Individual investors are at an additional disadvantage when investing in IPOs. Writes Burton Malkiel, "You will never be allowed to buy the really good IPOs at the initial offering price. The hot IPOs are snapped up by the big institutional investors or the very best wealthy clients of the underwriting firm." [46]

PRIVATE EQUITY

Private equity centers on investment in non-publicly traded companies. This can involve investing in the debt or equity of an existing private company, acquiring a private company or taking a public company private. A transaction involving buying a private company "a buyout," often involves significant amounts of debt. Capital raised by selling debt is what is used to buy out current stockholders and acquire a controlling interest in the company. Investment funds that sponsor private equity investments and transactions are sometimes called *buyout funds*.

Buyout funds are generally a poor investment for most investors, says David Swensen.[47]

The underlying company investments in buyout funds differ from their public market counterparts only in degree of balance sheet risk and in degree of liquidity. The higher debt and lower liquidity of buyout deals demand higher compensation in the form of superior returns to investors. Unfortunately for private equity investors, in recent decades buyout funds delivered lower returns than comparable marketable securities positions, even before adjusting for risk.[48]

Stock in private companies is also less frequently valued, from quarterly to annually, compared to public company stock which is valued by buyers and sellers every day markets are open. For private real estate, the intervals between valuations can be even longer.

Private equity managers typically invest in smaller and often more highly leveraged companies than the large, established companies that make up the S&P 500 Index. In addition, private companies are not able to access lower-cost financing provided by public capital markets. This makes the typical private equity investment inherently more volatile and riskier compared to companies constituting equity indexes such as the S&P 500. Writes Swensen,

> Leveraged-buyout transactions involve private ownership of mature corporate entities that have greater-than-usual levels of debt on their balance sheets. The high levels of leverage produce a correspondingly high degree of variability in outcomes, both good and bad. Leveraged-buyout investments, in the absence of value-adding activities by the transaction sponsor, simply increase the risk profile of the company.[49]

There is an argument that private companies benefit from having much more time and flexibility to implement their business models, and that private investments benefit from an illiquidity premium. An illiquidity premium is the additional return you may receive in exchange for locking up your money and not being able to sell or "liquidate" it readily for cash.

How significant and persistent illiquidity premiums are is a matter of academic debate. It has been suggested that institutional investors pay a higher price for a lower expected return in private investments because these infrequently priced investments have lower volatility and moderate paper drawdowns compared to publicly traded investments.[50] This illiquidity may help investors not sell at a market bottom, and also allows them to take on more risk because it's not as visible due to how it is priced.

With regard to the operating flexibility of private companies, there is some truth to this, but the advantages of private ownership are overstated. I remember Mark Walter, CEO of Guggenheim, who I worked under for a time at Guggenheim Investment Advisory, saying that there isn't that much difference between running a public and a private company. For a private company you still report to a board and have to produce results for investors in a reasonable time frame.

Some investors will cite return calculations showing that the average return of private equity funds outperforms an indexed equity investment, but that ignores the effect of leverage. That highly leveraged private equity may outperform indexed equity investments is not much of a boast given the higher inherent risk as Swensen notes. In addition, it is not practical for an investor to get the average return by indexing their private equity investments. An investor is forced to select a limited number of private equity funds, and as shown in **Chart 6.5**, that is a risky proposition because there is significant variability in the returns of private equity funds.

Investing in a private equity Fund of Funds which invests in a number of individual private equity funds is not a solution. The Fund of Funds' extra layer of fees and the more mediocre funds open to them make for unattractive returns relative to indexing the equity market.

If you face a banker or broker pitching a private equity product and how private equity outperforms, ask them for a compilation of the performance for all the private equity funds their firm has sponsored over the past 20 years. They won't have it. Which tells you something about what their priorities are: selling products and generating fees for themselves in the hope of good returns, not actually producing above-average long-term returns for their investors. They deal in enticing investors with the expectation of gaining superior returns, not consistently delivering them. Of course, the private equity offerings banks are pitching will sound appealing. Bankers and brokers are professional salespeople and know which buttons to push. "Investors require unusual self-confidence to ignore the widely

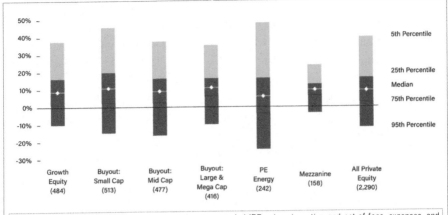

CHART 6.5 DISPERSION OF FUND-LEVEL RETURNS ACROSS PRIVATE EQUITY STRATEGIES
As of Second Quarter 2016, Vintage Years 1986-2014

Source: Cambridge Associates LLC. Private indexes are pooled IRRs since inception and net of fees, expenses, and carried interest. Number of funds included in groupings shown under label. Past performance is not indicative of future results.

hyped non-core investments and to embrace the quietly effective core investments," writes Swensen.[51]

Chances are private equity offerings will do worse than indexing equities. Writes Swensen:

> …in aggregate, buyout investments fail to match public market alternatives. After adjusting for the higher level of risk and the greater degree of illiquidity in buyout transactions, publicly traded equity securities gain a clear advantage.[52]

> Because buyout transactions by their very nature involve higher-than-market levels of leverage, the basic buyout-fund-to-marketable-security comparison fails the apples-to-apples standard. To produce a fair comparison, consider the impact of applying leverage to the hypothetical public market investments. Comparably timed, comparably sized, and comparably leveraged investments in the S&P 500 produced an astonishing 86% annual return. The risk-adjusted marketable security result exceeded the buyout result by 50 percentage points per year. [53]

But, because the riskier, more leveraged buyout positions
ought to generate higher returns, sensible investors recoil
at the buyout industry's deficit relative to public market
alternatives. On a risk-adjusted basis, marketable equities win
in a landslide. [54]

Treat private equity like the tempting candy bars at the checkout counter.
Remind yourself that they look appealing, but they are empty calories, and
not good for the health of your wealth. Look away and move on.

VENTURE CAPITAL

Venture capital returns are similar to public equity returns, but investing
in startup and late-stage venture companies is inherently more risky than
investing in large, established companies such as those in the S&P 500.
Venture investors do not receive returns adequately compensating for
this risk.[55] As with private equity, only if investors receive top-quartile,
or even top-decile, performance do venture capital returns justify the risk
incurred."[56] Swensen says,

> After adjustment for risk, the overwhelming majority of
> venture capital fails to produce acceptable risk-adjusted
> returns....[57] Suppliers of funds to the venture capital
> industry generally realize poor risk-adjusted returns.
> Sensible individual investors look elsewhere for investment
> performance. [58]

Accessing top-quartile or top-decile managers is hard to come by.
Top venture firms can pick and choose their investors, and often ration
investment even among their preferred investors—a handful of institutional
investors and wealthy individuals.[59] Says Swensen, "The top-tier venture
partnerships, essentially closed to new money, enjoy superior access to
deals, entrepreneurs, and capital markets. Exclusion from the venture
capital elite disadvantages all but the most long-standing, most successful
limited partners." [60]

Venture capital-backed start-ups care about the source of their funds. Investors with connections and helpful expertise are important to new companies looking to expand quickly. Venture capital funds that accept money from new investors may only have access to second-rate investment opportunities.[61]

Returns for venture capital funds are feast or famine. A few big winners offset the losses or ho-hum returns of most venture investments. Given the positive skewness of returns, that is returns dependent on a few winners, when a fund misses, it misses big, and the underperformance relative to equity market returns is severe.

HEDGE FUNDS

Having researched and invested in hedge funds for over twenty-five years for some of the largest institutional and private investors around the world, I would say the odds of you adding value to your portfolio return over time by investing in hedge funds is low, low to the point of it not being worth the effort. Few hedge fund managers generate an attractive risk-adjusted return after fees. The high fees are just too big a hurdle to overcome. And any portfolio diversification you might get is not worth the returns you give up. The risk/return of hedge funds is unattractive relative to the return you can get by investing passively in stocks and bonds via low-cost index funds.

There are a couple dozen hedge fund managers that generate true alpha, that is, return in excess of the risk taken by what they are investing in. Many are closed and you likely do not have access to them. Your chances, or any other person's chances, of consistently picking hedge funds that produce significant alpha going forward is about zero. You are missing nothing, therefore, if you check hedge funds and related alternative mutual funds and ETFs off your investment list.

HEDGE FUND FEES

Hedge funds average around 1.5-2% annually in management fees and 15-20% in incentive fees. Fund administrative costs, such as legal and accounting, can average around .25% annually, depending on the size of the fund. In addition, many institutional investors pay in-house staff or consultants or Fund of Funds (FOF) managers to research, recommend and manage their hedge fund investments. Fees for this range from 0.5% to 1% annually, sometimes higher in the case of FOFs receiving an incentive fee on returns (can be as much as 10%). There are also trading costs a hedge fund incurs in implementing its strategy. These costs can vary widely, from .5% to 5% or more annually. All in, hedge fund fees and costs are a back-breaking load for investors to bear.

CHART 6.6   SAMPLE ANNUAL COSTS FOR INVESTING IN HEDGE FUNDS

Management fee	1.5% – 2%
Administrative fee	0.25%
Consultant/FOF fee	0.5% – 1%
TOTAL Management Fees	2.25% – 3.25%
Trading Costs	0.5% – 5%
Incentive fee on gains	15% – 20%

By investing in hedge funds, therefore, you are starting each year 3-6% in the hole due to fees and costs. You are giving up a significant part of the return the market is willing to pay you for the passive provision of your capital. As noted, historically this has been 10% for equities and 5.5% for bonds, and 7.75% for a 50/50 mix. You are doing this in the hope that the hedge fund managers you invest in will consistently find enough marketplace inefficiencies—other people making suboptimal investment decisions or structural anomalies—to recoup the hedge funds' fees and costs, then match the market return, and then exceed the market return by some amount, year after year. It's wishful thinking.

After fees and costs, a hedge fund manager's security selections would have to generate about twice the return of a risk-equivalent indexed basket of stocks and bonds just to stay even with the index basket's return.

In **CHART 6.7** is a sample return calculation for a hedge fund investment.   »

After taxes, the hedge fund return relative to the passive market return is even less attractive, with the passive return being about 32% higher, 6.15% vs 4.65%.

7.75% net market return after tax = 6.15%
(assumes a 40% federal and state tax rate)

7.75% hedge fund return after tax = 4.65%
(assumes a 40% federal and state tax rate and taxes on
significant annual recognized short-term gains)

The odds of a group of hedge fund managers consistently
outperforming the market given such a high hurdle of fees are poor. Even
worse if you are a taxable investor.

HEDGE FUND RETURNS

You might take a flyer on hedge funds if there was convincing data
showing that hedge fund managers are strong performers who consistently
outperform the market. Evidence, however, is to the contrary. The most
objective research shows the same end result for hedge funds as for active
long equity and bond managers: they underperform market returns by
about the amount of their fees.[62] It's difficult even for an active hedge fund
manager with significant skill to outperform. Writes David Swensen, "Even
with substantial active management success (as defined by top-quartile
results), net returns to long/short hedge fund investors show only a modest
increment over money-market rates." [63]

CHART 6.7

15%	hedge fund manager return before fees and costs
-2%	management fee
-0.25%	administrative fee
-2%	trading costs
10.75%	return after management fees and costs
-2.15%	20% incentive fee
8.60%	return net of management fee, costs and incentive fee
-0.85%	consultant fee, FOF fee and in-house management costs
7.75%	hedge fund manager net return after all fees and costs

Foregoing the market return in the hope of hedge fund outperformance is a speculative, high risk bet that you are unlikely to win.

Another negative is that a successful hedge fund manager's returns usually decline over time and their performance reverts toward the mean. This is because success brings more investors and ever-larger amounts of capital to invest. It becomes increasingly difficult for a manager to find enough market inefficiencies to produce outsized returns. In addition, if a manager has a successful investment niche or trading strategy, others copy it or employees with know-how leave to start their own firms to exploit the opportunity. Even James Simons, who created excess returns for many years with his flagship hedge fund Renaissance Technologies, limited its capital to $10 billion, and that soon became employee-only money.[64]

A successful hedge fund's returns may also deteriorate because the fund becomes more conservative as it ages. This is partly due to the fund attracting institutional investors, who generally favor more consistent returns and have less demanding return expectations than private investors. Fund managers also reduce risk in their fund's investment strategy in order to preserve their valuable business. Reducing risk lessens the chances of large negative returns and falling out of favor with investors. But it also reduces the likelihood of high returns, and increases the chances that the manager's returns after fees will be mediocre at best. By lowering its expected return, but not reducing its management fees and costs commensurately, the manager's fund has an even greater chance of underperforming a risk-equivalent passive index return.

It is quite remarkable the number of multi-billion dollar hedge fund managers whose risk-adjusted returns are inferior to those of a simple indexed stock and bond portfolio. It is equally remarkable how many investors there are who are willing to pay 2/20 in fees for little more than hedged market beta, which you can access via an indexed stock and bond portfolio for next to nothing.

REPORTING BIAS, STALE PRICING AND FAT TAILS

Industry players point to hedge fund data showing that hedge funds as a group, and in particular certain hedge fund strategies, have outperformed traditional assets such as stocks and bonds over time both in terms of absolute and risk-adjusted returns. They also tout the low correlation of certain hedge fund strategies to equities, and that hedge funds improve the risk-adjusted returns of an investment portfolio. Institutional investors also sometimes refer to hedge funds as "Absolute Return," suggesting that hedge funds can generate returns irrespective of the market environment.

For starters, what you can be absolutely sure of is that there is no investment strategy with an absolute return, just as there is no perpetual motion machine (there is no motion without a source of energy). Whatever the hedge fund strategy, there is always a source of risk associated with its return. That an investor may not readily see the risk underlying the strategy does not mean it's not there. It's there. And the risks tend to reveal themselves at the worst possible times, such as during equity sell-offs and market illiquidity and volatility, when most of your other investments are also performing poorly.

What creeps into published hedge fund index returns is significant reporting bias, in the magnitude of several percentage points per year. "Public reports of hedge fund performance systematically overstate the realities of the hedge fund marketplace," writes Swensen.[65] Many analyses of hedge fund performance rely on hedge fund indices that are based on self-reported manager performance. The different indices are composed of whatever managers happen to report their returns at a given time. Managers who started a hedge fund that did not do well initially never report their returns to a database. Managers who initially do well may report after a year or two of good performance. Managers who start reporting and then perform poorly often stop reporting. Managers with lackluster performance who are closing their funds due to client withdrawals usually do not report their final monthly returns. These are often affected by write-downs of illiquid positions sold at fire-sale prices as the fund closes down its book.

A measure of the gap between perception and reality was the stated vs. actual performance of Long Term Capital Management, one of the most prominent hedge funds of the late 1990s skippered by some of the supposed best minds in finance—a gaggle of Nobel laureates and would-be financial masters of the universe.[66] In 1997-1998 LTCM blew up in a paroxysm of highly leveraged bets gone bad amidst market illiquidity related to the Russian debt crisis. There is a more detailed description of the event in Chapter 11. "The yawning chasm between Tremont's reported account of 32.4 percent per annum and LTCM's actual record of -27.0 percent per annum produces a staggering gap between perception and reality," writes Swensen.[67]

Turnover of managers in hedge fund indices has been around 15-20% a year, and is highest during market inflection points, such as the tech sell-off during the 2000-2002 period and the subprime mortgage crisis of 2007-2008. About every five years, then, most of the managers have "disappeared" from hedge fund indices. Many funds close down. Quite a few failed managers resurface at the helm of new funds with capital from impressionable investors with short or insufficient memories. Says Swensen,

> The profits interest typically paid by investors in hedge fund structures creates an option for managers that threatens investor interests. In the event of hedge fund gains, the manager shares in a substantial portion of profits. In the event of hedge fund losses, the investor bears the burden alone. The asymmetry of the profits-interest structure clearly favors the fund manager.[68]

As mentioned, hedge funds are often touted as having superior risk-adjusted returns compared to traditional assets such as stocks and bonds, particularly when the comparison is based on measures using standard deviation as a component, such as the Sharpe ratio. The Sharpe ratio is the most common measure that investment people use to assess the return you get on an investment for a given level of risk. **Chart 6.8** explains the calculation and how it allows you to have an apples-to-apples comparison of different investments' risk vs. return.

Be aware, though, that the Sharpe ratio is best used in comparing investments that are publicly traded. As mentioned in this chapter, asset classes such as private equity and venture capital are not suitable for comparison with funds investing in public markets, because the private investments are priced infrequently, and oftentimes held at cost for extended periods of time.

Some funds may appear less volatile than they actually are. A fund may have a track record of steady returns and an attractive Sharpe ratio, but its investment strategy may have a "fat tail." That is, once in a blue moon the fund may have very large, possibly catastrophic, negative returns. The Sharpe ratio of a fund like this camouflages the real risk of the fund's underlying investments.

Hedge fund returns often reflect smoothed performance based on how the investment positions are priced. Smoothed performance means that the published returns appear less volatile than the actual volatility of the fund's

CHART 6.8

Sharpe Ratio: Used for Calculating Risk-Adjusted Return

The higher the Sharpe ratio the better the return you have for a given level of risk

$$\text{Sharpe ratio} = \frac{Rp - Rf}{\sigma p}$$

Rp = return of portfolio
Rf = risk-free rate (Treasury bills)
σp = standard deviation (variability of return around its mean) of the portfolio's excess return

Example 1: Assume over time the stock market returns 10%, the risk-free rate is 3% and standard deviation of the market is 16%.

$$\text{Sharpe ratio} = \frac{10\% - 3\%}{16\%}$$

Sharpe ratio = 0.44

Example 2: Assume your investment fund returns 14%, the risk-free is 3% and standard deviation of your fund is 24%.

$$\text{Sharpe ratio} = \frac{14\% - 3\%}{24\%}$$

Sharpe ratio = 0.39

The stock market with a 0.44 Sharpe ratio provides a better risk-adjusted return than your fund which has a lower Sharpe ratio of 0.39. Your fund has a higher return than the market, but it also has a higher level of volatility (standard deviation).

underlying securities. By way of background, there are three basic tiers of priced securities: 1) those that are priced in public markets regularly, such as the stock of Apple and Microsoft, 2) those that are priced by broker quotes—what intermediaries say they are willing to buy or sell the security for at a given time, and 3) illiquid securities, such as private investments, where the manager has significant input on how the security is priced. Many hedge funds have some combination of these three forms of pricing, and with each step down the ladder of liquidity and transparency there is greater opportunity for and likelihood of dubious pricing by the hedge fund manager.

Bernie Madoff, the largest Ponzi scheme fraudster in history, was an extreme version of this. He just made up investor account values, which gave his fund the appearance of strong, stable returns, and he sent investors phony statements. There is a "soft fraud" version of this in some hedge fund and alternative strategies, and even long mutual funds, where managers bury less liquid and hard-to-price securities in special purpose vehicles where the manager either controls or has significant input on the pricing of the underlying illiquid securities. A hedge fund manager's risk/return statistics such as the Sharpe ratio can look very attractive compared to publicly traded securities when the manager or third parties they work closely with are pricing the less liquid securities in the manager's portfolio.

INADEQUATE DATA

Most investors in hedge funds and the consultants who advise them do not really know exactly how a manager is producing returns. It is disheartening the number of consultants and FOFs who do not independently confirm via account statements and trading logs how a manager achieved their stated past investment returns. They just take the manager's word for it. Even once invested, many investors do not have transparency into a hedge fund manager's actual investment positions. Some receive risk reports and third-party monitoring, but many just rely on the manager's self-reported data, often with a significant time lag. This is often the condition they have to accept to invest with a popular manager. Investors who have a hedge fund investment via a separate account have greater insight into exactly how a manager is producing returns, assuming the investor has the systems to analyze the data in a timely way. Many managers, however, do not offer separate accounts, and the minimums needed for a separate account eliminate all but the largest investors.

FIDUCIARIES KICKING THE PERFORMANCE CAN DOWN THE ROAD

Industry data supporting increased allocation to hedge funds plays into pension fund managers' fear of not meeting long-term return assumptions imbedded in their forecasting. Having an asset class with a holy-grail type name called "Absolute Return" with high return expectations and muted risk helps institutions justify their rosy long-term return projections and allows them to kick the can down the road on currently underfunded liabilities. This only makes the day of reckoning worse. All the active management fees institutions are paying to hedge funds and other alternative managers and the resulting underperformance makes it even less likely that the pension funds will achieve their long-term investment goals. The suspension of reality based on bad data and wishful thinking prevents the pensions, their beneficiaries, and the taxpayers who fund the pensions, from taking steps to address the shortfalls.

A fiduciary should think twice before betting taxpayer and beneficiary capital on such a speculative scheme as hedge funds. Would a prudent man take the sure win—what the market provides to you for providing your risk capital—or take the certain loss up front every year in the form of fees to hedge fund managers in the hope that active management can make up the loss and then provide some positive return beyond it? Concludes David Swensen,

> In the hedge fund world, as in the whole of the money management industry, consistent, superior active management constitutes a rare commodity. Assuming that active managers of hedge funds achieve success levels similar to active managers of traditional marketable securities, investors in hedge funds face dramatically higher levels of prospective failure due to the materially higher level of fees. [69]

PROTECTION ON THE DOWNSIDE

Another trope of the investment management industry is the "downside protection" that hedge funds will provide your portfolio in times of market turbulence. Hedge funds are said to be a good diversifier to stocks and bonds, and therefore a useful addition to an investment portfolio. The problem with this argument is that when hedge funds have really had the opportunity to show their low correlation and defensive attributes, they have failed miserably. 2008 was a good example of this, when hedge fund strategies were down approximately 18% or more. All strategies, with the exception of a handful of managed futures strategies and managers shorting the subprime mortgage market, had negative returns. A 50/50 stock and bond portfolio, which was down about 16% during 2008, provided more of a defensive hedge than hedge funds.

BEST OF THE BUNCH

Of the various hedge fund strategies, to me the two that have the most merit are distressed securities and activist concentrated equity. This is because these two are based on economic functions in a capitalist economy which should provide some return, in contrast to securities-trading strategies, which are a zero-sum game. Distressed managers buy securities from sellers who oftentimes are selling for non-economic reasons, such as they cannot hold non-investment-grade debt in their portfolios, or they do not have the expertise to deal with a company in bankruptcy. Activist managers in effect are supplementing corporate management, helping or forcing executives to improve the businesses they run and operate their businesses with higher levels of leverage. Given the typically long holding periods for these two strategies, they are also more attractive for a taxable investor.

Trend-following strategies, based on the momentum factor, which seems to relate to a persistent feature of human behavior, may be useful for investors looking for shorter-term portfolio risk mitigation. Trend-following strategies generally have low-to-negative correlation to the market. These strategies, however, generally are tax inefficient.

In sum, hedge funds are an expensive form of diversification unlikely to add much over time to your portfolio return. Concludes Swensen, "The high degree of dependence on active management and the expensive nature of fee arrangements combine to argue against incorporating long/short investment strategies in most investor portfolios." [70]

ANNUITIES

With an annuity, you hand over a pile of cash, typically to an insurance company, and in exchange you are promised payments for as long as you live. There are variations on this theme, but that's the basic model. It is a form of insurance against you living longer than expected. For the firms underwriting these contracts, enough annuitants die earlier than expected to pay for those living longer than expected and to provide the firm a profit.

The main problem with annuities is that in order to maximize the chance that they book a healthy profit, the annuity provider is discounting their long-term risk that you live longer than expected by a significant amount. What you receive in the form of returns is not particularly attractive relative to what you are likely to earn investing your assets yourself.

In addition, annuities can be complex,[71] and you are dependent on the annuity provider being around in 30-50 years, and also not rewriting the contract to decrease your benefits when they decide they have misjudged the risk. This could be years later in life when you need the annuity payment most.

Annuitization also gives you little flexibility to change your mind. If you find out you have terminal cancer at a young age and want to take a cruise around the world or do something else with your money, you are out of luck.[72]

Most annuity payments are not adjusted for inflation. They have constant payments over time, say $1,000 a month for as long as you live. The $1,000 a month payment you receive this year, however, may only purchase $500 of an equivalent basket of goods twenty years from now. You are in effect exchanging one risk: living longer than expected, for another risk: inflation being higher than expected. Some annuities include a cost-of-living adjustment (COLA) each year, but these annuities are more costly to purchase and the COLA is often capped, say to 2% per year. You bear the risk of inflation being higher than this.

These shortcomings notwithstanding, risk-averse investors may find it comforting to have a steady payment in retirement, and may want to put some of their savings into an annuity. As Burton Malkiel, notes, "At least partial annuitization usually does make sense. It is the only no-risk way of ensuring that you will not outlive your income." [73]

Keep in mind that Social Security is a form of inflation-adjusted annuity. The payment is based on your earnings over your lifetime and the age at which you start receiving benefits. Also, Social Security benefits receive cost-of-living adjustments based on increases in the Consumer Price Index.

LIFE INSURANCE

There are numerous forms of insurance that combine life insurance or long-term care insurance with investing. The range of these policies and their details are beyond the scope of this book. I suggest analyzing separately your need for insurance and your need for long-term wealth accumulation. Most people lean toward having term insurance for their insurance needs, keeping their retirement investing in a separate pot.

Life insurance is usually purchased to cover the period in a person's life when their unexpected death or disability would severely affect the lifestyle of those dependent upon them, such as a spouse or nonadult children. For this, term insurance is a low-cost and relatively easy-to-understand option.

Where the complexity arises and where the cost-benefit becomes much more difficult to ascertain is in the host of products that combine insurance with investing, such as whole, variable and variable universal life policies. Key differentiators among these products is how long the insurance is in effect, the variability of the premiums, and how much investment return risk the insured takes on and how much investment return risk the insurance company takes on.

A whole life policy does have some useful features, such as the interest and investment gains within the policy growing tax-deferred or tax-free, and the policyholder being able to borrow money against the policy's cash value.

Life insurance also can play a useful role in estate planning. Of particular benefit to wealthy individuals is that a policy's death benefit is transferred income-tax-free to beneficiaries.

Life insurance, though, is a costly way to invest. In addition to the cost of the insurance, you are paying the insurance salesperson a commission, which in effect comes out of your return, and then you are paying the insurance company. In the case where your policy has a guaranteed return, the insurance company is factoring in their profit margin and some margin for error in the expected return. All of this weighs on your return.

Any guaranteed return in an insurance policy, therefore, is likely to be on the lower end of the range of expected returns compared to what you might achieve if you competently managed the money yourself. That said, you might be more comfortable with a guaranteed return.

There are other risks to life insurance, such as the complexity of the insurance contract's terms. You need to fully understand things such as the ability of the insurance company to change the premium and the variability in the growth of the policy's cash value. Another risk is that after years of premium payments, the policy could lapse if you miss a payment.

Risk parity is an investment approach that tries to have equal risk exposure to several asset classes. If it were four asset classes—say stocks, bonds, real estate, and commodities—each would receive a 1/4 weight of the total portfolio's risk. The volatility and correlation of these asset classes are taken into account in order to have the risk equal-weighted among them. The thought is that you will have a more consistent return with equal exposure to investments with different underlying drivers. For example, earnings growth and expanding P/E ratios for stocks, and interest rates and credit risk for bonds.

As a simple example, if equities have an annualized risk of 17% and bonds have a risk of 8.5%, you would have a weight in bonds twice that of equities for each to have the same risk in the portfolio.

CHART 6.9

	Volatility	Portfolio Weight	Risk Weight
Bonds	8.5%	67%	50%
Stocks	17%	33%	50%
		100%	100%

This portfolio, 67% in bonds and 33% in equity, would usually underperform a typical traditional portfolio of say 60% equities and 40% bonds. Risk parity managers, therefore, use leverage to amplify the portfolio's exposure so that its risk is similar to that of the 60/40 portfolio.

Advocates of the risk parity approach believe a leveraged risk parity portfolio will outperform a traditional 60/40 portfolio given a comparable level of risk. This is largely due to the assumption that the risk-adjusted return of bonds is superior to that of equities (see **Chart 6.1**). Leveraging the bond exposure, it is believed, will give you a better overall risk-adjusted return. Otherwise, you would be better off just investing in stocks if you wanted to access a higher return for taking on higher risk.

Over certain time periods, risk parity looks attractive, because bonds have had better risk-adjusted returns than stocks. The last thirty years was a good period for bonds, with interest rates declining and inflation muted.

Whether bonds, with their current low interest rates as of 2021, will produce better risk-adjusted returns than equities going forward is anyone's guess. In addition, relative to a traditional allocation, a risk parity portfolio must overcome the hurdle of the cost of borrowing to leverage the portfolio and the management fees paid to the firm managing the risk parity portfolio.

The jury is still out on whether risk parity generates any excess risk-adjusted return compared to traditional stock and bond portfolios. Analyses based on different time periods produce varying results. As noted, in March of 2020, risk parity approaches such as that of the largest provider, Bridgewater Associates, underperformed and were down more than a traditional equity/bond portfolio. To date, the result of mixing various asset classes in equal amounts based on risk to produce excess performance is similar to that of mixing various colors of Play-Doh in the hope of creating something beautiful. It sounds intriguing and of great promise, but the actual result is more an uninspired gray. For now, better to go with a low-cost allocation of stocks and bonds.

ENVIRONMENTAL, SOCIAL, AND GOVERNANCE (ESG)

Environmental, social, and governance (ESG) investing screens company activities by selected ESG criteria. Environmental criteria centers on issues such as greenhouse gas emissions, fossil fuel production, clean water, and land use. Social criteria include how a company relates to employees, customers, and the communities where it operates. Governance centers on a company's diversity, incentive pay for executives, and treatment of shareholders.

There are no universal ESG definitions. They are a Rorschach test on the sensibilities of the investor using them. One investor may want to exclude all companies operating in the fossil fuel energy area, while another may approve of a company replacing coal-based energy with a less greenhouse gas emitting fuel such as natural gas. One may oppose nuclear energy as being a threat to the environment, and another may favor it as being a clean, non-carbon source of energy. Companies with a low carbon footprint, including large tech companies such as Google and Facebook, are favored in many ESG-oriented investment funds. Others dislike these companies for reasons related to social issues, such as invasion of privacy or censorship of communication.

The absence of universally accepted ESG definitions has resulted in a broad array of approaches. One study notes that the number of US stocks in sampled ESG funds totaled over 2,700, close to the 3,023 stocks in the Russell 3000 Index; so more than 90% of stocks in the US market apparently fit within some definition of ESG investing.[74]

There is no conclusive evidence of whether an ESG-oriented investment portfolio does any better or worse than a market-based portfolio. Some believe that a company's focus on ESG issues can have a positive effect on its financial results. They see a high ESG score for a company as an extension of the quality factor in equity investing, whereby stocks of companies with more stable earnings, stronger balance sheets and higher margins outperform low-quality stocks.[75]

Many ESG funds have outperformed the market in recent years given their overweight in technology and communications services stocks, such as Apple, Google, Microsoft and Facebook. These stocks have a low carbon footprint and also have outperformed the market, which has higher weights to energy and industrial companies, which generally have underperformed. Whether this relative outperformance continues going forward is unknown.

Investors should also note that investing in ESG funds may not meaningfully impact things such as climate change.[76] There is, for example, a difference between reduced greenhouse gas emissions exposure by companies in your portfolio, and actual emissions in the world.[77] You might not be holding fossil fuel energy company stocks, but someone else is. True, ESG-focused investors not buying these companies' stocks and bonds might increase their cost of capital. But by paying more for capital, these companies may be providing above-average investment returns to those investors who do not follow ESG mandates and buy their stocks and bonds. Alternatively, if ESG investors provide a large supply of capital to ESG-friendly companies, these companies may have to pay less for their capital, and therefore offer their investors a lower return given the high demand for their stocks and bonds.

CURRENCIES

There is no inherent return in currencies. Different currencies fluctuate in value relative to each other. Over time there should be no net benefit from investing in currencies. Some investors do seek profits from what is called a carry trade, where you borrow in a lower-yielding currency, such as the yen, and invest in a higher-yielding one, such as the Swiss franc. (See **Chart 8.9** for a summary of a yen carry trade.) There is risk in these trades, though, and they tend to perform worst during scenarios when markets are declining and there is a flight to quality.

CRYPTOCURRENCIES

Cryptocurrencies such as Bitcoin and Ether are stores of value and mediums of exchange, but volatile ones. Similar to gold, if people believe something is valuable then it is. Cryptocurrencies are less usable in most transactions than US dollars, but are more fungible than gold or frequent flyer miles.

How widely cryptocurrencies will be used is unknown. The more stable usage becomes, however, the more they will look and act like cash, and therefore be more a stable store of value with little expected return after inflation than an instrument for speculation and big returns.

Cryptocurrencies aren't really currencies. The IRS categorizes cryptocurrencies as property. To the IRS, transactions in virtual currencies like Bitcoin are taxable, just like transactions in any other property or capital asset, such as stocks. In addition, the IRS considers spending Bitcoin on purchases to be similar to selling it. You have similar issues in exchanging one cryptocurrency for another, say, Bitcoin for Ether.

If you buy or trade in cryptocurrencies, keep detailed records of your transactions. Best to document any receipts, sales, exchanges or other dispositions of cryptocurrencies, and the fair market value at the time of the transactions. Yes, it's a tedious task, but you want to avoid spending even more time and money later dealing with a tax compliance problem with the IRS.

Given that it is unlikely that world governments will cede control over the money supply to cryptocurrencies, there will likely be additional iterations and regulation related to cryptocurrencies before they are widely accepted in commercial transactions. They may also be supplanted by government-sponsored cryptocurrencies.

Government regulation of cryptocurrency transactions and reporting requirements for cryptocurrency exchanges are increasing. Crypto blockchain transactions are often made anonymously. That's the appeal to certain people of using cryptocurrencies—hiding their transactions. But the US government and other governments around the world are working to track these transactions.

The IRS and the Securities and Exchange Commission (SEC) are both looking to increase regulation of cryptocurrencies. The IRS is leaning heavily on Bitcoin exchanges such as Coinbase to provide details on their underlying wallet holders and the holders' Bitcoin transactions. Coinbase, for example, now reports crypto activity meeting certain criteria to the IRS. Similarly, the SEC is looking for a greater oversight and regulatory role regarding cryptocurrencies and transactions involving cryptocurrencies.

A positive for cryptocurrencies such as Bitcoin is that, like appreciated securities, they can be gifted to a charitable organization. This enables the donor to potentially benefit from avoiding capital gains taxes and obtaining a charitable donation deduction. There are a number of recordkeeping, valuation and IRS filing requirements and qualifications related to charitable tax deductions for cryptocurrencies. In addition, for a charity there are different requirements when accepting Bitcoin donations, such as whether the donations of cryptocurrency are accepted directly into the charity's own account or indirectly, such as via a donor advised fund. It's best for an investor or charitable organization to work closely with their tax professional on these issues.

CHART 6.10 BITCOIN US DOLLAR

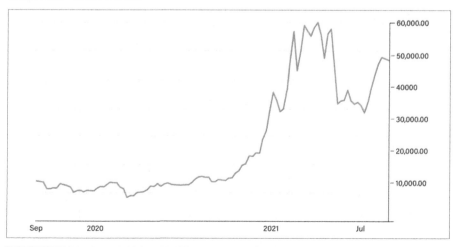

SUMMARY

You can have a sound investment plan and reach your investment goals without using non-core asset classes. If you want to use some non-core asset classes for additional portfolio diversification, and to speculate on outperformance, keep them to a smaller part of your allocation.

- Non-core asset classes are unlikely to meaningfully improve your return relative to a portfolio based on the core asset classes of stocks, bonds and cash.

- Unless you can consistently select top-performing private equity, venture capital and hedge fund managers, you risk significant underperformance relative to the Base Case.

CHAPTER 7

Active vs. Passive Investing

I learned from watching B horror movies as a kid that it was not a good idea to take the backroad shortcut. Usually there was some overbearing, know-it-all dude who convinces everyone else that the shortcut is the way to go even though he doesn't really know the area. It never ended well.

The same applies to taking a shortcut to your wealth goals by reaching for high returns through stock picking or betting on market moves. Some people think they are smarter than other investors, and that their superior ability is the golden ticket to outperformance. Some people think they or a manager they hire can consistently beat the Base Case by actively picking stocks or accurately predicting market moves. These people are generally wrong.

THE ILLUSION OF SKILL

In 44 BC Julius Caesar, emperor of the Western world, walks across the Forum in Rome toward the curia of Pompey. He is going there to meet resentful Senators bridling under his imperial control. Along the way he sees a grizzled soothsayer who had previously warned him, "Beware the ides of March." (March 15) As he strolls by on that very day, Caesar chirps to the soothsayer, "The ides of March are come." To which the soothsayer replies, "Ay, Caesar; but not gone." Caesar jauntily moves on, and shortly thereafter is stabbed to death in the curia by a group of senators, including Brutus, Caesar's protégé and alleged illegitimate son. "Et tu, Brute?" So writes Shakespeare in his play, *Julius Caesar*.

The Death of Julius Caesar by Vincenzo Camuccini
Photo Credit: Glasgow Museums

We don't know whether the soothsayer's timely warning to Caesar was due to clairvoyance or blind chance or inside information—the Roman senators' plot of regicide may have been percolating in certain circles of Rome's elite.

Odds are, though, that the soothsayer's augury was not due to any predictive skill on his part. That's because he was a member of the Haruspex, a group of well-respected and presumably well-paid Etruscan/Roman priests whose expertise was divining the future from animal entrails. Sheep livers were a favorite. The Liver of Piacenza, shown in the picture below, is a bronze, liver-shaped chart used by practitioners as a tool in developing their forecasts. Well-to-do Romans paid heaps of aureus gold coins for these liver-based prophecies.

Liver of Piacenza (bronze sculpture with Etruscan inscriptions in the shape of a sheep liver found near Piacenza, Italy) circa 200 BCE
Photo Credit: Lokilech, CC BY-SA 3.0 <http://creativecommons.org/licenses/by-sa/3.0/>, via Wikimedia Commons

We can shake our heads in disbelief and laugh at the silly, superstitious Romans relying on liver-based auguries when making decisions on business, politics and war. But we should not condescend. In our own time billions of dollars are spent each year on Wall Street forecasters and speculators whose ability to predict the future—the direction of markets and stocks—is no better than that of the Haruspex poring over their sheep livers. In 2019 the S&P 500 was up over 30%. No one forecasted that. In the first quarter of 2020 a coronavirus spread around the world and the S&P 500 declined over 30%. No one forecasted that. Then the market rebounded 70%. No one forecasted that.

Although many people in the financial industry believe, or pretend to believe, that they can accurately forecast the future, evidence shows that they fail to consistently do this. Sadly, investors continue to shower them with money, attention and, at times, adulation. This type of thing— educated, professional soothsayers profiting from people's desire for certainty and control over their world—thrives in our time as it did two thousand years ago in Rome. Today's investors putting faith in financial industry diviners, to paraphrase Malcolm Muggeridge, is "old news happening to new people."

Why all the attention paid to Wall Street forecasters? Says Nobel laureate Daniel Kahneman:

> An unbiased appreciation of uncertainty is a cornerstone of rationality—but it is not what people and organizations want…Extreme uncertainty is paralyzing under dangerous circumstances, and the admission that one is merely guessing is especially unacceptable when the stakes are high. Acting on pretended knowledge is often the preferred solution.[78]

As humans we dread uncertainty. Our brains try to bring order to the unpredictability of life.[79] Talking heads fill a need by making complex systems like our economy and the stock market seem explainable—and if these systems are explainable, they may be predictable, or even better, controllable.[80]

It doesn't much help that market forecasters and stock pickers today base their forward-looking views on the analysis of fact-based data, rather than spots on sheep livers. "The subjective experience of traders is that they are making sensible educated guesses in a situation of great uncertainty. In highly efficient markets, however, educated guesses are no more accurate than blind guesses," writes Kahneman.[81] When everyone has similar access to information, it is extremely difficult for a person to consistently outguess others.

The failure of the predictive ability of so-called experts is not unique to the investment industry. One study concluded that the ability of political experts to predict the course of political events was actually worse than random guessing—they were poorer forecasters than dart-throwing monkeys.[82]

In addition, the world can veer far off its current path and its expected path. In 1910, there had not been a war across Europe since the Napoleonic wars nearly 100 years earlier. Scientific progress was in full swing. Exciting new technologies and industries were in their infancy, including electricity, radio, automobiles and airplanes. The world was secure under the economic and military sway of two democracies, Great Britain and the United States. With regard to investing, in addition to the US and Britain, the emerging economic powers of Germany, Japan, Russia, and China looked to offer promising returns.

No one in 1910 would have predicted that over the next 40 years there would be not one, but two world wars, that a small ideology, communism, would take over two of the largest and most populous countries, Russia and China, and inspire socialist movements and nationalist expropriations around the world from Mexico to India, and that the British Empire would collapse. Before midcentury, any investments you had in Germany, Japan, Russia and China became worthless, or nearly worthless, due to the wars, inflation, and communist takeovers.

Any investment advisor predicting this course of events in 1910 would have been scoffed at as a lunatic. Someone today predicting similarly dramatic events over the next 40 years would also be dismissed as a doomsayer. But you never know, because change is not always gradual and the future is not predictable.

Also, do not mistake confidence for skill. A person's level of confidence in their market forecasts or stock picks is no predictor of accuracy. Think of CNBC's *Mad Money* host Jim Cramer. His energetic presentation of his stock picks makes for engaging TV. But the Action Alerts Plus portfolio that he co-manages has underperformed the S&P 500.[83]

Recommendations from a person with a high degree of confidence in their predictions should actually be avoided. That person often cannot see the limits of their own forecasting abilities.[84] Of course, people exhibiting strong, confident views are who financial news organizations like to showcase. Viewers are drawn to people who have the appearance of knowing something others don't. Writes Kahneman,

> It is wrong to blame anyone for failing to forecast accurately in an unpredictable world. However, it seems fair to blame professionals for believing they can succeed in an impossible task. Claims for correct intuitions in an unpredictable situation are self-delusional at best, sometimes worse. In the absence of valid cues, intuitive "hits" are due either to luck or to lies. If you find this conclusion surprising, you still have the lingering belief that intuition is magic. Remember this rule: intuition cannot be trusted in the absence of stable irregularities in the environment.[85]

By stable irregularities, Kahneman is referring to recognizable patterns, such as symptoms in newborns which indicate a particular underlying medical issue. You see enough babies and symptoms, and you develop a working knowledge and intuition about health issues a newborn may have.

In the investment world, there are no stable irregularities to learn from. The variables affecting companies and financial markets are innumerable. Human behavior varies, and the world constantly changes. The direction of an individual stock and the market as a whole is unpredictable. Who knows when the next infectious disease will plague the world, or whether war might break out between the US and China.

...a major industry appears to be built largely on an *illusion of skill*.

DANIEL KAHNEMAN

It is unlikely, then, that an active manager will have sustained success at picking stocks or that a Wall Street pundit will consistently and accurately predict future market movements. We can certainly understand, though, why overconfident stock pickers and forecasters like to think they can predict company prospects and the course of constantly changing markets, despite the overwhelming evidence to the contrary. Upton Sinclair summed it up well when he said, "It is difficult to get a man to understand something when his salary depends on his not understanding it." [86] Concludes Kahneman about the investment management industry, "a major industry appears to be built largely on an *illusion of skill*." [87]

BEATING THE BASE CASE

How have people who try to beat the Base Case by picking stocks rather than investing in the entire market done over time? Those who are educated and accustomed to achievement are inclined to believe that hard work and mental effort can result in superior performance. You would think that with the many intelligent, educated and experienced people in the investment world there would be a number who would be able to consistently outperform the market with their smarts and savvy. But it is not so.

Few investors consistently do better than the Base Case. Despite bold talk and wishful thinking, almost all active investors underperform the Base Case by about the amount it costs them to speculate—management fees, trading costs and administrative expenses. It is frustrating.

Why is this? The market return consists of the buying and selling activity of all of the investors in the market. The average investor gets the market return (the Base Case) before costs. After costs, an average return becomes a below-average return. This goes for both novice investors and professional money managers alike. It applies to both stock and bond investing.

Competition in the investment world is fierce, and markets are fairly efficient. Managers outperforming or underperforming the market is largely due to randomness.[88] Says Yale endowment CIO David Swensen, perhaps the greatest institutional investment manager of our time:

> Before management fees, before commissions, before market impact, before sales loads, before contingent fees and before taxes, investors in actively managed mutual funds face a coin flip. After all fees and expenses, investors experience a performance deficit. Rational mutual-fund investors avoid active management. [89]

FEES

"Performance comes, performance goes. Fees never falter." Words of wisdom from Warren Buffett.[90] If you can do one thing to improve your investment performance, keep your fees as low as possible. Investment firms have an incentive to maximize fees. You benefit from low fees, because the lower the fees the less drag there is on your investment returns. So you and the investment firm are fundamentally in conflict when it comes to fees.

Performance comes, performance goes. Fees never falter.

WARREN BUFFETT

To reduce your investment-related fees, eliminate as many people as possible that are between you and the end investment, such as an individual stock and bond. The more people and intermediaries, the higher your fees, and the worse your performance will likely be. "Sensible investors avoid the brokerage community, opting for the lower-cost, self-service alternative," says David Swensen.[91] Vanguard, for example, provides services to its member funds on an "at cost" basis. Decreases in costs flow through to investors in the form of lower fees.

Fees include management fees, administrative fees, and 12b-1 fees (which pay for marketing and distribution). For active equity funds, it has been estimated that management fees for portfolio management and administration account for 58 percent of the total, expenses for back-office functions such as transfer agents, custodians, and legal account for 20 percent of the total, and 12b-1 fees to promote distribution account for 21 percent of the total.[92]

Frequent trading by you or the active fund you invest in also racks up trading expenses, including brokerage commissions, bid-ask spreads, and market impact costs. Market makers, who provide liquidity in the buying and selling of stocks, profit from small differences between what they will buy a stock for (say $99.50 per share) and what they will sell a stock for (say $100 per share). Market impact costs relate to how trading may move the price of a stock, particularly one that is thinly traded. For example, assume you want to buy 100 shares of ABC company, currently trading at

$75 per share. If the lowest current offer by sellers of ABC stock to sell 100 shares is $75.25, your buying 100 shares will move the stock price up. And the cost to you in buying the 100 shares is not $7,500 (100 x $75), but $7,525 (100 x $75.25), or $25 higher.

Trading firms and new technology companies such as Robinhood Markets, Inc. have created attractive apps that entice you to trade. They get paid in part by directed brokerage, whereby firms executing your trades pay firms like Robinhood a fee to send trades their way. They make money on the spread between the buys and the sells. Many trades at relatively small spreads add up to billions of dollars for these firms. That's why they develop addictive apps to get you to trade.

Trading costs add up for mutual funds as well. One study of the 100 largest stock funds in defined-contribution plans found the median cost of trading to be 0.66%.[93] Another study on thousands of US stock funds estimated the average trading costs to be 1.44% of total assets, with an average of 0.14% in the bottom quintile and 2.96% in the top.[94]

Frequent trading also leads to recognition of capital gains, upon which taxable investors pay tax.

THE COST OF ACTIVE MANAGEMENT

You, the investor, are the one paying the costs of active management— the manager fees, trading costs and administrative expenses incurred in the speculative hope that through well-timed buying and selling of securities you will do better than the Base Case. People you pay to speculate for you are commonly called active managers. Whether they operate through a mutual fund or hedge fund or separate account, they are just people with some strategy that they think will do better than the Base Case. Regardless of whether the active manager succeeds or not in beating the Base Case, you pay.

Those who profit from your speculating: fund managers, stock exchanges, banks, brokers, investment data providers, pundits and financial news channels flacking stock ideas and market forecasts. Huge sums of investor wealth are shared among these players. They have enormous monetary incentives to encourage you to try to beat the Base Case by trading, watching their shows, and paying them to guess which stocks and bonds will outperform the others. Globally, investment management revenues in 2017 were $596 billion and profits were $62.7 billion. For investors, sadly, there is little to show for it.

CHART 7.1   ACTIVE MANAGERS TRY TO OUTGUESS THE MARKET

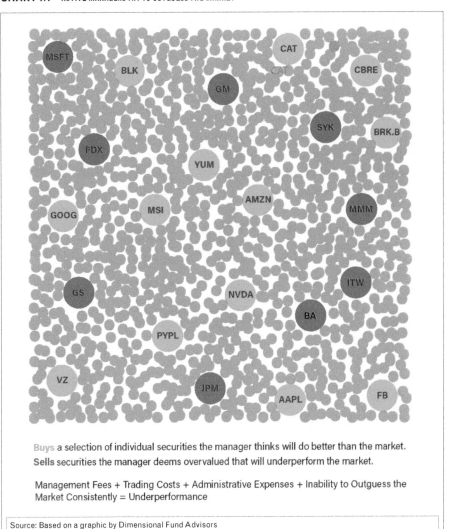

Buys a selection of individual securities the manager thinks will do better than the market.
Sells securities the manager deems overvalued that will underperform the market.

Management Fees + Trading Costs + Administrative Expenses + Inability to Outguess the
Market Consistently = Underperformance

Source: Based on a graphic by Dimensional Fund Advisors

Many investors pay fees of 0.5-1% or more annually to have a mutual
fund manager, or a 2% fee and 20% of profits in the case of a hedge fund
manager, to speculate in stocks, bonds and other securities on their behalf.
If an equal mix of stocks and bonds in the Base Case returns 7.75%, the
average investor who incurs 1% in active management costs would receive
an annual net return of 6.75%, assuming the manager they hired achieved
an average return.

A one-percent difference in return may not seem to be much of a difference, but it can make a huge difference in the growth of your wealth over time. The longer the time period, the larger the impact, given the effect of compounding. Say you are 35 years old and have $100,000 invested for your retirement in 30 years. Over 30 years your $100,000 compounding annually at 7.75% turns into $938,681 by the time you reach age 65. At a 6.75% rate of return, your $100,000 turns into $709,637. That's $229,044, or about 25%, less. Not good. It gets even worse when, as some investors do, you pay 2% of your assets annually for active investment advice, management fees and related trading costs. If your annual return is 5.75%, your $100,000 investment grows to $535,070 after 30 years, which is $403,611, or about 43% less than the 7.75% compounded return of the Base Case. That result is more than not good—it's really bad. And it happens to investors all the time.

CHART 7.2   RETURN ON A $100,000 INVESTMENT OVER 30 YEARS COMPOUNDED ANNUALLY

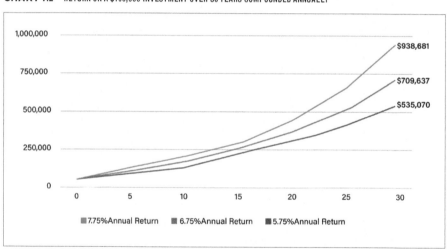

Another way of looking at the value proposition of an active manager is that you, the investor, will take a 2% loss every year to pay me, the active manager. I will then make up that loss, and then achieve the Base Case return of 7.75%. This means I need to earn a 9.75% return for you to break even with the Base Case return of 7.75%. Then, I will do even better than that, which will be outperformance for you, less any incentive fees I may charge. And you will take this bet every year. Upside for you—a small chance you will do slightly better than the Base Case. Downside for you—you consistently and significantly underperform the Base Case and you wind up with much less money over time than you would have had had you just invested in funds indexing the Base Case. Says David Swensen, "A minuscule 4 percent of funds produce market-beating after-tax results with a scant 0.6 percent (annual) margin of gain. The 96 percent of funds that fail to meet or beat the Vanguard 500 Index Fund lose by a wealth-destroying margin of 4.8 percent per annum." [95]

When you factor in other costs of active management, which can include sales loads and commissions, market impact on security prices caused by buying and selling, and taxes paid on realized capital gains from portfolio turnover, the end return to the investor is even worse than the example above.

Swensen, who could be talking about any actively managed investment product, whether it be a mutual fund, hedge fund, separate account, ETF, or private equity fund, says:

> The only reasonable course for individuals lies in avoiding for-profit investment management firms and turning away from the siren song of active management. After eliminating assets managed by profit-seeking firms and assets managed with market-beating aspirations, very little remains of today's mutual fund industry. Overwhelmingly, mutual funds extract enormous sums from investors in exchange for providing a shocking disservice. [96]

Ouch.

ODDS OF BEATING THE MARKET

With active management, you pay a high price to play a zero sum game. [97] When you buy a stock you think will go up more than the market average, the person selling it to you doesn't think so, or they wouldn't be selling it. Somebody's going to be wrong. If your portfolio is outperforming, someone else's is underperforming. They are transferring value to you.

In a world with some $75 trillion invested in stocks[98], of which active managers account for some 25% or $19 trillion[99], investors have to be transferring trillions of dollars in value regularly for active managers to

CHART 7.3 HIGH COSTS CAN REDUCE PERFORMANCE
Equity fund winners and losers based on expense ratios (%)

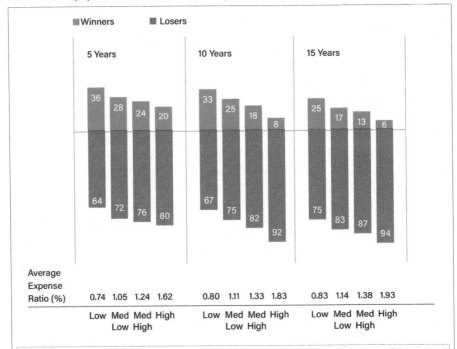

Average Expense Ratio (%)											
0.74	1.05	1.24	1.62	0.80	1.11	1.33	1.83	0.83	1.14	1.38	1.93
Low	Med Low	Med High	High	Low	Med Low	Med High	High	Low	Med Low	Med High	High

Source: Based on a graphic by Dimensional Fund Advisors. The sample includes funds at the beginning of the 5-, 10-, and 15-year periods ending December 31, 2017. Funds are sorted into quartiles within their category based on average turnover during the sample period. The chart shows the percentage of winner and loser funds by expense ratio quartile for each period. Winners are funds that survived and outperformed their respective Morningstar category index, and losers are funds that either did not survive or did not outperform their respective Morningstar category index. US-domiciled open-end mutual fund data is from Morningstar and Center for Research in Security Prices (CRSP) from the University of Chicago. Past performance is no guarantee of future results.

thrive. It is wishful and egotistical to think that other people are so dumb, careless, or incompetent that they will continually hand excess returns to you without a commensurate level of risk. Human beings have not survived for as long as they have on this planet by giving away stores of value for free. For those who did, their genes did not survive in the gene pool for long.

"Alpha," the ability of an active manager to generate returns above that of the market commensurate with risk has declined over time as financial markets have become more efficient. Temporary market inefficiencies and pricing arbitrages are quickly competed away.[100] More and more of the world's financial assets are managed by trained specialists who have similar levels of intelligence, education, access to data and technology.

CHART 7.4 HIGH TRADING COSTS CAN ALSO IMPACT RETURNS
Equity fund winners and losers based on turnover (%)

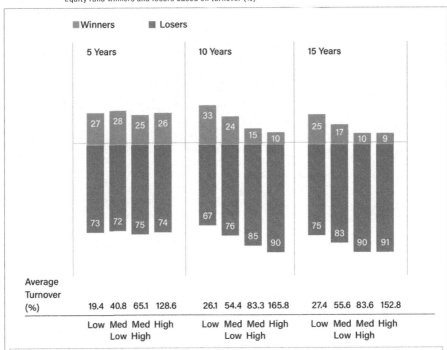

Source: Based on a graphic by Dimensional Fund Advisors. The sample includes funds at the beginning of the 5-, 10-, and 15-year periods ending December 31, 2017. Funds are sorted into quartiles within their category based on average turnover during the sample period. The chart shows the percentage of winner and loser funds by expense ratio quartile for each period. Winners are funds that survived and outperformed their respective Morningstar category index, and losers are funds that either did not survive or did not outperform their respective Morningstar category index. US-domiciled open-end mutual fund data is from Morningstar and Center for Research in Security Prices (CRSP) from the University of Chicago. Past performance is no guarantee of future results.

For example, over the past 75 years in the US, the percentage of the US stock market owned by individual investors has declined from about 90% to 35%, while the percentage of the stock market held in professionally-managed funds has climbed from 10% to over 40% (see **Chart 7.5**). An even greater percentage of trading on exchanges, in some cases over 90%, is done by hedge funds and other professional investors. The majority of this is algorithmic trading, which can flood exchanges with buy and sell orders and magnify price swings in individual stocks and in the overall market.[101]

Professionals are competing against other professionals to find market inefficiencies. It has been estimated that active managers account for most of the movement in stock prices, and that they trade $22 for every $1 traded by index funds.[102] It is an increasingly tough game in which to add

CHART 7.5   US DOMESTIC OWNERSHIP OF US CORPORATE EQUITIES

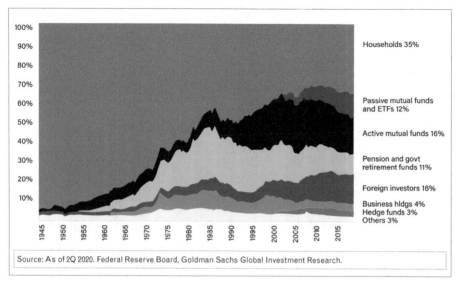

Source: As of 2Q 2020. Federal Reserve Board, Goldman Sachs Global Investment Research.

value, whether it be a long equity manager trying to pick stocks that will outperform, or a hedge fund manager trying to find pricing discrepancies across global equities, bonds, currencies and derivatives. As mediocre managers wash out due to below-average performance, the smarter, better managers remain, making the competition for excess returns even fiercer. Additionally, as discussed previously, managers with above-average returns, whether due to skill or luck, attract money from investors. It is more difficult to maintain above-average returns having to invest an ever-larger pool of capital, and returns inevitably trend toward the mean.

> ### Indeed, luck may be 99 percent responsible for the success of the very few people who have beaten the averages.
>
> **BURTON MALKIEL**

For active money managers, the odds are very low of overcoming the handicap of active management costs year after year. Think of a professional football team starting each game down two touchdowns. No matter how good the team is, the odds of it winning most of its games are low. The other teams have good players and coaches, too, and a two-touchdown deficit is too big a hurdle to overcome in a competitive arena. Similarly, most of the investment marketplace is made up of hardworking professional investors who are well-educated, well-informed and well-equipped with the technological tools of their trade. It is difficult to consistently overcome the cost hurdle of active management and outperform the Base Case when everyone else is about as capable as you are. Of those managers who have beaten the market, says Malkiel, "Indeed, luck may be 99 percent responsible for the success of the very few people who have beaten the averages." [103]

In addition, developments in technology and the speed of information flow have made markets increasingly more efficient. New information on companies, markets and the global economy is ever more quickly incorporated into security prices. Active manager fees have not gone down much over time relative to the increase in market efficiency, and any "alpha" or excess return a manager may generate is even harder to come by. And as information becomes more ubiquitous and readily available in real time, participants have ever shorter time frames in which to make investment decisions, which reduces the likelihood that they will consistently be right. Even trading on inside information in an attempt to beat the average becomes more perilous as regulatory tools for monitoring malfeasance become more sophisticated.

Also, do not confuse knowledge with unique knowledge. Your active manager may be smart and very knowledgeable about financial markets and securities. Of course they are. But unless a manager has unique knowledge about specific securities, that is, information which is not known by others, and the manager can consistently obtain such knowledge, they will not outperform the market. What they know is already reflected in security prices, and therefore there is no opportunity to outperform. As Professor Kahneman writes,

> Unfortunately, skill in evaluating the business prospects of a firm is not sufficient for successful stock trading, where the key question is whether the information about the firm is already incorporated in the price of the stock. Traders apparently lack the skill to answer this crucial question, but they appear to be ignorant of their ignorance.[104]

BEATING THE SPREAD

"Bear down, Chicago Bears, make every play clear the way to victory ..."[105] The rest of the lyrics to the Chicago Bears' fight song aren't much better, but if you are a die-hard Bears fan you will sing this until you are orange and blue in the face. In addition to your hometown enthusiasm, you may know quite a bit about football, and have solid reasons for believing that in this Sunday's matchup the Bears, with a record of 5-2, will beat the Packers, with a record of 3-4. You feel pretty good that you can predict the outcome of the game. And given that the odds are in your favor, the result is not all too surprising: Bears win!

But, for people in the marketplace of betting on professional football games, that the Bears are a good team and will likely win is not the question. The question is will the Bears beat the spread. Similarly, as mentioned above with regard to picking stocks that will outperform, what is important is not a company's business prospects, but whether those prospects are already incorporated into its stock price.

The betting spread for an NFL game incorporates the views of many other football enthusiasts, fanatics, and professional handicappers, who follow professional football as closely or more closely than you do. You can see in **Chart 7.6** that the odds of beating the spread are close to a toss-up. The wisdom of very knowledgeable people is incorporated into the spread, and it is difficult to consistently win bets given the spread. The same applies to the stock market, where available information is reflected in stock prices (see **Chart 7.7**). It is hard to say whether a stock is over or undervalued, and near impossible to consistently predict the directional move in its price, when that price reflects the opinion of many other well-informed market participants.

> ## There is general agreement among researchers that nearly all stock pickers, whether they know it or not— and few of them do—are playing a game of chance.
>
> ### DANIEL KAHNEMAN

Kahneman sums up what many academic studies have concluded on active managers outperforming the market through stock selection, "There is general agreement among researchers that nearly all stock pickers, whether they know it or not—and few of them do—are playing a game of chance."[106]

CHART 7.6 BEATING THE SPREAD

5-2

3-4

Who do you pick to win?

Who do you pick to beat the spread?
(Bears -10)

The spread is difficult to beat.

Favorites should beat the spread about half the time.

The favorite beat the spread:

–53% of the time in 45 Super Bowls [1]

–48% of the time in 5,000 NFL games [1]

–49% of the time in 8,000 NBA games [2]

Source: [1] Steven D. Leavitt, "Why Are Gambling Markets Organised So Differently From Financial Markets?" *The Economic Journal*, 114 (April 2004). [2] Rodney J. Paul and Andrew P. Weinbach, "Bettor Misperceptions in the NBA: The Overbetting of Large Favorites and the 'Hot Hand'," *Journal of Sports Economics*, 6 (November 2005).

CHART 7.7 INFORMATION REFLECTED IN STOCK PRICES

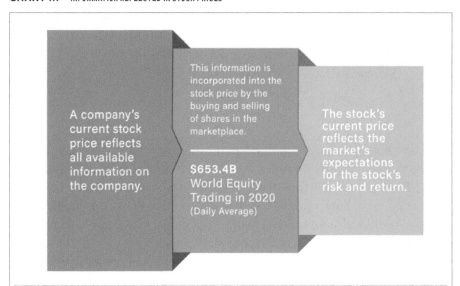

Source: Based on a graphic by Dimensional Fund Advisors. In US Dollars. Dimensional, using data from Bloomberg LP. Includes primary and secondary exchange trading volume globally for equities. ETFs and funds are excluded. Daily averages were computed by calculating the trading volume of each stock daily as the closing price multiplied by shares traded that day. All such trading volume is summed up and divided by 252 as an approximate number of annual trading days.

VALUE IS IN THE EYE OF THE BEHOLDER

The market price of a security is not "right" or "wrong," it just is. Your opinion may be that a stock is overpriced or underpriced, but what you think doesn't matter. What matters is what everyone else thinks. Says Burton Malkiel:

> Markets can be highly efficient even if they make errors. Some are doozies, as when internet stocks in the early 2000s appeared to discount not only the future but the hereafter. Forecasts are invariably incorrect. Moreover, investment risk is never clearly perceived, so the appropriate rate at which the future should be discounted is never certain. Thus, market prices must always be wrong. But at any particular time, it is not obvious to anyone whether they are too high or too low. . . . . professional investors are not able to adjust their portfolios so that they hold only "undervalued" stocks and avoid "overvalued" ones. The best and brightest on Wall Street cannot consistently distinguish correct valuations from incorrect ones. There is no evidence that anyone can generate excess returns by making consistently correct bets against the collective wisdom of the market. Markets are not always or even usually correct. But NO ONE PERSON OR INSTITUTION CONSISTENTLY KNOWS MORE THAN THE MARKET.[107]

LUCK OR SKILL

There have to be winners, right? Can't I find at least a few investment managers who regularly do better than the Base Case after their fees and costs? There are some investors who do better than the Base Case over time. Remarkably few, however, and the odds of you identifying them in advance are low. Additionally, you cannot really tell within a reasonable time period if their past outperformance was due to skill or luck.

For example, ten people play a game of heads or tails. After five flips of the coin, one person, Susan, remains. She picked heads or tails correctly each time. Would you say Susan was skilled at picking heads or tails? No. Similarly, among stock pickers, one person out of ten might have performed much better than the others, having picked a basket of stocks that outperformed the Base Case five years in a row. Do you know whether this was due to skill or chance? No. Would you bet your retirement savings that they will correctly predict the next five flips? No, unless you believe in clairvoyance.

CHART 7.8 PERCENTAGE OF US EQUITY FUNDS OUTPERFORMED BY BENCHMARKS (NET OF FEES)

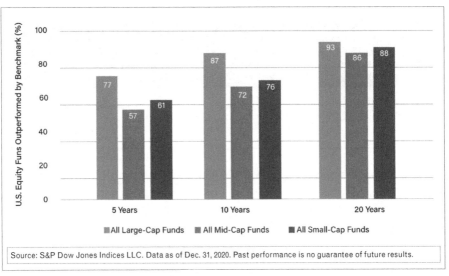

Source: S&P Dow Jones Indices LLC. Data as of Dec. 31, 2020. Past performance is no guarantee of future results.

CHART 7.9 FEW MUTUAL FUNDS SURVIVE AND BEAT THEIR BENCHMARKS
Period ending December 31, 2017

Equity Funds

2,828 Beginning
51% Survivors (1,442)
14% Winners (396)

Fixed Income Funds

1,599 Beginning
57% Survivors (911)
13% Winners (208)

Source: Dimensional Fund Advisors. In US Dollars. The sample includes funds at the beginning of the 15-year period ending December 31, 2017. Survivors are funds that had returns for every month in the sample period. Winners are funds that survived and outperformed their respective Morningstar category benchmark over the period. US-domiciled open-end mutual fund data is from Morningstar and Center for Research in Security Prices (CRSP) from the University of Chicago. Past performance is no guarantee of future results.

CHART 7.10   DOES ACTIVE MANAGEMENT ADD VALUE?

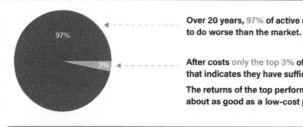

Over 20 years, 97% of active managers can be expected to do worse than the market.

After costs only the top 3% of managers produce a return that indicates they have sufficient skill to just cover the costs.

The returns of the top performers are expected to be only about as good as a low-cost passive index fund.

Conclusion

An investor doesn't have a prayer of picking a manager that can deliver true alpha. Even over a 20-year period, the past performance of an actively managed fund has a ton of random noise that makes it difficult, if not impossible, to distinguish luck from skill.

Source: Eugene F. Fama and Robert Litterman, "An Experienced View on Markets and Investing," *Financial Analysts Journal*, CFA Institute, 2012, Vol. 68, No. 6. 17.

Few managers outperform their benchmarks over time. Nobel laureate Eugene Fama concludes that after costs only the top 3% of managers produce a return that indicates they have skill to cover their costs (see **Chart 7.10**). Even these top performers are only expected to be about as good as a low-cost passive index fund.[108] David Swensen concurs: "A well-constructed academic study conservatively puts the pre-tax failure rate at 78 percent to 95 percent for periods ranging from ten to twenty years. The same study places the after-tax failure rate at 86 percent to 96 percent." [109]

Concludes Professor Fama, "an investor doesn't have a prayer of picking a manager that can deliver true alpha. Even over a 20-year period, the past performance of an actively managed fund has a ton of random noise that makes it difficult, if not impossible, to distinguish luck from skill." [110]

A HANDFUL OF STOCKS DRIVE RETURNS

In attempting to outperform the market by selecting stocks, you should ask yourself, "Do I feel lucky?" Only a handful of stocks drive market returns over time. According to finance Professor Hendrik Bessembinder, the best-performing 4% of listed companies explain the entire net gain of the US stock market since 1926. The other 96% of stocks collectively matched Treasury bills.[111] Says Bessembinder, "Simply put, large positive returns to a few stocks offset the modest or negative returns to more typical stocks." [112] Of the 25,300 companies in the CRSP (Center for Research in Security Prices) database from 1926 to 2016, just five firms—ExxonMobil, Apple, Microsoft, General Electric, and International Business Machines—account for 10% of the total net stock market wealth creation of some $35 trillion. [113] The 90 top-performing companies (about one-third of 1% of the companies) account for over half of the wealth creation, and the 1,092 top-performing companies (a bit more than 4% of the total), account for all of the net wealth creation. [114]

CHART 7.11 OF THE 25,300 COMPANIES IN THE CRSP DATABASE FROM 1925 TO 2016, JUST OVER 4% ACCOUNT FOR ALL THE STOCK MARKET NET WEALTH CREATION

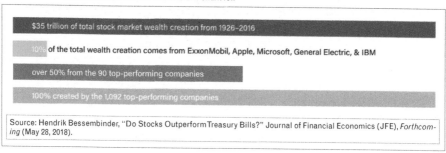

$35 trillion of total stock market wealth creation from 1926-2016

10% of the total wealth creation comes from ExxonMobil, Apple, Microsoft, General Electric, & IBM

over 50% from the 90 top-performing companies

100% created by the 1,092 top-performing companies

Source: Hendrik Bessembinder, "Do Stocks Outperform Treasury Bills?" Journal of Financial Economics (JFE), *Forthcoming* (May 28, 2018).

For an active manager with a concentrated stock portfolio, it's easy to get the stock selection wrong and underperform the market. "If you pick relatively few stocks as opposed to being broadly diversified," says Bessembinder, "there isn't a 50%-50% chance as to whether they'll over- or underperform the market. There's a greater than 50% chance they'll underperform." [115] Over their lifetimes, only 42.6% of stocks had a return greater than one-month Treasury bills. [116] In addition, the life of the average stock, at 7.5 years, is, borrowing from Thomas Hobbes, nasty, brutish and short. Only 36 stocks were in the database for all 90 years of the sample period 1926-2016. [117]

Getting one stock right or wrong can make a life-changing difference in your investment returns being great or grim. Of the few "home run" stocks that have had returns much greater than the mean, says Bessembinder, "It's easy for active stock pickers to miss these and wind up with a below-average performing portfolio. Better to invest in the entire market and ensure that you will participate in the market returns driven by these winners." [118]

PICKING A MANAGER THAT OUTPERFORMS THE MARKET

One estimate is that you would need over fifty years of monthly performance data to conclude whether an active manager's stock picking track record was due to skill or luck.[119] You and the manager likely don't have fifty years. In addition, the global economy and financial markets are constantly changing, and people change over time, too (we get old and feeble). This makes repeatability of past performance even more uncertain.

There is no way, then, in a reasonable time frame to conclude definitively that manager outperformance was due to skill, or that it will continue. We like to think it will continue. Our brains are geared toward pattern recognition,[120] so we intuitively think that a past series, such as a hot hand in basketball, will likely continue. More often than not, however, the returns are random.[121] As Kahneman writes with regard to cognitive illusions such as the hot hand fallacy, "We are far too willing to reject the belief that much of what we see in life is random." [122] And we are far too willing to take extreme actions based on assumed causation.

Kahneman tells a related story from when he worked for the Israeli air force. After he told a group of flight instructors that rewarding pilots for improved performance during their aerial combat training would work better than punishing them, one of the most seasoned instructors spoke up: "On many occasions I have praised flight cadets for clean execution of some aerobatic maneuver. The next time they try the same maneuver they usually do worse. On the other hand, I have often screamed into a cadet's earphone for bad execution, and in general he does better on his next try. So please don't tell us that reward works and punishment does not, because the opposite is true." [123] Says Kahneman of the instructor,

> The instructor was right—but he was also completely wrong!
> . . . What he had observed is known as *regression to the mean*, which in that case was due to random fluctuations in the quality of performance. Naturally, he praised only a cadet whose performance was far better than average. But the cadet was probably just lucky on that particular attempt and therefore likely to deteriorate regardless of whether or not he was praised. Similarly, the instructor would shout into a cadet's earphones only when the cadet's performance was unusually bad and therefore likely to improve regardless of

what the instructor did. The instructor had attached a causal interpretation to the inevitable fluctuations of a random process.[124]

Causal interpretation of a random process not only can get someone shouting into your earphone to do better, it can get someone ripping your heart out of your chest. The Aztecs of Mexico had the cultural practice of human sacrifice. The body count tended to rise when the weather wasn't good. El Niños would come along every two to seven years, making for wet winters and hot, dry summers. The unfavorable weather negatively affected the maize harvest, upon which everyone depended.

The Aztec high priests figured their gods were displeased if the weather was bad and the crops were failing, so to appease them the priests sacrificed men, women and children, and ever more of them, until the weather changed for the better. Eventually it did, and the priests no doubt patted themselves on the back for a job well done as they wiped the blood off the obsidian blades they used to slice open people's chests before reaching in and ripping out their beating hearts, basketfuls of which were offered up to their gods.

Human sacrifice in the Mendoza Codex.
Source: Unknown author Unknown author, Public domain, via Wikimedia Commons
Primary Source: Page of Codex Mendoza, 1542.
Document E: The illustrations in the Codex were drawn by Aztec artists.

You may think that an investment manager's recent outperformance is due to skill, but the odds are very high that it is just a random result, a deviation around a mean of performance like that of the Israeli pilots or the Aztec weather. Investors often make the mistake of allocating money to an investment manager when they are doing well and performing above their long-term mean, similar to the pilot luckily executing the perfect flight maneuver. They are disappointed, however, when the investment manager's performance reverts to the mean and comes crashing back to the average.

NO PERSISTENT SKILL

"Professional investors, including fund managers, fail a basic test of skill: persistent achievement. The diagnostic for the existence of any skill is the consistency of individual differences of achievement," writes Kahneman.[125]

There is little persistence in manager outperformance. Out of 556 US equity funds that were in the top-quartile of performance as of December 2016, less than 1% remained in the top quartile for the 5-year period ending December 2020.[126] Out of the 50 investment-grade intermediate bond funds that were in the top quartile of performance as of December 2016, none remained in the top quartile for the 5-year period ending December 2020, and of the 52 high yield funds, 5.8% remained in the top quartile.[127]

You can see in **Chart 7.12** that almost all equity and fixed income funds underperform their benchmarks over time. And that is before taxes are taken into account. Concludes Larry Swedroe in looking at the data, "The bottom line is that, basically, there was no evidence of persistence in performance greater than randomly expected among active equity managers. Making matters worse is that a stronger likelihood existed of the best-performing funds becoming the worse-performing funds than vice versa." [128]

No wonder then, that from 2018 to 2020, according to the Investment Company Institute, 2,038 mutual funds and ETFs closed.[129] Hope springs eternal, however, because over the same time period, 1,723 opened.[130] An unending cycle of life and death, profits for the industry and underperformance for investors.

If someone told you these were your odds in Vegas of winning, you would not enter the casino. The odds of winning in Vegas are actually much better than the odds of picking a winning mutual fund. Still, according to Thomson Reuters Lipper, active funds, including money market funds, manage approximately $15.4 trillion, which is 2.3 times the $6.7 trillion managed by index funds and ETFs.[131]

How about the handful of managers that outperform? Identifying them, and sticking with them over time, is near impossible for most investors. Morningstar examined the performance of a group of global active funds over a 15-year period, and found that of the funds that outperformed their benchmark, on average they trailed the benchmark for 10 years sometime during that period.[132] They also found that funds that ended up underperforming their benchmark over 15 years had stretches of outperformance of 11-12 years. A simulation of very skilled managers over

CHART 7.12

Percentage of Equity Funds Underperforming Their Benchmarks

Fund Category	Comparison Index	1-year	3-year	5-year	10-year	20-year
All US Funds	S&P Composite 1500	57.1	67.0	72.8	83.2	86.0
All US Large-Cap Funds	S&P 500	60.3	69.7	75.3	82.3	94.0
All US Mid-Cap Funds	S&P Midcap 400	50.7	53.5	59.7	72.8	88.0
All US Small-Cap Funds	S&P SmallCap 600	45.5	57.0	65.1	76.3	88.1
Real Estate Funds	S&P United States REIT	24.7	43.4	50.6	75.6	87.9
International Funds	S&P 700	54.6	63.3	74.4	79.5	91.3
Emerging Markets Funds	S&P/IFCI Composite	52.0	61.0	70.5	71.4	92.2

Percentage of Fixed Income Funds Underperforming Their Benchmarks

Fund Category	Comparison Index	1-year	3-year	5-year	10-year	20-year
Government Long Funds	Barclays US Gov't Long	94.3	98.0	98.1	98.7	98.0
Investment Grade Long Funds	Barclays US Gov't/Credit Long	94.4	97.7	97.8	98.4	97.1
Investment-Grade Int. Funds	Barclays US Gov't/Credit Intermediate	33.5	44.6	41.1	50.2	65.8
High Yield Funds	Barclays US Corporate High Yield	77.7	91.4	95.3	97.2	98.5
Emerging Markets Debt Funds	Barclays Emerging Markets	64.4	93.2	77.6	100.0	86.7
General Municipal Debt Funds	S&P National AMT-Free Municipal Bond	59.7	65.3	63.0	48.1	79.6
Loan Participation Funds	S&P/LSTA U.S. Leveraged Loan 100	90.6	100.0	91.7	96.0	100.0

Source: SPIVA® US Scorecard. S&P Dow Jones Indices LLC. Data as of Dec. 31, 2020. Returns shown are annualized. Past performance is no guarantee of future results. Table is provided for illustrative purposes.

You have a better chance of winning in Vegas than picking a winning mutual fund.

Images: Shutterstock

a 100-year period indicates that on average there would be a 25-year period of underperformance.[133]

Do you think you would retain a manager that had underperformed for 20 years? 10 years? 3 years?

Using a three-, five-, and even ten-year time period is far too short for effective manager evaluation. Many consultants and investors, however, replace managers who have underperformed their benchmarks over the preceding three-to-five-year period. They may well be throwing out the baby with the bathwater with regard to active managers that do produce alpha and outperform their benchmarks. As Swedroe notes,

> [Institutional investors] still engage in the practice of selling funds, or firing managers, once they have underperformed the market over the previous three years, typically replacing them with funds or managers that have recently outperformed. They do this while ignoring not only the evidence that past performance has almost no predictive value, but also that research has found the hired managers go on to underperform the fired managers.[134]

It is absurd that endowments, pension plans and investment consultants continue the charade of active manager selection. Pensioners and taxpayers should grab their pitchforks and storm the offices of their elected officials and pension boards, letting them know that in continuing to speculate with pension money via active managers, the boards are failing in their fiduciary duty. Some beneficiaries have taken notice, and taken action, by suing boards for excessive costs incurred in investing pension and endowment assets. Emory University settled a case in 2020 claiming the board had failed to efficiently administer the pension by investing in managers with excessive costs.[135]

In sum, investors, including professional investors, have little chance of picking active managers that consistently outperform their benchmarks. Investment consultant Charles Ellis noted that while you might win at the game of active management, the odds of doing so are so low that it would be foolish to try – which is why he called it "the loser's game." [136]

CHASING THE PAST

Chasing an investment manager's lofty past returns is not conducive to your achieving healthy future returns on your assets. You are looking at what was, not what is likely to be. As noted, reversion to the mean is the more likely course.

You also cannot rely on ratings schemes based on managers' past returns as a reliable method to sort the wheat from the chaff. Fund rating services such as Morningstar are of little use in picking active fund managers that will outperform in the future. Morningstar highly ranks funds that have performed well recently, and its rating system, according to David Swensen, is "hopelessly naïve" and "useless." [137]

> Even highly respected market observers focus far too much on past investment results. Morningstar's vaunted five-star rating system rests on the precarious foundation of historical performance numbers. Yet the assignment of a four-star or five-star rating to a mutual fund carries enormous influence on flows of investor funds. Just as in *The Wizard of Oz*, a pathetic little man stands behind the curtain.[138]

You may point to a certain manager's annualized returns as having beaten its benchmark over a long period of time. This too, however, may be a mirage. John Bogle gives an example:

> While the fund itself, often due to its success when its assets were small, has achieved a marvelous lifetime return on a *time-weighted* basis, the return it earns for its investors (the *dollar-weighted* return) often leaves much to be desired. Specifically, the standard *time*-weighted record published by the fund presents a decade-long compound return of +27.1% per year. The *dollar*-weighted return during that period, however, was about +5.5% per year. (Of course, it is the *time-weighted* record that is reported.) Put another way, while the *fund* appears to have made big money, its *investors* would have been better off with a simple bank deposit.[139]

MAGNITUDE OF UNDERPERFORMANCE

If there was a big reward for landing an active manager that outperforms the market, you might consider taking the bet. But there isn't. According to Professor Eugene Fama, only the top 3% of managers have skill, and that skill is just sufficient to cover the managers' costs.[140] From

CHART 7.13 PERCENTAGE OF US EQUITY FUNDS UNDERPERFORMING THEIR BENCHMARKS
% ANNUALIZED RETURN—YEAR-END 2020

Fund Category	5-year	10-year	20-year
All US Funds	12.9	10.9	6.5
S&P Composite 1500	15.0	13.7	7.7
% Manager Outperformance/Underperformance	-2.1	-2.8	-1.2
All US Large-Cap Funds	12.9	11.4	5.9
S&P 500	15.2	13.9	7.5
% Manager Outperformance/Underperformance	-2.4	-2.5	-1.6
All US Mid-Cap Funds	13.3	10.8	7.3
S&P MidCap 400	12.4	11.5	9.3
% Manager Outperformance/Underperformance	0.9	-0.7	-2.1
All US Small-Cap Funds	12.4	10.4	8.1
S&P SmallCap 600	12.4	11.9	9.8
% Manager Outperformance/Underperformance	0.0	-1.6	-1.7
Real Estate Funds	5.1	7.4	8.2
S&P United States REIT	4.6	8.2	9.5
% Manager Outperformance/Underperformance	0.5	-0.8	-1.3
International Funds	8.6	5.5	4.3
S&P 700	9.6	6.1	5.7
% Manager Outperformance/Underperformance	-1.0	-0.6	-1.3
Emerging Markets Funds	11.4	3.0	8.9
S&P/IFCI Composite	12.7	4.2	10.7
% Manager Outperformance/Underperformance	-1.4	-1.2	-1.9

Source: SPIVA® US Scorecard. S&P Dow Jones Indices LLC. Factset. Data as of Dec. 31, 2020. Returns shown are annualized. Past performance is no guarantee of future results. Table is provided for illustrative purposes.

Charts 7.13 and **7.14** you can see that over longer time periods active managers as a group underperform by about the amount of their fees and costs. In addition, notes David Swensen, managers that underperform the market do so by a greater margin (-2.6% per annum) than the margin (+1.4% per annum) of managers that outperform the market.[141]

CHART 7.13   PERCENTAGE OF FIXED INCOME FUNDS UNDERPERFORMING THEIR BENCHMARKS
% ANNUALIZED RETURN – YEAR-END 2020

Fund Category	5-year	10-year	20-year
Government Long Funds	3.2	2.9	3.6
Barclays US Government Long	7.8	7.7	7.1
% Manager Outperformance/Underperformance	-4.6	-4.8	-3.4
Investment Grade Long Funds	5.7	4.4	4.5
Barclays US Government/Credit Long	9.4	8.2	7.4
% Manager Outperformance/Underperformance	-3.7	-3.8	-2.9
Investment-Grade Intermediate Funds	4.1	3.3	3.6
Barclays US Government/Credit Intermediate	3.6	3.1	3.9
% Manager Outperformance/Underperformance	0.4	0.2	-0.3
High Yield Funds	6.4	5.2	5.3
Barclays US Corporate High Yield	8.6	6.8	7.5
% Manager Outperformance/Underperformance	-2.2	-1.7	-2.2
Emerging Markets Debt Funds	6.2	3.1	4.4
Barclays Emerging Markets	6.9	6.0	6.8
% Manager Outperformance/Underperformance	-0.8	-2.9	-2.4
General Municipal Debt Funds	3.4	4.1	3.6
S&P National AMT-Free Municipal Bond	3.7	4.5	4.2
% Manager Outperformance/Underperformance	-0.3	-0.3	-0.7
Loan Participation Funds	3.8	3.3	3.4
S&P/LSTA U.S. Leveraged Loan 100	5.3	4.0	4.5
% Manager Outperformance/Underperformance	-1.6	-0.8	-1.1

Source: SPIVA® US Scorecard. S&P Dow Jones Indices LLC. Factset. Data as of Dec. 31, 2020. Returns shown are annu-alized. Past performance is no guarantee of future results. Table is provided for illustrative purposes.

INSTITUTIONAL INVESTORS DO NO BETTER THAN ANYONE ELSE

Institutional investors—public and corporate pension plans, foundations and endowments—are no better than anyone else when it comes to investing. They cannot identify in advance investment managers that will outperform the market. A study that looked at the hiring and firing decisions of some 3,400 plan sponsors overseeing over $627 billion in investments found their timing to be terrible:

- Plan sponsors chase returns. They hire investment managers who have had strong returns in the prior three years.

- The hired managers do not have positive excess returns after being hired.

- Plan sponsors terminate investment managers after they underperform, but after being fired these managers often have positive excess returns.

- If plan sponsors had remained invested with the fired investment managers, their returns would have been higher than those delivered by the newly hired managers.

- The above results did not include any of the trading costs that would have resulted from moving from one manager to another.

- In sum, all of the hiring and firing of managers was counterproductive.[142]

It has been said that insanity is repeating the same mistakes and expecting different results. Plan sponsors keep making the same mistakes over and over in hiring and firing investment managers. It is both insane and inane for plan sponsors to squander beneficiaries' money on a kabuki dance of fulfilling their fiduciary duty by rotating managers every few years.

As Larry Swedroe writes of plan sponsors,

Most seem to never stop and ask the question: If the managers we hired based on their past outperformance have underperformed after being hired, why do we think the new managers we hire to replace them will outperform if we are using the very same criteria that has repeatedly failed? And, if we aren't doing anything different, why should we expect a different outcome? I've asked these very questions of many plan sponsors and never once received an answer—just blank stares.[143]

It is in your best interests to be more thoughtful than institutional investors. Acknowledge the unlikelihood that you will consistently pick winning managers, and invest accordingly.

TIMING MARKETS: YOU NEED TO GET AT LEAST TWO DECISIONS RIGHT

The odds of successfully timing markets are low, because you need to repeatedly get two decisions right: getting out at the right time to miss a falling market, and getting back in at the right time to catch a rising market. For example, after markets have been declining for a time, you might sell all your stocks and go to cash and miss the last 15% leg down of a market decline. However, you might be in cash during the three months when the market rebounds 25% off its low. In which case, you are behind where you would have been if you had just stayed fully invested.

Anecdotally, an investment advisor friend of mine told me the following story regarding a client of his during the crash of 2008. The advisor was investing $4 million for a wealthy individual, who we will call Tom. Tom had about half his money in equities, about $2 million. Tom went along with the advisor's recommendation to "stick to the plan" and keep money invested according to the agreed upon investment allocation.

Tom put up with some of the equity declines of 2008, but by early 2009 he feared the world was indeed collapsing, and in January he decided to go to cash. Tom's timing looked propitious, because between January 2009 and early March the market sold off. From a high of $2 million in equities in 2007, Tom's portfolio was down 20%, and was worth $1,600,000 in early March. If he had not sold in January, he would have been down 37%, leaving him with $1,260,000. So far so good for Tom.

From early March to early August 2009, the market rallied. The S&P 500 was up 45%. Tom was in cash, which wasn't earning much interest. Had he kept his money in stocks, he would have enjoyed the explosive uptick in the market, the best in forty years. Had he not sold in January and stayed invested in stocks, the $1,260,000 he would have had in early March would have appreciated to $1,827,000 by the end of August, leaving him 15% better off than going to cash and sitting on the $1,600,000.

Says David Swensen:

> Active market timers usually fail. Market timing requires taking relatively few, generally undiversifiable positions. Timing decisions involve the large questions of asset-class valuation, forcing short-term asset allocators to develop views on an impossibly broad range of factors. Even if the market timer overcomes the odds by making a correct call, notoriously fickle markets may fail to resolve valuation discrepancies in the short run. Serious investors avoid entering the market-timing morass.[144]

Not only is timing the market difficult, but the wind is in your face. Since the market goes up over time, it is best to stay invested, assuming you have a longer time horizon for your investment goals. Says Malkiel, "We have seen that market timing does not work." [145] Even sitting out of the market a few days can make a big difference in your long-term investment returns (see **Chart 7.15**).

After sharp market declines, the market usually rebounds in a short period of time, and therefore it is hazardous to the long-term compounding of your wealth to be out of the market at any time, especially times when the market outlook is gloomy (see **Chart 7.16**). "It's darkest before the dawn" certainly applies to financial markets.

A stunning example is the sharp market up and down in 2020. From February to March of 2020, global equities sold off 20% due to economic concerns related to the coronavirus. From April to December, the market rebounded over 47%. The chance you could have predicted the coronavirus and the down market and the magnitude of the rapid rebound was about zero. You do not want, therefore, to be out of the market when the rebound occurs, and the only way to be sure of that is not to leave in the first place.

CHART 7.15 REACTING CAN HURT PERFORMANCE
Performance of the S&P 500 Index 1990-2020

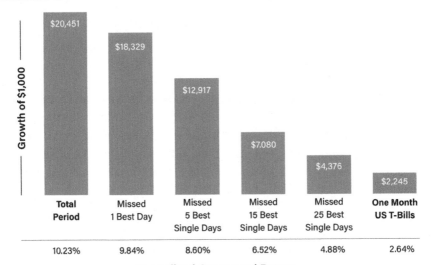

Source: Dimensional Fund Advisors. In US Dollars. The missed best day(s) examples assume that the hypothetical portfolio fully divested its holdings at the end of the day before the missed best day(s), held cash for the missed best day(s), and reinvested the entire portfolio in the S&P 500 at the end of the missed best day(s). Annualized returns for the missed best day(s) were calculated by substituting actual returns for the missed best day(s) with zero. S&P data copyright 2018 S&P Dow Jones Indices LLC, a division of S&P Global. All rights reserved. "One-Month US T-Bills" is the IA SBBI US 30 Day T Bill TR USD, provided by Ibbotson Associates via Morningstar Direct. Data is calculated off rounded daily index values. Indices are not available for direct investment. Their performance does not reflect the expenses associated with the management of an actual portfolio. Past performance is not a guarantee of future results.

CHART 7.16 THE MARKET'S RESPONSE TO CRISIS
Performance of a Balanced Strategy: 60% Stocks, 40% Bonds. Cumulative Total Return.

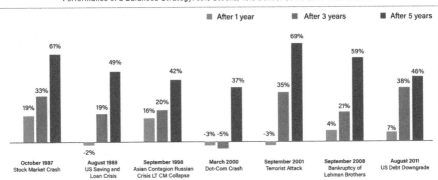

Source: Dimensional Fund Advisors. In US Dollars. Represents cumulative total returns of an Wealth Index Model invested on the first day of the following calendar month of the event noted. Assumes all strategies have been rebalanced monthly. All performance results of the Wealth Index Models are based on performance of indices with model/backtested asset allocations; the performance was achieved with the benefit of hindsight; it does not represent actual investment strategies. The model's performance does not reflect advisory fees or other expenses associated with the management of an actual portfolio. There are limitations inherent in model allocations. In particular, model performance may not reflect the impact that economic and market factors may have had on the advisor's decision-making if the advisor were actually managing client money. Past performance is no guarantee of future results. S&P data © 2020 S&P Dow Jones Indices LLC, a division of S&P Global. All rights reserved. Bloomberg Barclays data provided by Bloomberg.

TAXABLE INVESTORS

A taxable investor should look at their investments through the prism of after-tax returns. The taxes you pay on dividends, interest, and recognized short and long-term capital gains reduce your returns. What you have in your pocket after taxes is what you actually have.

Most taxable investors' portfolios are less tax efficient than they could be. Although it should not be the sole focus of an investment allocation, minimizing taxes should be of high priority, since taxes are a significant drag on investment returns. You may think, for example, that an active management strategy you are invested in has outperformed an index-type investment, only to find out that after taxes are figured in the active strategy has underperformed. Calculating after-tax returns is a gray area, though, because it relates to factors including your particular tax bracket and losses or loss carry-forwards you may have which can be used to offset gains.

Many investors do not fully appreciate the effect of turnover and tax inefficiency on their investment returns. Active management strategies generally have higher turnover, that is they change investment positions more frequently, and as a result recognize more taxable short-term and long-term gains, upon which you pay taxes. This is in contrast to more passive, index-type strategies, which turn over their positions less frequently and have fewer recognized gains and taxes owed on those gains.

The net, after-tax return of active strategies, then, is often lower than the net returns of index strategies, because of the greater tax payments produced by the active strategies. As indicated in **Chart 7.17**, high turnover managers' returns can be 35% lower than their pre-tax returns. As a taxable investor, you pay taxes on recognized gains assuming no offsetting losses.

Investors often pay taxes due on gains out of an account other than their investment account. Their investment account is generating taxes that are paid elsewhere, such as from a checking account. The investment account may look like it is doing well, but less well when you factor in all the money going to the IRS.

You can see in **Chart 7.18** that a significant part of a taxable investor's return goes to taxes. The after-tax shortfall in returns is a major contributor to investor underperformance relative to the Base Case returns. After taxes, the odds of significantly underperforming the Base Case far outweigh the odds of outperforming. **Chart 7.19** shows that over a 10-20 year time period, an investor investing with active managers had on average about a 10% chance of outperforming the market after taxes, and that outperformance would be by about 1 percentage point. You had a 90% chance of underperforming the market after tax by 4.2 percentage points. Would you want to take that bet? No.

CHART 7.17 TURNOVER IN A STOCK PORTFOLIO REDUCES AFTER-TAX RETURN

Turnover Rate	Pre-Tax Return	After-Tax Return	Difference
10%	10.3%	9.9%	-3.7%
25%	10.3%	9.3%	-9.3%
50%	10.3%	8.4%	-18.5%
100%	10.3%	6.5%	-37.0%

Assumed LT Capital Gains Tax Rate: 23.8%; ST Capital Gains and Ordinary Income Tax Rate:37%. Assumed tax rate on Stocks is a blended rate of 30.4%.

CHART 7.18 RETURNS AFTER TAXES AND INFLATION

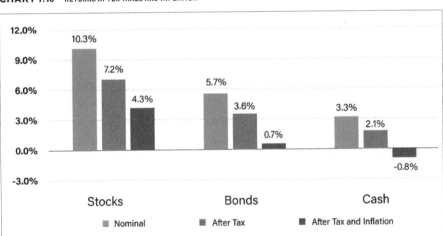

Source: In US Dollars. Stocks is the S&P 500 Index; Bonds is the 20-year US government bonds; Cash is One-Month US Treasury Bills; 1-Month Treasury Bills Index is the IA SBBI US 30 Day TBill TR USD. Treasury Index data sourced from Ibbotson Associates, via Morningstar. Inflation is the Consumer Price Index. CRSP data provided by the Center for Research in Security Prices. S&P data © 2020 S&P Dow Jones Indices LLC, a division of S&P Global. All rights reserved. Bonds, T-bills and inflation data provided by Morningstar. Assumed Long-Term Capital Gains Tax Rate: 23.8%; Short-Term Capital Gains and Ordinary Income Tax Rate: 37%. Assumed tax rate on Stocks is a blended rate of 30.4%. Assumed inflation is 2.9%. Past performance is no guarantee of future results. Indices are not available for direct investment. Their performance does not reflect the expenses associated with the management of an actual portfolio.

CHART 7.19 ODDS OF OUTPERFORMING THE MARKET AFTER TAXES
After-Tax Results relative to the Vanguard 500 Index Fund (Percent)

Period	Odds of Outperforming	Average Margin of Outperformance	Average Margin of Underperformance
10 years	9.0	1.8	-4.8
15 years	4.0	0.6	-4.8
20 years	14.0	1.3	-3.2

Source: Swensen, *Unconventional Success*, 217.

Given the bite taxes take out of your investment returns, you should certainly maximize contributions to your tax-advantaged accounts such as Individual Retirement Accounts (IRAs), 401(k) accounts, 403(b) accounts, Keogh accounts, and Simplified Employee Pensions (SEP).

ETFS, MUTUAL FUNDS AND DIRECT INDEXING

The tax advantages of investing in equities via an ETF is a gift that you should take advantage of. Of the different vehicles to invest in, such as ETFs, mutual funds, and separate accounts, ETFS generally are the most tax efficient over the long term. Because of how they are created and how units of investment are bought and sold, ETFs distribute out little recognized taxable gain on the equity securities they hold.

In contrast, in a mutual fund, net recognized gain is distributed out annually to shareholders. Mutual fund investors should be aware of how much unrecognized gain there is in the fund in which they are investing. You could be buying into significant potential tax liabilities due to accumulated unrealized capital gains in a mutual fund, because a buyer receives a pro rata share of unrecognized gains in the fund, even though they did not participate in the appreciation leading to those unrecognized gains. The new purchaser of a fund in effect takes on a share of the existing investors' tax liability.

Some investors also use direct indexing, where via a separate account they own individual stocks, such as those comprising the S&P 500 Index. Owning individual stocks provides more opportunities for tax-loss harvesting. You have more control over the recognition of capital gains, because you or the manager of the account can determine which securities to buy and sell and the timing of when gains and losses are recognized. Direct indexing accounts benefit from regular additions of fresh money, because this provides new opportunities to establish positions and recognize losses.

HIDDEN RISKS OF ACTIVE INVESTING

Active managers, in an attempt to outperform the market, may take on significantly more risk than you are aware of or expect. This includes both the volatility of the investment's return and the risk of a permanent loss of capital. The hedge fund and private credit and equity areas are full of managers and strategies that have "tail risk" or "fat tails"—strategies that may appear profitable and fairly stable in normal market environments, but which can produce catastrophic losses in extreme market environments (see **Chart 7.20**).

MODELING RISK

Oftentimes financially-engineered investments come from PhDs who spend considerable time away from the real world poring over data sets looking for profitable patterns. Subprime mortgage-backed credit in 2007-2008 is a good example of this. The financial modeling for these securities did not model in that they could be negatively affected by residential property values declining simultaneously across the entire US, because this had not occurred in the available historical data.[146] It was considered a one-in-a-thousand-year event.

The higher tranches of these mortgage-backed securities were given the highest rating, triple-A, by conflicted rating agencies. The rating agencies were hired by the issuers of the mortgage-backed securities, and the more agreeable your rating the more business you got from the issuers. Trusting investors around the world bought what they thought were safe investments. Of course, in fewer than a thousand years, the US housing bubble burst in 2007-2008 and real estate values declined precipitously. Foreclosure rates increased, and hundreds of billions of dollars of securities based on unsound subprime mortgages were downgraded to junk status. Fallout from the collapse of subprime mortgage-backed securities tanked global financial markets, and precipitated the greatest economic depression since the Great Depression of the 1930s.

CONCENTRATION RISK

Another risk managers will take is concentrated positions, such as where an active equity manager bets that a handful of chosen stocks will outperform the market. As noted by Professor Hendrik Bessembinder above, if you pick a few stocks opposed to a broad number, there isn't a 50%-50% chance that you will over- or underperform the market, there is a greater than 50% chance you'll underperform. Missing out on a couple of long-term stock winners can lead to significant underperformance. A manager making this lopsided and unattractive bet is either very confident or aggressive or both with regard to their views on the stocks they hold. Add to this their desire to produce market-beating returns which will attract assets to their firm and generate fees for them.

HIGH CORRELATION

For bond investments, active managers will often overweight credit risk in an attempt to outperform their benchmark. Riskier bonds and leveraged credit strategies have a high correlation to equity risk. In poor economic times and bad markets, these bond managers' funds do not provide a buffer to declining equity markets, the traditional role of bonds, but suffer negative returns along with equities.

As AQR Capital Management says of these managers, ". . . whatever it is they are doing (carry trades, overweighting securitized assets that embed credit risk, etc.) ends up providing the investor with something that resembles—and is highly correlated with—HY (high yield) exposure. This is hardly comforting for an investment into an asset class that is meant to provide diversification from equity markets." [147]

Active managers have an incentive, of course, to take risks with your money. Top-performing managers get far more recognition and compensation than middle-of-the-pack managers. They in effect have an option on outperformance. This is particularly true in the hedge fund space, where short, high-return track records can attract capital. Management fees and incentive fees can make a manager very rich in a short period of time. The lure of taking outsized risks to outperform and grab the golden ring is too much for many managers to resist.

Sometimes when they fail, and they have a big hole to dig out of in order to reach their high water mark and therefore be able to charge incentive fees on investor capital, managers close up shop. Then, a short

CHART 7.20   HIGHER TAIL RISK EVENTS IN NON-NORMAL DISTRIBUTIONS

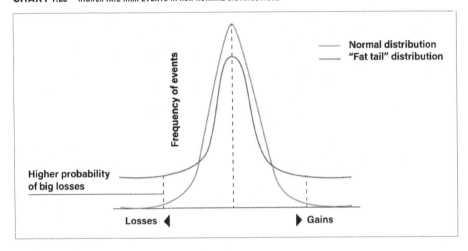

while later they start anew with new investors and a new high watermark. Investors have a short memory and do not hold to account as much as they should managers who fail, take a mulligan, and start over.

A notorious example of this is Amaranth Advisors LLC. Amaranth had about $9.2 billion under management before collapsing in 2006 due to a massive trading loss. The firm presented itself to investors as a multi-strategy fund, but apparently failed to let investors know that the fund's assets could be disproportionately bet on a handful of natural gas futures and could lose $6.5 billion in a week, which it did. Reports indicate that as the fund wound down, losses may have exceeded sixty-five percent of investors' capital. That wasn't the end of it.

Amaranth hired another hedge fund, Fortress, to liquidate its investments, and Amaranth investors were not allowed to redeem their investments. Ten years later, in 2016, investors were still waiting for the last 10% of their frozen assets to be returned. Interestingly, Amaranth's founder, Nick Maounis, had long since moved on. In 2010 he set up a new hedge fund called Verition Fund Management LLC, another multi-strategy investment management firm, which as of 2020 apparently managed over $5 billion. These types of phoenix-like rising-from the-ashes second (and third) acts for failed investment managers happens more often than you would hope.

A manager with a volatile return stream may also do well while you as an investor do not. In **Chart 7.21**, a manager of Portfolio 1 whose fund takes an incentive fee on returns would have a big payday in year 1, when the return was 50%. In Amaranth's case, if you have $9.2 billion under management, and you have a 50% year, you have made $4.6 billion, of which you keep 20% as your incentive fee, which is $920 million. You can understand why traders like Brian Hunter, who was the trader at Amaranth who made the outsized natural gas trades that destroyed the firm, swing not only for the fences, but for the street outside of the stadium. If the fund makes $920 million in one year, and blows out the next, the managers have made enough money for a lifetime, and either retire or start over with a new fund. They are fine. Their investors are not.

CHART 7.21 THE IMPACT OF VOLATILITY
Impact on a Hypothetical $100,000 Portfolio

	Year 1 Return	Year 2 Return	Average Return	Compound Return	Value at End of Year 2
Portfolio 1	50%	-50%	0%	-13.4%	$75,000
Portfolio 2	10%	-10%	0%	-0.5%	$99,000

Keep in mind that a fund generating large, outsized returns relative to the market almost always means that the manager is taking large, outsized risks with your money. In my experience, manager's claiming outperformance usually are manipulating their portfolios vis-a-vis their benchmarks, or have benchmarks that are not really representative of the exposures and risk of the manager's portfolio.

For example, large cap equity managers are notorious for including more volatile, and theoretically higher performing, mid and small cap stocks in their portfolios. Bond managers which compare themselves to an investment-grade bond index such as the Barclays Aggregate often have riskier, less liquid and lower quality credits in their portfolios. They also amplify credit and interest rate exposures using derivatives in an attempt to outperform their benchmark.

It's a soft fraud upon which many managers' outperformance is based. It will be difficult for you to understand these risks, either due to a lack of transparency on the manager's part, or your inability to understand the embedded risk in a manager's many positions. Best to stick to something simple that you can understand, won't surprise you, and for which you can have a reasonable expectation as to how it will perform in good times and bad.

YOUR SAVINGS AS A FORM OF ENTERTAINMENT

You may view stock picking as a form of entertainment and excitement. Or there may be some psychic return for you, such as the enjoyment one gets daydreaming about how amazing life would be if they won the lottery. Be mindful, though, that like betting against the house in Vegas, if you play the active manager game long enough you have very high odds of losing— losing here being underperformance relative to the Base Case and having less wealth than you might have had. As Nobel laureate Paul Samuelson said, "Investing should be more like watching paint dry or watching grass grow. If you want excitement, take $800 and go to Las Vegas."

After the deductions of the costs of investing, beating the stock market is a loser's game.

JOHN BOGLE

The best way to avoid losing relative to the Base Case is by not playing the active management game. As legendary index pioneer Jack Bogle wrote, "*Our financial croupiers always win.* In the casino, the house always wins. In horse racing, the track always wins. In the powerball lottery, the state always wins. Investing is no different. *After the deductions of the costs of investing, beating the stock market is a loser's game.*" [148]

Bogle's sentiments are echoed by Samuelson, who told Congress, "I decided that there was only one place to make money in the mutual fund business, as there is only one place for a temperate man to be in a saloon: behind the bar and not in front of it." [149] So don't use your money, at least not much of it, as a form of entertainment. If you want thrills, ride a rollercoaster, canoe down the Amazon, or go gambling in Vegas.

When it comes to investing for your retirement, take your ball of money and go home. You are not a wimp, but a pragmatist who will not be goaded into playing a game in which you are likely to be worse off than if you hadn't. Warren Buffett wrote that if you aren't certain that you understand and can value stocks far better than the market, you don't belong in the game. He adds, "As they say in poker, 'If you've been in the game 30 minutes and you don't know who the patsy is, *you're* the patsy.'" [150]

In the active management investment game, you the investor are the patsy. If you find yourself being swayed by some authoritative-sounding financial pundit on TV or online, just picture them holding the Liver of Piacenza (above in this chapter) trying to predict the future, and you'll turn it off and do something more productive with your time. If you think you might be missing something from all this theatrical punditry, heed Warren Buffett's advice: "We've long felt that the only value of stock forecasters is to make fortune tellers look good. Even now, Charlie [Munger] and I continue to believe that short-term market forecasts are poison and should be kept locked up in a safe place, away from children and also from grown-ups who behave in the market like children." [151]

If you feel compelled to speculate in individual securities or with active managers, do it with a small amount of your money, say 5% or 10%, and take your shot. Don't invest with a manager who has dozens of positions and is hugging an equity or fixed income index. Put it with a manager who has real conviction on a handful of positions, or select a handful of stocks yourself. Who knows, you might get lucky. Or put it with a manager who is investing in something off the beaten path, an exposure you are unlikely to see in a traded fund. This might include deep distressed credit or startup companies via venture capital. At least if you get it right, or are lucky, the reward will be worthwhile.

Also, if you decide to speculate with some of your money, set it up in a separate account, away from your main investment assets. Don't combine your "stay rich" or "stay retired" money with your "get rich" money. You do not want to succumb to the temptation of doubling down on losing speculative positions with assets from your main retirement assets. The easy reach of new chips is a slippery slope to wrecking your long-term investment plan. Have a separate account for your play money. Speculate to your heart's content, but if you lose a lot, do not replenish the account. Work your way back. The longer the better, as it will keep you out of trouble.

SUMMARY

Treat active management for what it is, an expensive form of speculation, and allocate your capital accordingly. Whatever value some financial experts can produce through the application of their expertise is usually more than offset by the costs incurred for their services. They are not good enough at picking stocks or market timing to consistently offset the drag of their fees and trading costs. This is unlikely to change. As managers fail to beat the market and their funds close, new participants boldly step forward to take up the challenge and the chance to reap the huge payouts given to those who outperform the market, even for a time. There are always people willing to take their swing at the plate to earn these outsized rewards. Unfortunately, many individual and institutional investors continue to give them money to do so.

Mark Twain summed it up well, "There are two times in a man's life when he should not speculate: when he can't afford it, and when he can." [152]

With regard to active management:

• Few funds outperform the market on a risk-equivalent basis over time.

• There is little persistence among top-performing managers and funds.

• Management, trading, and administrative costs and taxes weigh down active manager performance to the point of underperformance.

• Markets are pretty efficient, and getting increasingly efficient, at aggregating investor knowledge and expectations into market prices.

• An investment that you cannot completely see and understand may have a fat tail of risk and should be avoided.

• If you feel the need to speculate in stocks, do so with a small part of your wealth.

CHAPTER 8

Factor-Based Investing

$\mathbf{S}$hould you do anything other than just buy a broad basket of indexed equities and bonds and sit on it? That would certainly be a reasonable choice. There are a few things, however, that may produce additional return beyond indexing the market. These center around market "factors," which are anomalies from the norm of efficient markets, where return is directly proportionate to risk. Contrary to the expectation of market efficiency, factors provide above-market returns (called premiums) across a range of securities.

Academics claim to have found hundreds of these factors, a virtual "zoo of factors." The most prominent and persistent factors are market beta, size, value, momentum, profitability, and quality (see **Chart 8.1**). These are discussed in this chapter. For more detail, a very good book on factors and factor-based investing, and upon which this chapter draws significantly upon, is *Your Complete Guide to Factor-Based Investing* by Andrew Berkin and Larry Swedroe. You can also find useful information on Dimensional Fund Advisors' website.[153]

Advance warning: this chapter is rather heavy going. It's near a 10 on the scale of eyes glazing over. So feel free to skip it. I would suggest that if you would like to consider factor-based investments for your portfolio, you should enlist the help of an investment advisor with experience in the area.

WHY FACTORS?

Although the academic debate on why factors exist is ongoing, two main explanations are that 1) factors have inherently greater risk, hence the higher returns, and 2) quirks of human behavior in financial markets create deviations from market efficiency. Anomalies are considered factors when they are: [154]

- **persistent** (they hold across long periods of time and different economic regimes),

- **pervasive** (they hold across countries, regions, sectors and asset classes),

- **robust** (they hold for various definitions, such as price-to-book (P/B) and price-to-earnings (P/E)),

- **investable** (they remain after trading costs are considered) and

- **intuitive** (there are logical risk-based or behavioral-based explanations for the premiums and why they should continue to exist).

Should you tilt your investment portfolio toward factors? You don't need to. As noted, you'll do just fine buying the entire stock and bond market through indexing. But if you believe the arguments concerning factors, and believe that they will persist, you could weight your portfolio toward them. Your end result will be similar to indexing, and you may do somewhat better.[155]

There is no certainty, though, that factors will persist, because investors are now aware of them. In addition, given higher turnover and tax inefficiency in implementing certain factor-based strategies, it may be preferable to keep them in tax-advantaged accounts.

CHART 8.1 RETURN AND RISK

	Mean Return (%)	Standard Deviation (%)	Sharpe Ratio
Market Beta	8.3	20.6	0.40
Size	3.3	13.9	0.24
Value	4.8	14.1	0.34
Momentum	9.6	15.7	0.61
Profitability	3.1	9.3	0.33
Quality	3.8	10.0	0.38

Source: Andrew L. Berkin and Larry E. Swedroe, *Your Complete Guide to Factor-Based Investing: The Way Smart Money Invests Today* (St. Louis, MO: BAM Alliance Press, 2016), 189.

CHART 8.2 MARKET BETA, SIZE, VALUE, MOMENTUM, PROFITABILITY, AND QUALITY (1927-2015)

	MB	SIZE	VAL.	MOM.	PROF.	QUAL.
Annual Premium (%)	8.3	3.3	4.8	9.6	3.1	3.8
Sharpe Ratio	0.40	0.24	0.34	0.61	0.33	0.38
1-Year Odds of Outperformance (%)	66	59	63	73	63	65
3-Year Odds of Outperformance (%)	76	66	72	86	72	75
5-Year Odds of Outperformance (%)	82	70	78	91	77	80
10-Year Odds of Outperformance (%)	90	77	86	97	85	89
20-Year Odds of Outperformance (%)	96	86	94	100	93	96

Source: Andrew L. Berkin and Larry E. Swedroe, *Your Complete Guide to Factor-Based Investing: The Way Smart Money Invests Today* (St. Louis, MO: BAM Alliance Press, 2016), 133.

CHART 8.3   HISTORICAL CORRELATIONS (1964-2015)

FACTOR	MARKET BETA	SIZE	VALUE	MOMENTUM	PROFITABILITY	QUALITY
Market Beta	1.00	0.29	-0.27	-0.17	-0.27	-0.52
Size	0.29	1.00	0.01	-0.12	-0.22	-0.53
Value	-0.27	0.01	1.00	-0.20	0.09	0.04
Momentum	-0.17	-0.12	-0.20	1.00	0.08	0.30
Profitability	-0.27	-0.22	0.09	0.08	1.00	0.74
Quality	-0.52	-0.53	0.04	0.30	0.74	1.00

Source: Andrew L. Berkin and Larry E. Swedroe, *Your Complete Guide to Factor-Based Investing: The Way Smart Money Invests Today* (St. Louis, MO: BAM Alliance Press, 2016), 186.

MARKET BETA

Market beta is the degree to which a security moves with the market. A portfolio composed of all the stocks in the market would have a beta of one. A stock with a beta of greater than one would have greater volatility (a measure of risk) than the market, and a stock with a beta of less than one would have less volatility (and less risk) than the market. The premium for market beta shown in **Chart 8.2** is the difference between the average annual return of the market (US stock market) and the average annual return of one-month US Treasury bills. From 1927 through 2015, the US market beta premium has been 8.3 percent.[156] The beta premium has been positive in about two-thirds of the years (1927-2015). In addition, the Sharpe ratio (measure of risk-adjusted returns) for beta has been 0.4, the second highest of all the factor premiums.[157]

The reason you get paid a premium for market beta is due to the uncertainty and the volatility of the return. When investing in the stock market, you can go for long time periods with disappointing performance. At 10-year time frames, for example, the market beta premium was negative 10% of the time, and at 20-year time frames, was negative 4% of the time.[158]

In addition, the volatility of the stock market, as measured by standard deviation, has been about 20% for the US stock market and 3 percent for one-month US Treasury bills.[159] The worst one-year return for the total US stock market was -43.5% in 1931. In contrast, the one-month US Treasury bill has never had a loss in a calendar year. The worst peak-to-valley loss in the US stock market was more than 83% from September 1929 through June 1932. During that period, the one-month US Treasury bill returned 6%.[160]

For portfolios with different investment returns, market beta explains about two-thirds of the difference. The remaining third needs to be explained by something else—luck, skill, or other factors, such as those described in **Chart 8.4.**[161]

See **CHART 8.4** »

SIZE

The size factor is the difference between the return of small company stocks and large company stocks. It's referred to as small minus big (SMB). The stocks of small companies historically have been riskier, more volatile and less liquid than stocks of large companies. Because of this an investor has been paid more to hold small cap stocks. Some reasons why small cap stocks may have higher returns and higher volatility than large cap stocks include:

1) Less stable businesses: Compared to large companies, small companies tend to have higher leverage than large companies, less ability to raise capital, less product diversity, newer business models, more volatile earnings, and lower profitability.

CHART 8.5 ANNUALIZED RETURNS BY MARKET CAP (1926-2015)
Largest to Smallest

CRSP Market Capitalization Deciles	1-2	3-5	6-8	9-10
Annualized Return %	9.82	11.15	11.54	12.15

Source: CRSP data provided by the Center for Research in Security Prices.

CHART 8.4   HISTORICAL CORRELATIONS (1964-2015)

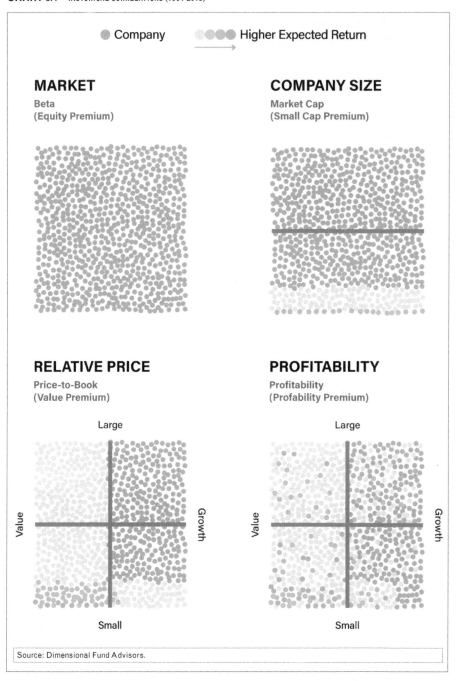

Source: Dimensional Fund Advisors.

2) Worse Performance in Periods of Economic Distress: Small companies are less resilient than large companies in a bad economy. During recessions and depressions, stocks of small companies generally underperform stocks of large companies, which have more stable business models and better access to financing. For example, when monetary policy is more restrictive, and the economic environment is poor, small value companies are more likely to wind up in bankruptcy. In good economic times, small cap stocks tend to appreciate faster than large cap stocks. These are often periods when monetary policy is accommodative, the economy is doing well, credit is readily available and corporate profits are high.

3) Less Liquid: Small cap stocks are less liquid, and therefore more costly to trade and have more volatile price swings than large cap stocks. Investors earn a premium for bearing the risks related to illiquidity. From 1927 through 2015, the standard deviation (variability around a mean return) of small cap stocks has been about 30%, compared to 20% for large cap stocks (a relative difference of 50%).

It should be noted that small cap growth stocks have underperformed over time. Academics believe this may be due to investors' attraction to "lottery-type" stocks, where there is the chance to "win big." [162] Like lottery tickets, these growth stocks are oversubscribed relative to their likely return, and therefore they have lower returns over time.[163] Small cap growth stock performance is similar to IPOs, which provide below-market returns as a group, but may provide a big payoff to the handful of investors who invest in a winning stock. (See **Chart 2.2** for a comparison of the distribution of returns of small cap stocks compared to large cap stocks.)

Small cap stock portfolios that have a quality screen which eliminates the stocks of "junk" companies have done well over time. The junk stocks are very small companies that typically are distressed or illiquid securities, or penny stocks that are fodder for stock touts and boiler room operations. The preference, then, is for small, more liquid value stocks with a quality tilt. Small cap portfolios of this sort have outperformed large cap stocks over time.

VALUE

Analysts break stocks into three main styles: value, core and growth. Value stocks pay higher dividends and trade at lower price-to-earnings (P/E) ratios and lower price-to-book (P/B) values than growth stocks, which have higher P/E and P/B ratios and above-average earnings growth rates. Core stocks are in between value and growth.

Over long periods of time, value stocks have outperformed growth stocks. The value factor, or value premium, is the annual average return of value stocks minus the annual average return of growth stocks. From 1927 through 2015, the annual US value premium has been 4.8%.[164] The value premium extends across international markets as well.[165] And it has been found in bonds, commodities and currencies.[166]

Although one would expect that any excess return provided by value stocks would be quickly eliminated as investors pile into a strategy providing excess returns, the value premium seems to persist.[167] Why is this? The short answer is no one knows for sure, but here are a couple explanations.

VALUE STOCKS ARE RISKIER

One logical reason for the value premium is that value stocks are riskier (see **Chart 8.6**). They have weaker and more volatile earnings, have more debt, greater sunk costs in capital investment, less certain cash flows, and are more susceptible than growth stock to bad economic environments. Because of their greater risks, value stocks should earn a higher return relative to growth stocks.[168] Value stocks carry more debt than growth stocks, and value companies' earnings are more than twice as volatile as those of growth companies.[169] Companies with high leverage, or debt, tend to operate with less of a financial cushion and are more often distressed or bankrupt than firms generally.

Value stocks are a bit less risky than growth stocks in good economic environments, and much riskier in bad economic environments.[170] Their returns tend to correlate to the market cycle, and therefore are less attractive than growth stocks in that they perform worse in down markets, when an investor's other investments, and possibly their business and job prospects, may also be faring poorly. Therefore, given this unattractive dynamic, value stocks should pay a higher premium than growth stocks, which hold up better in a bad economy. This was demonstrated in the recession from December 2007 to June 2009, when the value premium was -0.44 percent per month.[171] In 2008 large cap value stocks were down 42.8%, whereas large cap growth stocks were down 30.9%.[172]

STOCKS AS LOTTERY TICKETS

One other explanation for the value premium is that investors are unduly pessimistic about the prospects for value companies, and overly optimistic about the prospects for growth companies. As noted previously, people will pay up for the chance of a big score, however remote, on a lottery-type stock. In research jargon, people have a preference for stocks that have positive skewness, where values to the right of (greater than) the mean are fewer but farther from it than values to the left of (less than) the mean. You are more likely to have a loser, but a small chance of having a massive winner. Growth stocks have more of a lottery-type payoff, because they may be the next Amazon, Facebook or Google. And because people are paying up for the chance of a big payoff, growth stocks often can be overpriced relative to value stocks, with the value stocks then providing a better long-term return. Investors' partiality for positively skewed assets explains other anomalies such as the below-average return on IPOs.

In addition, growth stocks, such as internet and technology stocks, are "story stocks." They attract higher levels of media attention and investor interest than stodgy value companies, such as banks, utilities and manufacturing companies. The genius of a Steve Jobs and the creative disruption of new companies like Google and Facebook makes for more interesting reading and images than the CEO at a utility company improving margins. Investors can get carried away with over-optimistic projections on a story stock company's future earnings potential and overpay for the stock. They may "anchor" to a company's high growth rate and unduly project the high growth rate continuing for many years, even though growth inevitably declines as the company grows bigger in size and its growth reverts towards the mean. Additionally, people are susceptible to recency bias, in that they tend to invest in companies that they are familiar with, because they see them most often in their daily lives and in the news (Facebook, Amazon, Apple, Netflix, and Google).

CRITICS OF THE VALUE PREMIUM

Some noteworthy investors do not view the value premium as a distinct investment advantage. They see value and growth varying in return over time, but neither outperforming. John Bogle, founder of Vanguard, has argued that "neither strategy—growth or value—has an inherent long-term edge" and "there is no reason to expect either style to outpace the other over time." Bogle notes that academic studies concluding that value outperforms growth are period dependent.[173]

> In the very long run, the cycles have ironed themselves out and, at least in my view, there is no reason to expect either style to outpace the other over time (despite the important tax advantage for the growth investor)…[174]

> …I'm a firm believer that RTM [return to the mean] is a pervasive investment principle. So place me in the camp of those who believe that neither strategy, Growth or Value, has an inherent long-term edge.[175]

Warren Buffett has said that "Market commentators and investment managers who glibly refer to 'growth' and 'value' styles as contrasting approaches to investment are displaying their ignorance, not their sophistication. Growth is simply a component—usually a plus, sometimes a minus—in the value equation." [176]

Value can underperform growth over long periods. This is particularly a risk for investors with short-to-intermediate investment time horizons. In addition, value stocks are less tax efficient than growth stocks. Growth companies, to maintain and take advantage of their high growth rates, tend to reinvest more of their earnings rather than pay them out as dividends to stockholders. Therefore, the return of growth stocks comes more from capital appreciation, which is more tax efficient for an investor who is taxed on dividend income. Growth stocks may have an after-tax advantage of 1% to 2% in annual return compared to value stocks, a significant long-term advantage for an investor in a high tax bracket.[177]

CHART 8.6 PERFORMANCE OF VALUE VS GROWTH ANNUALIZED (1975-2020)

	Return %	Std. Deviation	Sharpe Ratio
Large Cap US Stocks	12.5	18.1	0.45
Large Cap US Growth Stocks	13.0	15.8	0.54
Large Cap US Value Stocks	14.1	21.9	0.44
Small Cap US Stocks	15.5	24.2	0.46
Small Cap US Growth Stocks	15.3	20.8	0.52
Small Cap US Value Stocks	17.3	28.4	0.45

Source: Dimensional Fund Advisors

MOMENTUM

Momentum describes the tendency of a rising stock price to continue to rise, and a falling stock price to continue to fall. Writes Burton Malkiel, "Some patterns appear to exist in the development of stock prices. Over the short holdings periods, there is some evidence of momentum in the stock market. Increases in stock prices are slightly more likely to be followed by further increases than by price declines. For longer holding periods, reversion to the mean appears to be the pattern." [178]

Research on the momentum factor shows that stocks that had positive momentum for 6 months and were held for the next 6 months achieved a compound annual growth rate of 12.01%, outperforming the S&P 500's average annual return of 10%.[179] From 1927 through 2015, the annual average return of the momentum factor was 9.6%, and from 1994 through 2015 it was 6.3%.[180] The momentum premium has been strong across geographies, and is particularly strong in small cap and microcap stocks.

Cliff Asness and his colleagues at AQR Capital Management believe there has been a momentum premium in US equities since 1801, and in the UK since the Victorian age.[181] They conclude that momentum exists in other asset classes as well: "Some of this evidence predates academic research in financial economics, suggesting that the momentum premium has been a part of markets for as long as there have been markets." [182]

It is not clear why the momentum anomaly persists, but one explanation is that it is due to human behavioral tendencies called cognitive biases. There is evidence that investors tend to underreact to new information about a company. For example, it takes a while for investors to process positive news about a company and incorporate it into its stock price. So over several months the stock rises. The momentum from the positive news and the rising stock price causes other investors to follow the herd and to become overly optimistic about the company's prospects, leading to further appreciation in the company's shares.

Another cognitive bias, recency bias, may also play a part in the momentum premium. Due to the media coverage of the stock, the stock more quickly comes to mind when investors are deciding which stocks to invest in. People invest in what is familiar to them and what they can more readily recall (Apple, Amazon, Facebook), and this contributes to momentum in the stock of a high profile company. In time the stock's price appreciation reverts toward the mean as the good news fades and the company fails to meet the rosy investor projections.

Momentum stocks may have higher risk as well, because they tend to have sharp drawdowns when trends reverse. Negative returns, those below the mean, are fewer but farther from the mean compared to positive returns, those above the mean.[183] The momentum premium, therefore, is compensation for an investor on occasion enduring very significant declines, which tend to occur during periods of economic weakness or market shocks, when market trends reverse. In addition, momentum strategies have significant turnover, which increases transaction costs and recognized capital gains, making the strategy less attractive to a taxable investor.

PROFITABILITY & QUALITY

The stocks of highly profitable companies produce higher returns than stocks of less-profitable companies, even though the stocks of highly profitable companies may have higher valuations.[184] Gross profitability (sales minus the cost of goods sold) is a good predictor of future earnings growth. The profitability factor takes the annual average return of the top 30 percent of firms with high profitability minus the returns of the bottom 30 percent of firms with low profitability (referred to in academic literature as robust-minus-weak, or RMW).

One explanation for the profitability premium is that firms with strong profitability are mainly growth companies, which have earnings projected farther into the future, and far-off returns are less predictable and therefore more risky. In addition, high profits attract competition. As a high growth, high profit business attracts competition, there is significant risk that a company's advantage in the marketplace may be superseded more quickly than anticipated. Think of companies such as Motorola and Nokia, which were the leading players in the mobile phone industry in the early 2000s, but were surpassed in under a decade by competitors such as Samsung, Apple and Huawei.

Another explanation for the profitability premium is that investors overestimate how quickly the performance of profitable firms will mean revert, that is, how long it will take for a company's profitability to deteriorate due to competition or obsolescence. Investors think the returns will mean revert faster than they actually do. Also, as noted above, investors underreact to news on company profitability, and therefore underprice the company's stock.

The profitability factor, a growth strategy, complements investment strategies based on the value factor and the momentum factor. Profitable firms do relatively well in recessions when equity markets do poorly and value strategies underperform and momentum strategies suffer losses due to trend reversals. A stock's profitability is the single most significant predictor of low volatility.[185]

The quality factor (quality minus junk or QMJ) measures the returns of high-quality companies minus the returns of low-quality companies. It includes profitability and several other elements. High quality companies exhibit stable earnings, high margins, low leverage, and strong balance sheets.[186] Companies meeting these criteria have produced high returns and performed well in down markets.

TERM PREMIUM AND DEFAULT PREMIUM

Most of the differences between bonds can be explained by two factors: term risk, also known as duration, and default risk, also called credit risk. For the period 1927 through 2015, the premium earned for term risk, defined as the annual average return on long-term (20-year) US government bonds minus the annual average return on the one-month US Treasury bill, was 2.5 percent.[187] The longer the maturity of bonds, the higher the premium. The term premium historically has had better odds of generating outperformance than the risk premium (see **Chart 8.7**).

CHART 8.7 TERM PREMIUM AND DEFAULT PREMIUM ODDS OF OUTPERFORMANCE (%)
1927-2015

	1-Year	3-Year	5-Year	10-Year	20-Year
Term	64	74	80	88	95
Default	53	54	56	58	61

Source: Andrew L. Berkin and Larry E. Swedroe, *Your Complete Guide to Factor-Based Investing: The Way Smart Money Invests Today* (St. Louis, MO: BAM Alliance Press, 2016), 190.

The term premium provides a diversification benefit as it has low-to-negative correlation to other factors. "For the period from 1964 through 2015, its correlation to the other factors has been: market beta: 0.12; size: 0.12; value: 0.01; momentum: 0.08; profitability: 0.06; and default: -0.42." [188] Correlation of US Treasury bonds of any term has been about zero.

The default risk premium is the return on long-term investment-grade bonds (20-year)[189] minus the return on long-term government bonds (20-year).[190] Taking credit risk has not been rewarded much historically. From 1927 through 2015, the annual average premium was 0.3 percent. Corporate bonds have higher yields than government issues of the same maturity, but the incremental yield historically has been offset by credit losses, higher expense ratios of corporate bond funds relative to government bond funds (resulting from the need to analyze the credit risk of corporate issuers), and other features incorporated into corporate bonds, such as call options.[191] A call option gives the issuer the right to call in (prepay) the bonds. The issuer will do so if interest rates drop sufficiently to warrant the expense of the recall and reissuance of new bonds at the then-prevailing lower interest rate. The investor holding the higher-yielding bond that is paid off early will then have to purchase a new bond yielding a lower interest rate. There are very few US Treasury issues with call features.[192] In addition, US government securities are not taxed at the state and local levels, whereas interest on corporate debt is.

Default risk also has a high correlation to bad economic and equity market environments (see **Chart 8.8**). Much of the return of high yield debt is explained by risk premiums of equities rather than debt.[193] All but short-maturity corporate bonds carry equity-like risks. In addition, high yield debt does not have a normal return distribution. It exhibits negative skewness and has excess kurtosis (fat tails)—a higher percentage of very low and very high returns than would be expected in a normal distribution. The very high kurtosis exhibited by high yield debt reflects the risk of downgrades, defaults and bankruptcies.

CHART 8.8   HIGH YIELD BOND RETURNS IN BAD EQUITY MARKETS

	2008 Return (%)	1Q 2020 Return (%)
S&P 500 Index	-37.0	-19.6
U.S. High Yield Corporate Bonds	-26.2	-12.7
U.S. Treasury Bonds - Intermediate	11.4	5.3

Source: S&P 500 Index, Bloomberg Barclays US Treasury Bond Index Intermediate, Bloomberg Barclays US. High Yield Corporate Bond Index.

The higher yield of low-grade bonds makes their duration shorter and less sensitive to movements in interest rates than investment-grade bonds. And their effective duration is lower because they are often called earlier by issuers (they have weaker call protection than investment-grade bonds).

CARRY FACTOR

The carry factor is the propensity of higher-yielding assets to produce higher returns than lower-yielding assets. Common strategies in this area include going long currencies of countries with high interest rates and shorting those with low interest rates.

This anomaly may be due to the market actions of non-profit-seeking participants such as central banks, who may be focused on interest rates or employment, and commercial hedgers, such as food manufacturers hedging the price of wheat. Central bank mandates include promoting stable currencies and full employment, and actions supporting these policies may contribute to the carry factor. In addition, companies with earnings in foreign currencies hedge this exposure in order to provide more stable earnings in the currency in which they report for their financial statements.

The risk in carry is when investment relationships change quickly, such as in crisis environments when capital flees to low-yielding "safe haven" currencies. The higher-yielding currencies are in some ways riskier, as they are more correlated with equity market risk in bad economic environments when stocks decline and there is a flight to higher quality and more liquid assets. Flight to quality and liquidity favors more stable, lower-yielding currencies. The premium, then, is closely linked to the fact that it performs poorly in down markets and is closely linked to global macroeconomic risk.

An example of this would be the yen carry trade in the early 2000s through the economic crisis of 2008. With the widening spread between US and Japanese rates from 2004-2007, the yen-carry trade grew, as investors borrowed in lower-yielding yen and invested in higher-yielding dollar-denominated assets, thereby capturing the spread or difference between the two. Investments included riskier assets such as US subprime residential mortgage-backed securities (RMBS) and collateralized debt obligations (CDOs). As the prices of these securities declined in 2007-2008 and shook the global financial system, the US Federal Reserve cut interest rates aggressively, eliminating the difference between Japanese and US rates. Traders tried to unwind their leveraged yen-carry trades by selling RMBS, CDOs and other securities for dollars to buy yen, leading to the appreciation of the yen against other currencies. This caused considerable volatility in currency markets and losses for investors. As the yen appreciated, investors in the carry trade lost money because their yen costs increased while their dollar-denominated investments decreased in value.

CHART 8.9 YEN CARRY TRADE

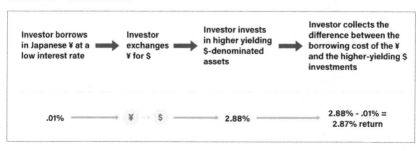

TREND FOLLOWING

Trend-following strategies are related to momentum in that they tend to buy a security when its price is rising, and sell it when its price is falling. These strategies may try to profit from trends in security prices over different time intervals, from hours to days to weeks to months. Reasons for trends in markets include behavioral biases of investors, transactional cost frictions, demands from market hedgers, and interventions by central banks and governments.

Trend-following strategies, which are common in the managed futures space, have almost no correlation to stocks and bonds, which makes them attractive from a portfolio diversification standpoint. They also have a tail-risk hedge aspect in that they tend to do well in times of expanding market volatility that accompanies sustained equity market sell-offs.

Returns for trend-following strategies, however, are generally low. For most investors, the lower standard deviation of their portfolio return obtained by the diversification provided by trend following strategies is more than offset by lower total portfolio return over time.

Also, a significant part of the return of trend-following strategies historically has come from the interest on cash and Treasuries used as collateral for futures trades by trend-following managers. Returns for the strategy are even worse, therefore, in low-rate environments. In addition, trend-following strategies are high turnover and relatively tax inefficient.

DETERIORATION OF FACTOR PREMIUMS

It would be reasonable to expect that factor premiums will be lower going forward because they are now well known by institutional investors. The drivers of factor premiums have been highlighted by academic studies, and as factor-based investments expand in popularity, it is more likely that the excess return provided by these factors will diminish. There seems to be evidence of this. Increased institutional trading after publication of anomalies is related to the post-publication decay in their returns.[194]

One study points to a 32% reduction in factor returns after publication, and post-publication there has been a reduction in nine of the fourteen anomalies.[195] Berkin and Swedroe note that from 1927 to 1981, the annual size premium (small compared to large) was 4.7%. In the post-publication period, from 1982 to 2015, the premium was only 1 percent. Institutional awareness, increasing speed in analyzing data, and lower trading costs are some of the reasons for why factor premiums are likely to shrink. Relatedly, some experts believe that much of what has passed for active manager skill was "loading" on these factors and premiums, and as they decline, active manager returns should also decline across all asset classes.

There is evidence, however, that some anomalies may persist. Factor-based premiums that are more costly to arbitrage due to trading costs or lack of liquidity may decline less even though the marketplace is aware of them. These friction costs may prevent the factor premiums from disappearing entirely. In addition, where risk is central to the factor, premiums should remain.

Also, it takes time for many factors to provide outperformance, which may be too long to wait for investors who benchmark themselves to a popular index such as the S&P 500. Investors who overweighted the value factor were disappointed when the S&P 500 outperformed value stocks for the period 2010-2020. Many investors find it difficult to endure the psychological pain of underperforming a benchmark for long periods, and therefore may not be suitable for factor-based investing.

Factor premiums have experienced long periods of negative returns. The market beta premium, for example, has been negative in 9% of 10-year periods and in 3% of 20-year periods.[196] Additionally, adding factors may increase portfolio turnover, thereby increasing trading costs and making a portfolio less tax efficient.

SUMMARY

• Factors are anomalies from the expectation of efficient markets.

• The premiums, or excess returns, from factors historically have been persistent across securities and geographies.

• Now widely researched by academics and invested in by institutional investors, there is no assurance that factor premiums will persist and if so to what extent.

CHART 8.10 DIMENSIONS OF EXPECTED RETURNS
Historical premiums and returns (annualized): US, Developed ex US, and Emerging Markets

Company Size

Relative performance
of small cap stocks vs.
large cap stocks (%)

Relative Price

Relative performance
of value stocks vs.
growth stocks (%)

Profitability

Relative performance
of high profitability
stocks vs. low profitability
stocks (%)

US Stocks

1928-2020

1.94 | 11.95 | 10.01

Small minus Large | Small | Large
| Annualized Returns

1928-2020

2.80 | 12.39 | 9.59

Value minus Growth | Value | Growth
| Annualized Returns

1964-2020

3.49 | 11.90 | 8.41

High Prof. minus Low Prof. | High Prof. | Low Prof.
| Annualized Returns

Developed ex US Markets Stocks

1970-2020

4.85 | 14.18 | 9.32

Small minus Large | Small | Large
| Annualized Returns

1975-2020

3.98 | 12.92 | 8.94

Value minus Growth | Value | Growth
| Annualized Returns

1991-2020

3.98 | 12.92 | 8.94

High Prof. minus Low Prof. | High Prof. | Low Prof.
| Annualized Returns

Emerging Markets Stocks

1989-2020

2.32 | 12.42 | 10.10

Small minus Large | Small | Large
| Annualized Returns

1990-2020

3.97 | 10.97 | 6.99

Value minus Growth | Value | Growth
| Annualized Returns

1992-2020

3.52 | 9.79 | 6.27

High Prof. minus Low Prof. | High Prof. | Low Prof.
| Annualized Returns

CHART 8.11 HISTORICAL PERFORMANCE OF PREMIUMS OVER ROLLING PERIODS
US Markets

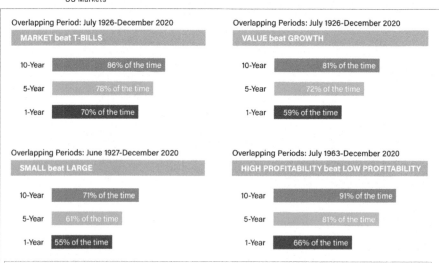

Overlapping Period: July 1926-December 2020

MARKET beat T-BILLS

10-Year	86% of the time
5-Year	78% of the time
1-Year	70% of the time

Overlapping Periods: July 1926-December 2020

VALUE beat GROWTH

10-Year	81% of the time
5-Year	72% of the time
1-Year	59% of the time

Overlapping Periods: June 1927-December 2020

SMALL beat LARGE

10-Year	71% of the time
5-Year	61% of the time
1-Year	55% of the time

Overlapping Periods: July 1963-December 2020

HIGH PROFITABILITY beat LOW PROFITABILITY

10-Year	91% of the time
5-Year	81% of the time
1-Year	66% of the time

Source: Dimensional Fund Advisors. Past performance is no guarantee of future results. Actual returns may be lower. In USD. Indices are not available for direct investment. Index returns are not representative of actual portfolios and do not reflect costs and fees associated with an actual investment. Based on monthly rolling differences in annualized returns over the periods listed. Rolling multiyear periods overlap and are not independent. Indices are not available for direct investment. Index returns are not representative of actual portfolios and do not reflect costs and fees associated with an actual investment. "One-Month Treasury Bills" is the IA SBBI US 30 Day TBill TR USD, provided by Morningstar. S&P data © 2021 S&P Dow Jones Indices LLC, a division of S&P Global. All rights reserved. See "Index Descriptions" in the appendix for descriptions of Dimensional and Fama/French index data. Market is Fama/French Total US Market Research Index. T-Bills is One-Month US Treasury Bills. There are 1,015 overlapping 10-year periods, 1,075 overlapping 5-year periods, and 1,123 overlapping 1-year periods. Value is Fama/French US Value Research Index. Growth is Fama/French US Growth Research Index. There are 1,015 overlapping 10-year periods, 1,075 overlapping 5-year periods, and 1,123 overlapping 1-year periods. Small is Dimensional US Small Cap Index. Large is S&P 500 Index. There are 1,004 overlapping 10-year periods, 1,064 overlapping 5-year periods, and 1,112 overlapping 1-year periods. High is Fama/French US High Profitability Index. Low is Fama/French US Low Profitability Index. There are 571 overlapping 10-year periods, 631 overlapping 5-year periods, and 679 overlapping 1-year periods.

Risks

Like nightmares, there are as many investment risks for an investor to worry about as an active imagination can conjure. A reoccurring one for many people is the stock market cratering. There are, however, other risks to consider. I highlight a few in this chapter, including inflation, longevity, shortfall, regret and cognitive decline.

INVESTMENT VOLATILITY

Stocks can certainly go down 50% or more in a given year. But as highlighted in **Chart 2.7**, stocks and bonds converge around their long-term Base Case returns the longer you hold them. Risk therefore can be looked at as time dependent. The longer your time horizon, the less you need to be concerned with short-term ups and downs in the stock market.

Professional investors often focus on the volatility of investments, and use standard deviation as a measure of this. As noted, standard deviation, the dispersion around the mean return, is a component of the Sharpe ratio (see **Chart 6.8**), which is a measure of the return of an investment relative to its volatility. The higher the Sharpe ratio, the more attractive an investment theoretically is given the risk you are taking. Many fund managers will tout their funds as having low standard deviation and high Sharpe ratios.

What matters for a long-term investor, however, is not an investment's Sharpe ratio but its long-term return. If you can look past the short-term volatility of your investments and focus on the total return, and for taxable investors the total after-tax return, you can avoid overconcentration on short-term volatility. This is easier said than done, particularly when the stock market is tanking. Some investors pay a premium in terms of high management fees, and often experience lower risk-adjusted returns, to invest in less liquid asset classes such as private equity and private real estate which are priced less frequently than publicly traded securities and therefore have lower price volatility. If you can tune out the regular volatility of your investment portfolio, however, and focus on the long term, you will improve your chances of reaching your investment goals.

If you are nearing or in retirement, your time frame is shorter. It's often-times not that short, as many people have retirements of 30 years or longer. But you need to consider volatility, particularly if you are drawing down on your assets at a fairly constant rate. This is called *sequence of returns risk.* If you start your retirement at the beginning of a bear market in equities and are using your saved wealth at a constant rate, you may in effect be using a higher percentage of your total assets than you had planned.

For example, assume you have $2,000,000 in retirement savings and were planning on spending 5% annually ($100,000). Your investment portfolio is half in stocks ($1,000,000) and half in bonds ($1,000,000). If the stock market goes down 50%, your stock portfolio is now worth $500,000 and your total portfolio $1,500,000. Your $100,000 in annual spending is now 6.7% of your portfolio. If this goes on for a few years without a rebound in stocks, your above-target spending will reduce the ability of your retirement assets to sustain your planned spending over the longer term. Of course, you could reduce your spending in line with the reduction in your retirement savings, but not everyone can easily do that. Therefore, scenarios like this should be factored into retirement planning.

INFLATION

Inflation risk is where your wealth does not retain its purchasing power after inflation. In **Chart 9.1** you can see that what cost $1 in 1964 cost $8.80 in 2020. The risk of not keeping up with inflation is what provides an incentive to invest at least part of your portfolio in equities. Equity returns historically have outpaced inflation over longer time periods.

See CHART 9.1 »

CHART 9.1   INFLATION: MONEY TODAY WILL LIKELY BUY LESS TOMORROW

1960	1980	2000	2020
$1.00	$2.65	$5.75	$8.80

Source: US Bureau of Labor Statistics CPI Inflation Calculator

---

LONGEVITY RISK

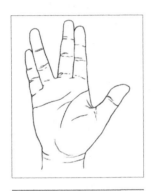

An icon from my youth, the half-Vulcan Mr. Spock from the television show *Star Trek*, would say as part of the Vulcan salutation, "live long and prosper" ("dif-tor heh smusma" in the Vulcan language). Spock's words, a blessing of sorts, are apropos for a human living on retirement savings, because if you live a long time you will need your investments to prosper.

Outliving one's assets is probably the greatest investment risk most people face. In having your wealth last should you reach a very old age, you are between a rock and a hard place. On one hand, your investment allocation cannot take the volatility of an all-stock portfolio, where you could go years without a return, all the while drawing down on your assets for living expenses. On the other hand, you need to take some equity risk to provide for the growth of your assets after inflation.

For example, if you seek to preserve your capital by buying secure, short-term investments such as Treasury bills, you run the risk that inflation will be higher than what the bills are returning. Over time the purchasing power of your wealth will diminish. If $1 today purchases half of what it did 15 years ago, you have in effect lost half your wealth (see **Chart 9.1**). If your money is not growing at the rate of inflation, which over the last century in the US has averaged about 3%, your standard of living will decline. You will either need to reduce your spending, or spend down your capital to support your standard of living.

Individuals have to constantly battle the twin nemeses of inflation, which erodes the purchasing power of wealth, and volatile markets, which can result in significant drawdowns on wealth. It's a bit of a pickle. Having your assets keep up with inflation is a focus, but alternatively, if you attempt to outrun inflation and your own wealth consumption by investing in riskier assets such as stocks, you run the risk of drawing down your assets during a period of negative or flat equity market returns.

Over your retirement years, to provide a steady investment return you will need some balance of equities and bonds, complemented by Social Security and perhaps an annuity. You will want to plan this carefully, and working with an advisor or financial planner may be in order.

The timing of your retirement also affects what money you will need should you live a very long life. Your retirement projections will be different if you retire right before a period when financial returns are subpar. There have been lengthy periods, 10-20 years, when equity investments and fixed income investments produced low-to-negative returns after inflation. High return periods typically are followed by periods of underperformance. The bull market of the 1950s to mid-60s was preceded by the depression and wars years of the 1930s and 1940s. The strong equity markets of the mid-1980s and 1990s were preceded by the stagflation years of 1968-1982, when both equities and bonds performed poorly. The bull market from 2009 to 2019 was preceded by a ten-year period following the dot.com bust when the return for the S&P 500 was negative.

Save generously and assume low investment returns. If your investment returns turn out better than expected, you will be pleasantly surprised. If not, you will not be disappointed. Being in control of your fate through disciplined saving and conservative return assumptions, rather than hoping high investment returns will bail out your retirement, will help you rest easy. You will not worry about your assets being able to support you should you live an extra-long life.

Along these lines is a story about Albert Einstein. Einstein was on a lecture tour in Japan after having won the 1921 Nobel Prize for physics. He was staying at the Imperial Hotel in Tokyo, when a local courier delivered a message. Einstein apparently had no cash to tip the courier, so he gave him short notes on the hotel's stationery. One of the notes read, in Einstein's native German, "A calm and modest life brings more happiness than the pursuit of success combined with constant restlessness." [197] A calm and modest approach to your finances, based on savings and moderate assumptions for investment returns, is a good plan for financial contentedness.

SHORTFALL RISK

The front-and-center risk for you as an investor is that you do not reach your investment goals. This is also called shortfall risk. An example would be where you do not have enough assets to retire on at age 65. This can be due to chance, something extreme that happens in your life—disability or job loss—or in the world economy—prolonged economic depression or lower-than-average stock and bond returns.

Assuming your life is fairly normal with regard to health, and the world economy continues to grow, the biggest variables in your reaching your wealth goals will be your savings and how successful you are at managing the wealth you have. To reach your financial goals safely and on time, there is a balance between taking enough risk so that you reach your goals and not too much risk so that you may suffer a setback that is difficult to recover from.

Consider your portfolio from the perspective of "liability driven investing." Institutional investors use the term to describe an approach whereby their investments are determined by their liabilities. If a pension plan, for example, knows it needs to achieve a 7% return to meet the payments due its beneficiaries in 10 years, the pension manager will develop an investment plan that will maximize the chance of having enough cash in 10 years to meet its obligations, and do so taking the least amount of risk to achieve the 7% return.

Think about what is the least amount of risk you need to take to achieve your investment goals. If you can achieve your goals by being 70% in bonds rather than 70% in equities, then you may decide to forego the additional volatility of equities and go with bonds, as it achieves your investment goal with the least amount of risk. Alternatively, if your plan calls for achieving a 7% annual portfolio return after inflation, you are likely going to need to take significant equity risk to achieve that goal.

REGRET

People regret when an investment they made goes bad, or an investment they decided not to make does well. Emotions including regret can wreak havoc with the best-intentioned investment plan, so be aware, and develop habits of investing that will help you avoid second-guessing and the pang of regret. These can include developing a lifemap and sticking to a long-term investment plan, avoiding the temptation to speculate in individual securities, limiting how often you look at the value of your investment portfolio, and other techniques to shift your focus from the immediate and emotional to the longer-term and dispassionate.

Years ago I managed a conservative muni bond portfolio for Oprah Winfrey at an investment firm at which I worked. It was, according to her advisor, Oprah's "stay rich" money. Putting your investments into a "stay rich" bond and cash bucket and a "get rich" equity bucket is a useful way of mentally accounting for your varied investment goals. It is backed by behavioral research. Mentally separating these two pots of money, and better yet having them in separate accounts, can help you keep your emotions on a more even keel with regard to your investments. When the stock market is doing well, you can feel good looking at the strong gains in your "get rich" equity account. When stock prices are falling, you can feel good that you have a safe stash of money in your "stay rich" conservative bond and cash account.

COGNITIVE DECLINE

As a person ages, their brain's ability to effectively process information declines. You may be sharp as a tack now, but the future you, the one in 10 or 20 or 30 years, may not be. Mental decline may be mild, with cases of forgetfulness and senior moments, or extreme, with debilitating dementia.

Making sound investment decisions, a fairly high-level mental activity, often suffers with age. And you may not be fully aware of your own decline. One study indicates that even as people's financial literacy declines, they remain overconfident in their abilities.[198]

See CHART 9.2 »

CHART 9.2   FINANCIAL LITERACY DECLINES WITH AGE WHILE CONFIDENCE REMAINS HIGH

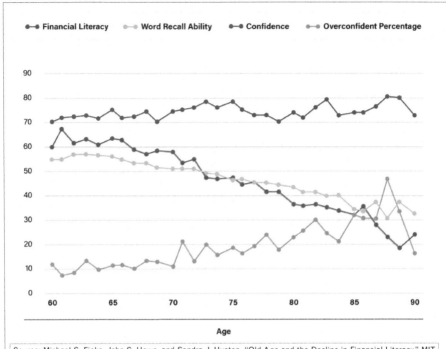

Source: Michael S. Finke, John S. Howe, and Sandra J. Huston, "Old Age and the Decline in Financial Literacy," MIT Center for Finance & Policy, September 2015.

Scientific evidence suggests people are happier as they age, are more prone to being generous, and are less easily ruffled by the minor day-to-day annoyances of life. Having a more sanguine mental outlook may be something to look forward to in one's older years.

These general tendencies, however, may put an older person at greater financial risk. They may be less discerning and more gullible. Here are some examples:

1) Being less skeptical of sales pitches for investment products, whether it be TV pitches or sales calls regarding "help" with your retirement benefits, annuities, reverse mortgages, gold coins, etc.,

2) Being taken advantage of financially by a caregiver, or even a family member, who may be helping you pay your bills,

3) Being open to risky, long shot investments, such as small company penny or "pink sheet" stocks, when all you need for a comfortable retirement are more conservative, stable investments, and

4) Being too generous financially with children and grandchildren, or with charities, thereby jeopardizing the assets you need in retirement.

Being on top of financial competency is particularly important when one spouse is dependent on the other spouse's handling of their joint finances. One spouse may be unaware that the other is making unwise decisions which are undermining the couple's financial security.

People like a good ending to a story. You don't want your story to be that the wealth you worked so hard for during your lifetime was frittered away at the end.

TEAM OF ADVISORS

I suggest you build a small team of trusted advisors who have insight into your finances. This group can include family members. But it should also include people who have a professional responsibility to act as a fiduciary, that is, in your best interests. This could be an accountant, an investment advisor, or an attorney.

Get this group together at least once a year to review your overall financial, tax and estate situation. This will ensure multiple eyes on your finances. They will know you, and since they interact with you less frequently, say, than family members, they may more readily see changes in your mental acuity over time. Tell them you want them to speak up if they see a noticeable change. With the regular review, they will also be in a position to spot changes in your investment activity or expenditures that may be of concern.

CONSOLIDATE ASSETS & FINANCIAL INFORMATION

If you have several IRA and 401(k) accounts, consider consolidating them. This will make it easier for you to manage and easier for others to manage if they need to take over from you in the event of your incapacity. It would also enhance the safety of your assets if you consolidated them in fiduciary-protected accounts.

It is also prudent to have your account information, related passwords, and provider contact information in a safe but accessible place. Should something happen to you, you want your spouse or partner or whoever takes over your financial matters to know where everything is located. In a time of crisis, which is what it will be if something unexpected happens to you, you want cash and other financial resources to be available.

DURABLE POWER OF ATTORNEY

You should have a durable power of attorney in place as part of your overall estate planning. A durable power of attorney authorizes someone to act on your behalf in legal, business and financial matters in the event you are incapacitated. Should you become mentally incapacitated, you want a responsible person to oversee your financial affairs. Put this in place now. You may not use it, but better safe than sorry.

None of us likes to plan for our physical and mental decline, and eventual end. But better to do so when you are still capable. You don't want to leave a financial mess that will create stress for and perhaps conflict among your family members. It should give you peace of mind that your financial affairs will be in order whatever may come.

SUMMARY

• Accept that volatility is part of investing, but plan to achieve your investment goals with the least amount of volatility possible.

• Inflation is a form of negative return on your investments, because it reduces the purchasing power of money. Your investment plan should take into account the real, after-inflation, growth of your wealth.

• Have the risk/return profile of your portfolio tailored so that you are taking enough risk to maintain the purchasing power of your wealth after inflation, but no more than is needed to achieve your retirement goals.

• Regret is a powerful emotion. If it helps you stick to a disciplined investment plan, mentally bucket your investments into your "stay rich" bond and cash allocation, which will fare well in times of market declines, and your "get rich" equity allocation, which will help you grow the after-inflation value of your wealth.

• Establish a plan for the management of your life should you experience significant cognitive decline. Put in place a durable power of attorney for a person to handle your finances should you become mentally incapacitated. Also, build a team of trusted advisors to review your finances at least annually, and who can step in and help in the event you experience mental decline that could jeopardize your financial well-being.

CHAPTER 10

Using an
Investment Advisor

On the road to financial security you may feel that you would like a guide to accompany you, someone to ride shotgun. You might ask yourself, should I hire someone to help me manage my money? And if so, whom?

TO MANAGE OR NOT TO MANAGE YOUR MONEY YOURSELF

You are the chief executive officer of your life. You should be on top of planning your financial future and achieving your goals. If you take the time to learn a core amount of investment knowledge, you can do a good job managing your money yourself. Of course, some people are better equipped to do this than others. For example, you may be the type of person who is disciplined about diet and exercise, or you may do better working with a personal trainer or dietician to achieve your fitness goals. "A lot of people are too intimidated, too busy, or just can't be bothered to devote time and effort to their finances," writes Jason Zweig.[199] With regard to wealth management, about half of adults use an investment advisor to help navigate financial issues.

Key reasons for using a financial advisor:

1) Saving time for other things. Time is precious and becomes dearer as one gets older. You may not want to spend what limited time you have on Earth learning the ropes of investing and handling your finances. Just as you may hire an accountant to do your taxes in order to save time and benefit from their specialized knowledge, you may similarly want to hire an investment advisor to help you with your finances.

2) Getting the job done. People often procrastinate to avoid the mental strain of having to make important financial decisions. The sooner you develop a well-constructed financial plan, though, the better your long-term results are likely to be. Small things make a difference in investing and in the compounding of returns. An investment advisor can help you define your financial goals and stay on task.

3) Making good decisions and avoiding mistakes. You may not feel confident enough to make investment decisions which affect you and your family's well-being. You may find it reassuring to have an experienced investment professional help you plan for retirement, coach you through despair during market sell-offs, and step up to help during life events such as job loss, divorce, retirement, infirmity, and death. The advisor's fees are a direct cost and a drag on your investment returns over time, but the added cost may be worth it to you because you can offload financial decisions to your advisor. This may help you avoid investment mistakes, and the advisor may more effectively invest your assets than you would.

4) Avoiding feelings of regret. You may want to avoid feelings of regret related to financial decisions. For example, assume US stocks have outperformed emerging markets stocks over the last 10 years, and you shift all your money into US stocks. Three years later you look back and see emerging markets have had double the return of US stocks. You feel regret. Here's another: you back up the truck on a whiz-bang technology company stock you hear is a "sure thing." It plummets 50%. You feel regret. Lastly, in the throes of a market swoon, you sell all your stock investments and go to cash. The market rebounds 30% over the next six months. You feel regret. And if the investment program recommended by your advisor does not work out as well as you would like or expect, you have someone to blame other than yourself.

If some of the above reasons resonate with you, then you may value having an investment advisor as the chief investment officer in the lifelong business of managing your wealth.

YOUR INVESTMENT PERSONALITY

Here are a few personality profiles to try on for size in the context of managing your finances yourself or having an advisor help you.

1) DO IT YOURSELF: Self-Assured Sally and Sam. You like controlling things, are willing to spend time learning about investments, are a fairly calm person, and tend to think long term. The rational side of your brain can maintain executive control over the emotional, impulsive side of your brain. You believe you have the discipline to handle challenging investment decisions and volatile markets.

PROS: You have detailed knowledge and control over your investments. Since you will need little or no help from an advisor in managing your money, your investment costs will be minimal. You benefit from not paying investment advisory fees, which are a drag on the compounding of returns on your money over time.

CONS: It's all on you. If you don't like the result, you have no one to look to but yourself, and you may experience regret if you make subpar investment decisions. In addition, you will have no one to bounce ideas off of or to provide moral support during dark times in financial markets. If you are an overconfident type, you may compound investment mistake upon mistake, which will have a deleterious effect on the growth of your wealth.

2) CONSULTATIVE ADVICE: Agreeable Kay and Ray. You like to understand your investments and where you are headed financially, but do not consider yourself knowledgeable enough to manage them alone. You value the advice of an expert, seeing an advisor or financial planner as a partner and sounding board. You are generally willing to accept an advisor's investment recommendations, but you want to make the final decision on how your money is invested.

PROS: You will have a professional helping you with financial planning and investments. You believe the advice you are getting is worthwhile, and that the benefits will outweigh the costs over time. If the advisor can help you invest a bit more efficiently and help you avoid making a significant investment mistake or two over time, their fees will be justified. In addition, you may value their help on retirement, tax and estate planning.

CONS: You will pay for the investment advice, the cost of which may reduce the compounding of your wealth over time.

3) TURNING OVER THE KEYS: Harried Hanna and Henry. You are not comfortable making investment decisions, and do not want to spend your time learning or thinking about investments. You may doubt your self-control or ability to maintain a steady allocation in times of market euphoria and market despair. You would like to turn investment decisions over to an advisor. You would be happy, and relieved, to check in once a year with your advisor and be told that everything is on track with regard to your financial goals.

PROS: You will have a professional formulating and implementing your investment plan. You will be able to shift worry and responsibility for financial decision-making onto your advisor.

CONS: You will pay for the investment advice, the cost of which may reduce the compounding of your wealth over time. You are dependent on the advisor being competent and acting in your best interests.

If you think you are like Sally and Sam, and are willing to put some effort into studying investing (reading this book would be a good indicator that you are), have good self-control, and a fairly simple wealth and estate profile, then you are a good candidate for managing your own wealth. You may need modest, if any, input from an advisor or financial planner.

If you are more like Kay and Ray and Hanna and Henry, then you may value having an advisor as a partner in helping you plan your financial future, make investment decisions, and coach you on investment matters. And you may like shifting the mental burden of financial decision-making onto an advisor. If you fit these profiles, then you are a good candidate to work with an investment advisor or financial planner.

WHAT ADVISORS CANNOT DO FOR YOU

In thinking about whether or not to hire a financial advisor, you should understand what a financial advisor can do for you, rather than what you hope they can do for you or what advisors sometimes suggest they can do for you.

An investment advisor is not really going to help you beat the market or do better than the Base Case with regard to investment returns. Advisors are knowledgeable investors, but they are not superior investors. This is not because they do not know a considerable amount about markets and investments. They do. You have seen, however, in Chapter 7 in the discussion on active managers, that unless a person has unique knowledge about an investment, which few do, or can foresee the future, which no one can, a person has a low probability of outperforming the market. An investment advisor, who is a form of active manager, has little chance of outperforming the market with stock selection, sector rotation, asset class timing, or picking managers that can do any of those things consistently.

If you are looking for an advisor to make investment recommendations that outperform the market on a risk-equivalent basis, therefore, you are asking them to do something they have little likelihood of achieving. Some advisors may suggest they can outperform the market with their alchemy of investments, but then they are either ignorant of the chances stacked against them, are deceitful, or are willing to risk underperformance to you by speculating with your money. Dumb, dishonest or foolhardy—none are attractive qualities, and not what you want in an advisor.

WHAT ADVISORS CAN DO FOR YOU

What an advisor can do is help you select a sensible investment allocation given your investment goals, tolerance for volatility and time frame. And since asset allocation drives 90-100% of long-term investment returns, this is all they need to do to do a competent job for you. An advisor will help you select an allocation of stocks, bonds and cash best suited to your objectives and risk tolerance, and help you stick with it through up and down markets.

In addition, for taxable investors, an advisor can help you efficiently allocate assets among taxable, tax-deferred and tax-exempt accounts. They can also harvest tax losses in your accounts to increase your after-tax returns. And when you are in retirement and living off your savings, they can help you draw down your assets in a tax-efficient manner.

It's okay if an investment advisor helps you achieve an average, Base Case-type investment result. Being a coach and giving you confidence in your investment plan is a useful service. It is possible that on your own you might make decisions that could lead to a below-average result, such as buying at market highs and selling at market lows, or chasing shiny objects—buying into hot stocks, sectors, and investment strategies at the wrong time. You might also not have your assets optimally allocated by taxable and tax-exempt or tax-deferred accounts, or know what might be most advantageous in the order you draw down on your assets. In addition, having an advisor is an insurance policy in the event that you are incapacitated or die. Your advisor will be there to help your loved ones navigate through a difficult period and potentially changed financial circumstances.

An advisor can help you in a number of areas:

- Talk through your investment goals with you and then draft a written statement regarding these and your plan of investment designed to achieve them (this is often called an *investment policy statement*).

- Model all your investments into a total portfolio, and show you possible return paths for your investments over the course of your life and in different market environments (*scenario analysis*). This helps you develop reasonable expectations as to what is achievable with regard to the growth of your wealth, how long it will take, and the effect of average, above-average and below-average portfolio returns on the growth of your wealth and the likelihood of you achieving your investment goals.

• Rebalance your portfolio and various accounts as needed. This helps keep your investment plan on track and saves you from having to worry about executing the plan.

• Allocate your assets optimally between taxable and tax-exempt or tax-deferred accounts.

• Tax-loss harvest to reduce taxes paid on capital gains.

• Comprehensively review your investments, taxes, insurance, real estate, estate planning, retirement planning, and charitable gifting to find solutions specific to your situation.

• Coordinate your overall financial plan with your other advisors, such as your accountant and estate attorney.

THE ULYSSES FACTOR

Ulysses and the Sirens
By Herbert James Draper. The Bridgeman Art Library, Object 96235, Public Domain, https://commons.wikimedia.org/w/index.php?curid=4226713

Another story from my youth, which has relevance to why you may want to use an investment advisor, is Homer's tale of Ulysses and his encounter with the sirens. Ulysses, on a very long journey home following the Trojan War, is told by the goddess Circe that he will pass the island of the sirens. The sirens are monsters pretending to be beautiful women. Their amazingly beautiful voices and melodies lure sailors to their deaths upon the island's rocky shores. She tells Ulysses to block his men's ears with beeswax so as not to hear the sirens' song. Ulysses does this, but he wants to hear the song himself, so he has his men lash him to the mast of their ship. Long story short, hearing the enchanting song of the sirens, Ulysses wants to jump into the sea and swim to shore to be with them, but the ropes hold fast and Ulysses and his men safely pass by the island.

How does Ulysses' ordeal relate to you, your investments, and an investment advisor? Tell your advisor you want them to keep you from the sirens' song of outwardly appealing but likely suboptimal investments. They should lash you to the mast of your simple, low-cost, long-term investment program. Tell your advisor in advance that you want to avoid shiny objects of hot stocks, "in" investment sectors and strategies, and "flavors of the month" investment approaches. Tell them that even though you may plead from time to time for something more exciting, you want them to keep you tied to a rational, steady, long-term investment plan.

You can do this upfront commitment as an insurance policy of sorts against your own lack of resolve. You never really know how you will react when you are losing large sums of capital to sliding markets, or when your brother-in-law tells you how he earned ten times his money on a hot stock, and that "smart people know how to pick 'em." Hiring an advisor can be an expensive form of insurance, but avoiding just one fateful investment episode, one momentary lapse, may mean the difference between safely passing temptation and arriving on the golden shores of financial security, or, because of an impulsive decision, your financial ship lying wrecked upon the rocks.

THE .7 PERCENT SOLUTION

If you decide to hire an advisor, you want them to be motivated to do a good job for you. Therefore you will want to pay them accordingly. You do not, however, want to be an annuity on autopilot for the advisor. You want to fairly pay, but not overpay, for their help. In talking to an advisor about their services and fees, you are at a disadvantage, because you probably are thinking you need financial advice (or you wouldn't be talking to an advisor), and they are experienced at giving prospective clients reasons to hire them and rationales justifying their fees. It's like someone who walks into an auto dealership—the person is likely there because they are thinking of buying a car. The salesman knows this, knows what buttons to push, and how to arrange things at the purchase to maximize profit for the dealership.

My suggestions below help level the playing field between you and an investment advisor or financial planner, and hopefully will enable you to get the most out of the money you spend on investment and financial planning advice.

Whether it be fees paid to an investment advisor, financial planner, bank, brokerage firm, robo-advisor or investment manager, it is important to keep the total cost you pay the lowest possible as a percentage of your investable wealth. Fees are a drag on returns, and you want to have the highest possible investment returns to maximize the growth of your wealth.

Advisors have different ways of getting paid. Investment advisors typically get paid as a percentage of assets under management. Broker-dealers get paid commissions for buying and selling securities and funds, and ongoing payments related to those. Financial planners may get hourly fees, per project fees, or annual retainer fees. Some firms are hybrids, and get paid in several different ways. In the below example I am using a fee on assets under management (AUM) model, because most advisors charge a fee based on AUM. The same principle, though, applies to a financial planner charging an hourly fee or a broker charging transactional fees.

However an advisor or broker or financial planner is getting paid, you want to limit it to a fixed amount. I would anchor this amount to a percentage of your investable assets. It could also be a set dollar amount. As a general rule, I would say that for basic investment advice, which includes asset allocation, fund selection, asset location and financial planning, you should target to pay not more than .5% (1/2 of 1%) annually on your investable wealth. In addition, you should target to limit all underlying manager, fund and ETF fees, trading charges, commissions, third-party fees, and administrative costs to no more than .2% (1/5 of 1%) of your wealth annually.

Target about .7% (7/10 of 1%) of your assets annually for all investment-related advice and services. Whatever the advisor's fee for service is, whether it be a percentage of AUM, hourly fees, retainers or flat fees, keep it and underlying fund costs to .7% or less. This is about 10% of the Base Case return of 7.75%. By limiting your costs, your assets will compound at a higher rate of return.

You should tell whoever is providing you investment advice that .7% is the maximum total cost all in that you will pay, and that they will represent to you each year that this amount has not been exceeded. If the advisor is providing services other than investment advice and management, such as doing your taxes or serving as corporate trustee, you can pay additional fees for these extra services.

Limiting your advisory and investment management costs to .7% will do two things for you. It will eliminate any advisor who is looking to make more off of you than they are worth. It will also encourage them to take a simple, low-cost approach to investing your assets, which is what you want. To meet the .2% manager and trading cost threshold, for example, the advisor will have to mostly avoid active managers, and instead put you in low-cost index funds. You won't have to monitor every investment the advisor is making for you, because you have set up the guardrails which will keep them in index funds.

Some investment firms, particularly banks and brokerage firms that sell their own products, have an incentive to sell you more expensive products and to assess more opaque costs, such as administrative fees and per share trading charges. If you have them commit in writing not to exceed .7% all in, however, you will not have to worry about figuring out the myriad of ways they charge you fees, which is a game you will not win and shouldn't spend your time playing. Save yourself the vexation and put the onus on the advisor to show that their costs, and those of the underlying managers and funds they use, are in line with your .7% target.

Despite what any investment manager or advisor says, they can provide all the investment advice you need for .7%. If they say for whatever reason it's not possible, find another advisor. Investment advice is largely a commodity service, anyway, and there are plenty of investment advisors, financial planners and brokers to choose from.

In addition, many people of working age have most of their retirement savings in a 401(k) plan. These plans often have free tools to help employees evaluate different investment options, including index funds and target date funds, and select a portfolio appropriate for their age and risk tolerance.[200]

YOUNGER PERSON EXAMPLE

Example of a younger person starting out: If you don't yet have a treasure trove of wealth, say your savings are around $100,000, your needs are fairly simple and your annual budget for investment advice reflects this ($100,000 x .7% = $700). This should buy you several hours of a financial planner's time, which can run from around $150-$300 per hour. They can provide you a basic financial plan and invest assets in your IRA or taxable account in a few index funds. If you have a 401(k), they should be able to look at the offerings in the plan and make a few suggestions, such as index funds or target date funds, if your firm's 401(k) plan does not already provide that service.

The advisor or financial planner should do this work, even if it takes some extra time, because their expectation should be that you will be a long-term client and that your assets will grow over time and hence so will their fee. In addition, as they do a good job for you, you may be a source of referrals to them of other prospective clients.

OLDER PERSON EXAMPLE

Example of an older person with more investable wealth: If you have $2 million to invest, your fee would be higher ($2,000,000 x .7% = $14,000). You may have several accounts, maybe 529 plans for your kids if you have any, and taxes to consider. This fee amount should buy you asset allocation among your accounts, fund selection, comprehensive financial planning, insurance review, estate planning review, portfolio reporting, and coordination with your other providers, such as accountant and estate attorney.

Advisors' work tends to be front-end loaded. They spend the most time at the start getting up to speed on your financial situation, developing a plan and implementing it. After that, the work is usually more modest, involving rebalancing, maybe some tax-loss harvesting and portfolio reporting for tax purposes, and making changes around significant life events. Financial planning software makes the planning process efficient, and portfolio software automates account aggregation and performance and tax reporting on your investments. In addition, a basic index portfolio does not take much of an advisor's time to monitor and manage.

LOWER-COST PROVIDERS

If you want to work with an advisor, but you don't need as much personal service regarding financial, tax or estate planning, you may find appealing an offering such as Vanguard's Personal Advisor Services, which provides you consultation with an advisor and a financial plan for an annual fee of 0.3% of assets (with an account minimum of $50,000 as of 2021). Similarly, robo-advisor firms such as Betterment provide investment management for an annual fee of 0.25%-0.5% of assets, depending on your account balance.[201] Lower-cost independent investment advisors and financial planners can provide a somewhat more personal service at a similar cost.

Another cost-saving approach is to pay a financial planner to do a comprehensive financial plan for you, including a general asset allocation, and you do the investing. This is a paint-by-number approach to investment planning, where they provide the asset allocation outline and you fill it in with index funds. An a la carte comprehensive financial plan often ranges from $2,000-$5,000. The index funds as discussed cost very little on an ongoing basis. Financial plans usually do not have to be done every year, just updated from time to time, particularly around important life events, such as retirement. Or pay the planner for a couple hours of review each year. This can be a very cost-effective way of accessing financial expertise.

ADVISOR HACK:
—— SPLITTING YOUR ASSETS BETWEEN FEE AND NON-FEE ACCOUNTS ——

If you want to use an advisor who balks at your cost parameter of .7%, you can still meet this objective by giving them part of your money to manage and invest the other part yourself in index funds. This is what I call the advisor fee hack.

Here is an example for a client with a $2 million dollar investment portfolio. The advisor says their lowest fee on assets up to $3 million, including their advisory fee, underlying manager fees and trading costs is approximately 1.4%. That's above your .7% total cost target.

So, you invest $1 million in index funds directly, say through Vanguard, in broad-based funds such as Vanguard's Total World Stock ETF and Total Bond Market Fund, $500,000 each. The cost of these funds are low, around .05%.

Give your second $1 million to the advisor to manage, and have them model into their allocation your assets at Vanguard. Most advisors will model your "away" assets into your overall investment plan. The advisor will charge you 1.4% on the $1 million. The blended cost, between what the advisor is managing and what you have at Vanguard, will in total be about .7%, your overall cost target.

Again, if the advisor doesn't like this, then find another advisor. You will find someone who will do a very competent job for you investing $1 million and providing financial planning for you while incorporating your other $1 million in Vanguard investments into your overall investment plan.

WHO SHOULD I USE?

I will not go into a general description of the differences between investment advisors, financial planners, brokers, robo-advisors, etc., but will make a couple of general observations about who you might choose as your advisor.

In selecting an advisor, I would focus less on what they are called— registered investment advisor, financial planner, broker-dealer, online robo-advisor—and more on what suits you. Financial advisors, whatever they are called, offer a similar type of service centered around an investment allocation tailored to your particular goals, complemented by financial planning, which usually incorporates tax, estate and insurance planning. Advisors generally will accommodate how you like to communicate—in person, by phone, video call, online chat, email or some combination of these.

With regard to technology, and using a robo-advisor, for example, keep in mind that all advisors use some form of technology to complement their offering. Additionally, robo-advisors are increasingly making humans available to clients for more personal and nuanced service. Traditional advisors' and robo-advisors' service offerings, then, are converging, and the differences are one of degree rather than of kind.

If you prefer working with a person, find someone you relate to well personally and who has sound investment and financial planning qualifications and experience. I would also look for someone who will adhere to the cost restrictions of the .7% solution outlined above, which will likely be a financial planner, RIA or robo-advisor. They will be more likely to work within your fee constraint, as they are not in general incentivized to invest your assets in high cost, active management products, as may be the case with brokers at large banks.

The more complex your investment scenario, the more likely you are to want to have as your advisor a person who knows you and your financial situation very well. You will want someone to coordinate with your other advisors, such as your estate planning attorney and accountant, and you will want someone available to answer questions and handle issues such as retirement planning, charitable gifting, and cash flow management. If you have a more complex financial situation, with various moving parts and a complex tax and estate situation, then a registered investment advisor, and then a financial planner, would likely be a preferred choice.

You should definitely check the background of anyone you are considering working with for regulatory violations or client complaints.[202] For advisors with a dodgy history, bad behavior usually follows a pattern, and you do not want to be their next mark.

ADVICE IS NEVER ENTIRELY OBJECTIVE

Whether you use an RIA, a financial planner, bank, broker-dealer, or robo-advisor, there is always some bias in the financial advice they are providing. It centers on, you will not be surprised to hear, their profitability. Brokers may want to sell you products upon which they receive commissions or trailing (12b-1) fees. Investment advisors will advocate investment plans which place more of your assets under their fee schedule. Financial planners may recommend investments upon which they receive incentive compensation, and robo-advisors may put you in a portfolio or direct trades in your account that fits their business model. Some advisors may substitute investment complexity for efficiency in an attempt to convince you of their value and to charge you higher fees. Your money will wind up in a too complex, too high cost and too tax-inefficient portfolio. Says David Swensen:

> Most investors have scant access to truly unbiased, objective investment advice. Brokers push high-commission products. Investment companies tout trendy mutual-fund offerings. Even the most ethical purveyors of financial products sometimes confuse the best route for the client with the most profitable path for the service provider. The all-too-prevalent charlatans never suffer from confusion about which road to take.[203]

FIDUCIARY STANDARD

Some advisors highlight that they are a "fiduciary" or always take into account "your best interests." In the current state of affairs, registered investment advisors (RIAs) have a fiduciary duty to act in your best interests, whereas a broker-dealer only has to recommend investments "suitable" to you. That said, you can find broker-dealers with high integrity, and as noted, RIAs have their own biases. In addition, laws are changing to, in effect, require any professional providing investment advice to act as a fiduciary.

Many advisors are ethical and will do a good job for you. But you should always keep in mind that their businesses and personal interests in making money prod them into doing what is best for them within the tolerance of your retaining their services. As noted, if you set the frame for an advisor with a .7% fee maximum for all investment-related fees and expenses, you constrain their behavior. As former President Ronald Reagan said when doing arms control agreements with the Soviet Union, "Trust, but verify."

An advisor's objective is to make their firm and themselves money. Their livelihood and that of their families depends on them selling you their product or service, so do not expect to get an entirely complete and objective view. That doesn't mean they don't want you to make money, too—they do. It is just that they want to make sure that they make money for themselves first. The firm to which you give your money has an incentive to extract as much value for themselves at the lowest cost required to keep you as a client. You and the person selling you their product or service are in a dance, and they are leading, as they have done the dance a thousand times. Many are masterful salespeople, and they are able to direct your focus to how you will benefit from their offering.

Dump a mental bucket of cold water over your head to reorient your thinking from how you are going to benefit from their services to how they are going to benefit. Thinking in this way helps take the breathy expectations out of an investment firm's offering, and puts your mind into a more sober state. You realize that the affable salesperson, broker or advisor is not your new best friend or an all-knowing expert, but a businessperson offering a service or product. How does the advisor make money, and are their interests aligned with yours? Shiny objects dangled in sales pitches dazzle less when you focus on the fees the advisor is receiving, and that they may profit no matter how well your investments do.

The more closely an investment firm's financial success is tied to your long-term financial success, the better value their service is likely to be. In the 17th century, for example, European investors would fund commercial ship voyages to the Far East to buy spices, and then sell the cargos for great profit at ports across Europe. It was no doubt reassuring for investors to know that the ship's captain had a significant stake in the outcome. If the ship foundered, the captain not only lost his stake in the profits, but often his life. That was a good motivator for the captain to take care with the investor's capital and for the enterprise to be a success. You want to have your money with people who have an incentive for your money to grow and multiply over the long term, not people using hyperbole and ruses to divert your money into their pockets via short-term investment schemes.

As discussed above with regard to the services advisors provide, you will have to determine what services you really need. And then you have to determine whether or not the service is worth the cost.

DON'T HASSLE YOUR ADVISOR

If you hire an investment advisor, to have them do the best job possible for you, agree on an investment plan, and then let them do their job. Do not nitpick every security or manager selection, or ask them all the time why certain investments are doing worse compared to some reference point, such as the S&P 500 Index.

In a diversified portfolio of assets, which is what you want for your investment portfolio, there will always be something that is performing worse than your reference point. Also, the stock market and the value of your portfolio will go up and down many times over your lifetime. On occasion, shockingly so. This is part of investing—as noted previously, if there was no volatility or uncertainty in markets, there would be little return. The average return of the US stock market over a long period of time has been around 10%, but that is made up of annual returns from up 50% to down 40%—rarely is the return in any given year actually 10%, so you should not expect it to be like clockwork.

Your advisor does not have control over the market going up or down, and they cannot predict the future, so don't leave them thinking that you think they should. It will just worry them that you are going to dump them as your advisor. That is not the mental state you want your advisor to be in. The one thing your advisor fears more than a bad stock market is losing your business. Advisors are human and self-interested, and if they think you may pull your account because of a poorly performing investment, they may make suboptimal investment decisions which will cost you money in the long run.

If you focus on a particular investment or even that your overall portfolio isn't doing well—maybe hasn't done well for several years relative to your reference point—your advisor may be inclined to remove the investment or change your portfolio allocation to placate your concern and to show action on their part. This is usually at the worst time, just before the underperforming security or allocation is about to rebound by reverting to the mean. Remember the story from Chapter 7 about the Israeli air force pilots reverting to the mean in performance? You may on occasion get out of the way of a falling knife, but more often than not what you sold will outperform whatever you buy in its stead over the intermediate term.

The more you pressure your advisor about poor performers or why they aren't more invested in something that is performing better than other things they have you invested in, the more likely they will be inclined to chase returns—buying assets that have done well recently and are now at above-average valuations, and selling assets that have underperformed recently and now are at below-average valuations. That is a near-certain recipe for long-term underperformance of your investment assets.

Stay on top of your advisor, make sure they are paying attention to your portfolio and are up-to-date on any changes in your life or financial situation. But do not badger them. You hired them for their judgment. So let them use it.

SUMMARY

Whether you do it yourself or hire a financial advisor, succeeding at investing and reaching your financial goals include having a plan that you can stick with in good markets and bad, keeping your costs and taxes down and understanding what you and a financial advisor can realistically achieve with regard to the growth of your wealth over time.

- Determine if investing your wealth and planning for your financial future is something you want to do yourself or to work on with a financial advisor.

- Investment advisors, whether they be an RIA, financial planner, broker-dealer, bank, or robo-advisor, provide a similar service.

- Understand the profit motive for a particular type of advisor's advice.

- Select an advisor that suits your personality, goals and preferred style of working.

- Put up guardrails on advisory and investment management fees.

- Be realistic about what your financial advisor can and can't do for you, and let them do their job without you backseat driving or Monday-morning quarterbacking.

CHAPTER 11

Guideposts for Managing Your Wealth

Reaching your wealth goals is less about outracing other people and more about avoiding personal behavioral potholes. This chapter has some thoughts that may help you better navigate the road ahead and reach your goals on time and as planned.

BRAIN BOUNDS

The biggest challenge to growing your wealth is not other people or the market or the world. It's you, specifically, your brain. Your brain is designed to make snap judgments based on immediate data, rough approximations, and emotional intuition. It's a great tool for surviving in nature and dealing with other humans, but it's a poor tool for sticking to a long-term investment plan. It's like driving a Formula One race car down a logging road. The race car, like your brain, is a spectacular machine, but it wasn't designed for the task.

Your brain is essentially a bag of chemicals generating a menagerie of thoughts, feelings, and responses, much of which is automatic and subconscious.[204] Brains are easily distracted and affected by things irrelevant and even detrimental to long-term investment success.[205] Your brain may make different decisions depending on the time of day, whether you are tired or hungry, happy or sad, how the issue you are considering is worded, and even the color of the room you happen to be in when making a decision. Writes Kahneman,

We know from studies of priming that unnoticed stimuli in our environment have a substantial influence on our thoughts and actions. These influences fluctuate from moment to moment. The brief pleasure of a cool breeze on a hot day may make you slightly more positive and optimistic about whatever you are evaluating at the time. The prospects of a convict being granted parole may change significantly during the time that elapses between successive food breaks in the parole judges' schedule.[206]

Put some distance between your brain and your investments. Go on an investment decision-making diet. Feed your brain as few investment-related temptations as possible. Do not give your brain the opportunity to make an impulsive decision that may impair the long-term growth of your wealth.

This includes tuning out financial media and Wall Street sales pitches. Remember Ulysses having his men put beeswax in their ears so they would not hear the sirens' song. Financial media are people trying to get you to watch their shows by making you feel that you need to constantly

CHART 11.1   THE HUMAN BRAIN IS NOT WIRED FOR DISCIPLINED INVESTING
Humans often apply biased and faulty reasoning to investing

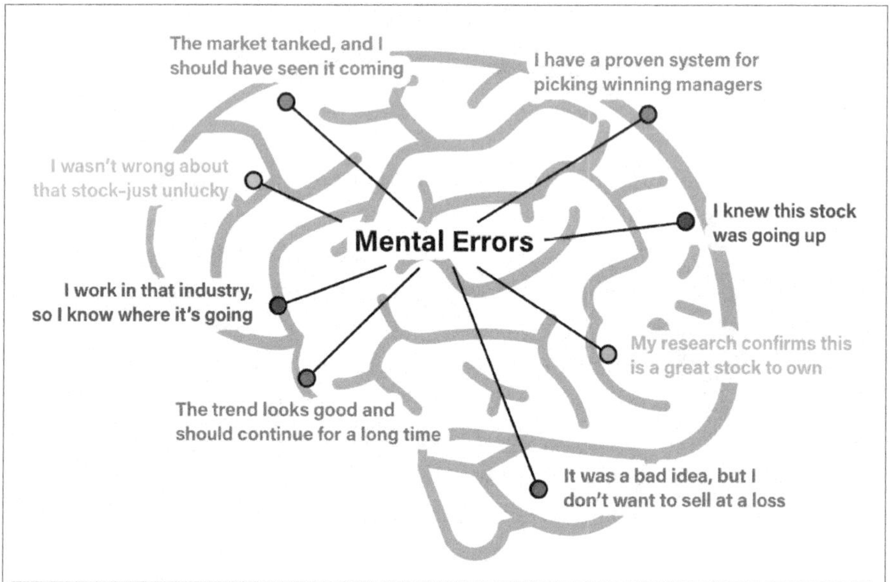

The market tanked, and I should have seen it coming

I have a proven system for picking winning managers

I wasn't wrong about that stock—just unlucky

Mental Errors

I knew this stock was going up

I work in that industry, so I know where it's going

My research confirms this is a great stock to own

The trend looks good and should continue for a long time

It was a bad idea, but I don't want to sell at a loss

Source: Dimensional Fund Advisors

be on guard and doing something, namely buying or selling an investment promoted by the show's sponsors. It's how they make money. They are constantly pushing information on you in the hope you will take the bait and make an investment.[207] In addition, avoid the fool's gold displayed before you by Wall Street: Hot Stocks to Buy Now, Winning at Investing, The Secret Sauce of Investing Success, Investments with a Big Upside and Low Downside, What Smart Money is Buying. It is exhausting trying to resist fiddling with your portfolio in the face of a media barrage of hot stock tips and market chat. Processing all the stimuli literally drains your body of energy-generating glucose. When your glucose level is low you feel tired and are more prone to acquiesce to the impulsive part of your brain rather than the deliberative one.

You have a limited reserve of self-control, so don't overtax it. "Self-control and deliberate thought apparently draw on the same limited budget of effort," writes Kahneman on what is called "ego depletion." He gives an example of an experiment where people were first ego depleted by having to eat vegetables while resisting the temptation to eat chocolate and rich cookies set in front of them. Exercising self-control to not eat the chocolate and cookies was a mentally draining experience for the test subjects. Kahneman notes, "Later, these people will give up earlier than normal when faced with a difficult cognitive task." [209]

An investor needs to do very few things right as long as he or she avoids big mistakes.

WARREN BUFFETT

Stick to a set of rules that minimize emotional reactions and emphasize thoughtful deliberation and self-control. Says Warren Buffett: "What counts for most people in investing is not how much they know, but rather how realistically they define what they don't know. An investor needs to do very few things right as long as he or she avoids big mistakes." [210] Here's a technique for investment discipline based on Thomas Jefferson's maxim of "When angry, count to 10 before you speak; if very angry, count to 100." Whenever you are excited and tempted to significantly change your investment portfolio, wait 10 days. If very excited, wait 100 days. Scratch the days off like a castaway on a deserted island. You may find that your initial enthusiasm for action fades, and what seemed like a good idea at the time may in retrospect seem like an emotional, impulsive reaction.

A useful tool for maintaining investment discipline is to be an advisor to yourself. Pretend you are giving another person advice.[211] For example, Martia. Doing so provides perspective and reduces the effect of your ego on decisions. You may find your recommendation to the imaginary person to have a less optimistic outcome than what you envision for yourself. That is a good check on your own overconfidence. "Knowing, or even imagining, that someone else is relying on your advice can make you feel more accountable, forcing you to go beyond your gut feelings and fortify your opinions with factual evidence," writes Jason Zweig.[212] Says Kahneman, " … it is easier to recognize other people's mistakes than our own." [213]

Another useful approach is to imagine that someone whose opinion you care about will see the results. For example, your children or grandchildren will be given a full accounting. This tends to pull you away from egotistical self-indulgence and toward more deliberative, considered thought.

LESS IS MORE

I grew up in Chicago, where Ludwig Mies van der Rohe created world-renowned architecture, and the Bauhaus movement bloomed in the glass-box skyscrapers of the Loop and Magnificent Mile. "Less is more," Mies said of the sophisticated simplicity of his work. "Less is more" is also a useful touchstone for investing. As discussed in prior chapters, you only need a handful of investments in a simple portfolio to access the Base Case. Benjamin Graham's comments on how to be a successful investor are apt. "People don't need extraordinary insight or intelligence. What they need most is the character to adopt simple rules and stick to them." [214]

The less you look at your investments, and the less you trade them, the more likely you are to achieve your investment goals. "Lethargy bordering on sloth remains the best investment style. The correct holding period for the stock market is forever," says Buffett, echoing his teacher, Ben Graham, who said it helped him to view markets "from the standpoint of eternity, rather than day-to-day." [215] Adds Buffett, "A willingness to look unimaginative for a sustained period—or even to look foolish—is also essential." [216]

Despite the sage advice of Buffett and Graham, pathological peeking at investment returns is endemic among investors. In a survey by *Money* magazine, 22% of investors said they check the prices of their investments every day, and 49% said they check them at least once a week.[217]

Looking at the value of your investments going up and down hourly, daily, monthly or quarterly does not hasten your reaching your investment goals. You cannot will your investments higher. Securities don't care how often you look at them, think about them or pray with regard to them. And "watching over" your investments doesn't make them any more secure and has no effect on their long-term return.

Here is a formula for disciplined investing:

The number of days you do not think about your investments

~minus~

The number of days you think about your investments

The higher the number, the more likely you will successfully stick to a long-term investment plan.

If you have an intermediate-term investment objective, say buying a house in 10 years, does it make sense to look at your investments daily? Even quarterly? Checking your portfolio every year or so should be often enough. "If owning stocks is a long-term project for you," says Kahneman, "following their changes constantly is a very, very bad idea. It's the worst possible thing you can do, because people are so sensitive to short-term losses. If you count your money every day, you'll be miserable." [218]

If you count your money every day, you'll be miserable.

DANIEL KAHNEMAN

Constantly looking at your investments increases the likelihood that in an emotional moment, say when the stock market is screaming upward or crashing downward, you will make a decision that will undermine the long-term growth of your wealth. You will buy high and sell low. It only takes one really bad decision to throw your investment plan off course for a lifetime. As noted in **Chart 2.6**, despite many crises, the stock market has moved up steadily over time.

In addition, the more you look at your investments, the more likely you are to trade them, and the more you trade them, the more likely you are to underperform the Base Case. Says Buffett, "For investors as a whole, returns decrease as motion increases." [219] In one study, the more people traded stocks, the worse they did. Not surprisingly, given their testosterone-driven competitiveness, men traded more than women and had the worse results. One study found that individual investors who traded the most earned 6.5% less annually than those who traded the least.[220]

You will also want to avoid the roller coaster of emotions summarized in **Chart 10.2**.

Let other people trade stocks and bonds in the hope of buying cheap and selling dear. Their buying and selling helps make markets more efficient, and the cost of doing so comes out of their pocket.[221]

In times of market turmoil you may feel the urge to "take action" and change your portfolio allocation, such as reducing your exposure to equities and increasing cash. As discussed in Chapter 7, to come out ahead doing this, rather than staying with your long-term allocation, you have to get two decisions right: exiting the market before it falls, and then re-entering the market before it rises. The odds of getting both of these more right than wrong, particularly over several market cycles, is low, because strong

CHART 11.2 THE EMOTIONAL & RATIONAL CURVE OF INVESTING

Source: Dimensional Fund Advisors

market upswings and downswings often occur in short periods of time. The coronavirus market crash of February-March 2020, down 20%, and the rapid rebound from April through December, up over 47%, is a good reminder of this.

Lastly, reducing how often you look at your investments may well improve your health. You will avoid years of mental anxiety and stress created by your amygdala reacting to your wealth gyrating up and down with market fluctuations. You will have more time to spend on enjoyable, productive and healthful activities. It is a great understanding, and an uplifting feeling, to know that in investing, less is more. By doing little and just efficiently tapping the Base Case, your wealth will likely grow more than that of people who spend each day thinking about their investments and worrying about the market.

───────── **MR. VINEGAR: A WEALTH MANAGEMENT BEDTIME STORY** ─────────

When I was growing up, children's stories were not about how you are a winner, how anyone can achieve their dreams, or how good triumphs over evil. They were, for the most part, frightful tales of how life is a struggle in a world full of dangers—"Little Red Riding Hood" (young girl is nearly eaten by a wolf pretending to be her grandmother), "Goldilocks and the Three Bears" (reckless young female home invader has rude awakening from food coma), "Jack and the Beanstalk" (impoverished boy who is stealing from a giant's home almost becomes the giant's lunch), "The Little Match Girl" (destitute girl afraid to go home to an abusive stepfather freezes to death in an alley), just about anything from the Brothers Grimm—"Hansel & Gretel" (children abandoned in the woods by their vicious stepmother narrowly avoid being baked and eaten by a cannibalistic witch).

One of the most educational stories for investors ever written is "Mr. Vinegar."

> Mr. Vinegar happened upon a pile of gold guineas, the loot of several thieves who Mr. Vinegar had inadvertently scared away in a forest. He had a fortune in his lap. So his wife told him to take the guineas to a local fair and buy a cow, and from that they would make butter and cheese to sell and live comfortably.

Mr. Vinegar agrees and goes off to the fair, where he sees
a beautiful red milk cow. Mr. Vinegar thought, "Oh! if I
only had that cow, I should be the happiest man alive," and
he buys the cow for 40 guineas. Proudly walking back and
forth with his new cow, Mr. Vinegar sees a man playing the
bagpipes, with children following him and pocketing money
on all sides. "Well," thought Mr. Vinegar, "if I had but that
beautiful instrument I should be the happiest man alive—my
fortune would be made." So he went up to the man, and said,
"Friend, what a beautiful instrument that is, and what a lot
of money you must make." "Why, yes," said the man, "I
make a great deal of money, to be sure, and it is a wonderful
instrument." "Oh!" cried Mr. Vinegar, "how I should like to
possess it." "Well," said the man, "as you are a friend, you
shall have it for that red cow." "Done," said the delighted
Mr. Vinegar; so he exchanged the beautiful red cow for the
bagpipes. He walked up and down with his purchase, but
he couldn't play a tune, and instead of pocketing pence,
the boys followed him hooting and laughing. Mr. Vinegar's
fingers grew very cold, and very much ashamed, he was
leaving the town, when he met a man with a fine thick pair of
gloves. "Oh, my fingers are so very cold," said Mr. Vinegar
to himself; "if I only had those beautiful gloves I should be
the happiest man alive." He went up to the man, and said
to him, "Friend, you have a capital pair of gloves there."
"Yes, truly!" cried the man, "and my hands are as warm
as toast." "Well," said Mr. Vinegar, "I should like to have
them." "What will you give?" said the man, and, "As you are
a friend, you may have them for those bagpipes." "Done,"
cried Mr. Vinegar. He put on the gloves, and felt very happy
as he walked homeward. At last he grew very tired, when
he saw a man coming toward him with a good stout stick in
his hand. "Oh," said Mr. Vinegar, "if I had but that stick; I
should then be the happiest man alive." He spoke to the man:
"Friend, what a fine stick you have there." "Yes," said the
man, "I have used it for many a long mile, and a good friend
it has been; but if you have a fancy for it, I don't mind letting
you have it for that pair of gloves." Mr. Vinegar's hands now

being warm, and his legs tired, he gladly made the exchange.

As he drew near to the wood where he had left his wife, he heard a parrot on a tree calling out to him: "Mr. Vinegar, you foolish man, you simpleton! You laid out all your money at the fair in buying a cow; not content with that, you changed it for bagpipes, on which you could not play, and which were not worth one tenth of the money. You no sooner had the bagpipes than you changed them for the gloves, which were not worth one-quarter of the money, and when you had the gloves, you changed them for a miserable stick, which you might have cut in any hedge." The bird burst into laughter, and Mr. Vinegar, being very angry, threw the stick at its head. The stick lodged in the tree, and he returned to his wife without money, cow, bagpipes, gloves, or stick.

When it comes to investing based on emotions in the moment, there is a bit of Mr. Vinegar in all of us. Don't be Mr. Vinegar with your savings. And read Mr. Vinegar to your children and grandchildren. It's good to learn early in life the consequences of foolish wealth management.

YOU ARE LIKELY an AVERAGE INVESTOR

You may think you can pick stocks and bonds or managers who can pick stocks and bonds better than the next person. But as discussed in Chapter 7, you are likely mistaken. If you think you are much better than average, you may well be susceptible to confidence bias, one of a host of biases (sometimes called heuristics) that make the human brain not well-suited to long-term investing. I will not summarize all of these biases in this book, as a number of experts have covered this area very well.

No one really likes to think they are average, but when it comes to investing, you are. Or at least I'm about 98% sure you are. It doesn't mean you aren't smart and talented in your own way. People, and particularly people for whom things have worked out in life, tend to think that their judgment is better than average. This encourages them to think that they can also select investments or managers that are better than average. "People overestimate their own knowledge, underestimate the risks involved and exaggerate their ability to control events," writes Burton Malkiel.[222]

Here are a couple examples of confidence bias by investors:

- Investors expected their personal portfolios to do 1.5 percentage points better than the market, no matter how well the market did.[223]

- A survey of 750 investors found that 74% thought that their mutual funds would "consistently beat the S&P 500 every year"—even though most funds underperform the market.[224]

Martin Zweig notes that in a survey conducted by *Money* magazine, nearly a third of the people interviewed said that their stock funds had beaten the market by at least 5%, and 1 of 6 said they had outperformed by more than 10%. When the research team checked their actual performance, however, it turned out that 88% had exaggerated their returns. Over a third of the people who thought they had beaten the market actually lagged it by at least 5%, and a fourth of all of those who thought they did better than the market were at least 15% behind it.[225]

People overestimate their own knowledge, underestimate the risks involved and exaggerate their ability to control events.

BURTON MALKIEL

Lastly, should you have any doubts about people's overconfident perceptions of themselves, 64% of Americans believe they will go to heaven, and only one-half of one percent believe they will go to hell.[226] Martin Zweig sums up,

In short, to evaluate ourselves is to lie to ourselves, especially when the evaluation requires us to compare ourselves to the average person. Inside each of us, there lurks a con artist who is forever cajoling us into an inflated sense of our own powers. The less skilled or experienced you are at something, the harder your inner con man works at convincing you that you are brilliant at it.[227]

Being what we call mentally healthy means boosting our self-esteem by deceiving ourselves that we are better than we are. People who see themselves most accurately are the clinically depressed.

Given that most people are average, your investing acumen is likely to be average and therefore produce average results. As unappealing as that may sound to you, it is a good approach to take, because it helps you avoid making costly investment decisions emanating from your overconfidence.

You will make better investment decisions if before you make a decision you remind yourself that, 1) "I don't know as much about a situation—a company's prospects, why the stock market went up or down yesterday, where the economy is headed—as I may think I do," and 2) "my knowledge is likely no greater than others in the market and therefore whatever information or insight I may have is likely already priced into the market and the investment I am considering."

Just because you are successful in your line of work—business, law, accounting, medicine, etc.—does not mean you will be successful at picking investments or investment managers. It doesn't help when people around you tell you how smart you are and that you are a genius in your line of work. It doesn't build a healthy skepticism, and reinforces one's over-inflated self-image. It's a common failing of smart, talented people who have achieved success. They insufficiently discount the part of their success that was due to timing and circumstance, more generally called luck, or that their expertise is based on a stable set of knowledge or a modest number of variables. Writes Kahneman, "Luck plays a large role in every story of success; it is almost always easy to identify a small change in the story that would have turned a remarkable achievement into a mediocre outcome."[228]

Unlike other aspects of life, such as playing the piano, in investing there is no direct correlation between time and effort spent on the activity and achievement of favorable results. Additionally, just because you have had some success at investing in the past does not mean it is likely to continue.

Says David Swensen,

Individual investors possess neither the time nor the resources to succeed in active management of marketable securities portfolios. Sophisticated institutional investors dominate the marketable security landscape, aggressively competing to unearth the rare security that promises risk-adjusted excess returns. Individuals who attempt to compete with resource-rich money management organizations simply provide fodder for large institutional cannon.[229]

As discussed in prior chapters, the odds of your active security selections, or those of managers you hire, doing better than average are low. You have about a 90% chance of underperforming an index investor over a 10-year time frame, and 95%-97% chance of underperforming over a 20-30 year time frame. This does not take into account all the time you will spend managing your assets and managing the people who may be managing your assets.

Human nature being what it is, you probably remember your winners more than your losers, or mentally bucket your losers in a category of "I haven't lost money, I am going to sell them when I get back to even." When you make an investment and it loses money, you want to make it back. Your mind anchors to the higher value of what you paid for the investment, and it mentally hurts to accept the loss of value. As noted, people feel the pain of losses about twice as much as they feel joy in gains. Not selling means that, in your mind, it isn't officially a loss yet. Regret and pride work against you. You are prone to sell winners, which confirms a win, boosting your self-esteem. And you are inclined to hold onto losers, which avoids the hit to your self-esteem and the pain of confirming the loss. If you are a taxable investor, selling losers is usually a better strategy, because you recognize the tax loss which can be used to offset recognized gains. Holding winners— letting your winners run—also is generally a better strategy.

Invest your ego into something you are more likely to win at, such as your career, or building a strong relationship with your spouse, significant other, or children. When a student at the University of Nebraska Omaha asked Warren Buffett what aspect of investing, in his leisure time, the student should be studying, Buffett said, "For most people, the bulk of their income is going to come from earning power in their chosen profession. Therefore, from the standpoint of building wealth, free time is better spent sharpening one's professional skills rather than studying investing." [230] You don't want to look back on your life and see all the time you spent researching investments as a fool's errand and a waste of precious time.

Below are several examples from my own experience of where the very smartest and most successful people in our world, who had every reason to think that they would be able to outperform the market, did not. I would like these examples to at least give you pause to think that if this individual, firm or industry failed despite the highest level of knowledge and intelligence, you should maybe be more circumspect about your chances of being smarter than the market and betting your retirement savings on a hunch.

LONG-TERM CAPITAL MANAGEMENT

When I first started following hedge funds in the mid-1990s, one of the managers that was the talk of the town was Long-Term Capital Management ("LTCM"). LTCM raised over $1 billion in capital for its launch in February 1994. The firm was founded by John Meriwether, the former vice-chairman and head of Salomon Brothers' bond arbitrage group (highlighted in Michael Lewis' book *Liar's Poker*). Also onboard were a number of Wall Street whizzes, as well as Nobel laureates Myron Scholes and Robert Merton, who were on the board of directors.

LTCM's strategy was basically to make a variety of trades based on small perceived price discrepancies among securities. LTCM did this first in government bonds, and then across a range of securities. The main bet was that LTCM would profit when these small pricing dislocations reverted to their historical norms. To turn these small profits into big profits, LTCM leveraged its trades. In 1998 LTCM borrowed $124 billion upon its equity capital base of $4.7 billion, for a debt-to-equity ratio of over 25 to 1.

As sometimes happens in cases where failure is deemed near impossible (think *Titanic*), after several years of successful trading, the once-in-a-thousand-years scenario befell LTCM. This sprung from the 1997 Asian financial crisis and the 1998 Russian debt crisis, when Russia defaulted on its domestic ruble-denominated bonds. There was a global flight to quality. Pricing dislocations widened, rather than narrowed, and LTCM's trades went against it.

Despite the complexity and vast number of its trades, LTCM was in effect long risk and short liquidity and volatility. The firm lost a good portion of its capital. Given its losses, LTCM could not raise new capital from investors, and the firm was taken over by Wall Street banks under the supervision of the Federal Reserve Bank of New York. LTCM's leveraged positions were wound down and the firm was liquidated in 2000.

Catastrophic failures of investment firms run by very smart people usually center around hubris and technical models that underestimate the ability of humans to create unique and unpredictable economic events far afield from the assumptions upon which the models are based. In addition, greed, the impetus for using extreme leverage to maximize profits, risks the total or near total loss of capital, which is what happened to LTCM's investors. Says Warren Buffett, "My partner Charlie [Munger] says there is only three ways a smart person can go broke: liquor, ladies and leverage. Now the truth is — the first two he just added because they started with L — it's leverage." [231]

PAUL ALLEN [232]

Paul Allen was a genius who had the good fortune of working with another genius. Paul and his friend two years his junior, Bill Gates, won the lottery of the PC revolution by co-founding in 1975 the company that came to dominate desktop computer software. Microsoft's software was for businesses what water is for humans—you had to have it. Gates and Allen had a 64/36 partnership in Microsoft, and after the company went public in 1986 Allen's share was worth billions. Bill Gates always acknowledged Paul's key role in Microsoft's success. The media's focus, though, was mainly on Gates after Allen reduced his duties at Microsoft in 1983 due to health issues.[234]

Notwithstanding the lack of media accolades, Paul's Microsoft billions allowed him to pursue pretty much whatever he was interested in. There were, of course, endeavors that only an eclectic billionaire could fund: a Frank Gehry designed interactive music museum, an array of radio telescopes to search for extraterrestrial life, and an institute dedicated to brain research.

Paul's status in the technology world and his billions also gave him a front row seat to the nascent technology companies of the 1990s. If anyone had access to top venture capital firms and promising dot.com start-ups, it was Paul. Allen invested in dozens of technology-oriented companies as part of his "wired world" vision.

Allen bet large on this theme in 1998 when he bought Marcus Cable for $2.8 billion and a month later bought Charter Communications for $4.5 billion.[235] Allen became Charter's chairman and fifty-one percent stakeholder in the company. Said Allen at the time, "For over 20 years, I have been talking about and investing in the 'wired world,' a connected future marked by the merger of high-bandwidth data channels, the power of the personal computer, and the availability of compelling content. . . . I will finally have some wires for my wired world."[236] Cable had the pipes to deliver high bandwidth internet services to consumers. Charter went public in 1999, completed a number of acquisitions and became the fourth-largest cable TV operator in the US.

Allen's investment timing in Charter was unfortunate. The company took on significant debt with its acquisitions, paying high prices at the top of the dot.com euphoria in 1999. Charter's earnings were eaten up by the large interest payments on its debt, and when technology stocks crashed in 2000-2002, Charter struggled to remain competitive under its heavy debt load.[237] The company ultimately declared bankruptcy in 2009, and Allen's investment was worth cents on the dollar post-bankruptcy restructuring. His loss at the time was estimated to be $7 billion. Allen was pilloried in the press for this massive destruction of capital. *Forbes* called it "one of the most stunning individual investment losses ever." [238] Some called Allen the "accidental billionaire."

There should have been no expectation, however, that Allen would have the kind of success with Charter or any of his other tech investments that he had with Microsoft. Lightning rarely strikes twice. Microsoft was a one-in-a-many-million occurrence. Foreseeing the direction of the rapidly-changing technology landscape in the late 1990s was uncertain, even for people like Allen, despite great intelligence and experience, and plenty of capital and access to top tech executives.

Just because you are smart and have had success in an area does not mean you will do better than everyone else in that area again, or any other area you invest in, for that matter. As noted previously, notwithstanding your opinion of yourself and the confidence you have in a particular investment, your expectation should be that the returns will be no better than average. Luck and timing play a big part.

Allen may have been ahead of his time. What he said in 1999 was predictive of the world we live in today. "The enabling technologies are falling into place. We can already see a future where high-bandwidth access to information is cheap, where there is plenty of computing power to manipulate that information, and where most of us are connected. . . . I think the most exciting things happening have to do with content. We have only begun to invent what will be possible." [239]

Although he was a technology expert and innovator, Allen had more success post-Microsoft with non-technology investments. Despite the Charter debacle, Allen did well with his ownership of the Seattle Seahawks and Portland Trailblazers, and real estate development in downtown Seattle. But I would guess, although I have no unique insight, that the overall returns on money Allen invested from the sales proceeds of his Microsoft stock did no better than the S&P 500, and perhaps worse.

2007-2008 CRASH OF ASSET-BACKED SECURITIES

A tale of overconfidence and industry-wide delusion is that of mortgage-backed securities in the mid-2000s. The models upon which mortgage-backed debt products were based did not envision that house prices around the country could in unison depreciate by 20% or more. It was not modeled in, because it had not happened before in recorded history. It was not in the data, and the eggheads building the models for these products used available data. But "has not happened before" does not mean "cannot happen."

That house prices had not ever depreciated by more than 3% prior to 2007 was statistically true. It should have been accompanied with an asterisk that historically mortgages required a down payment and were accompanied by meaningful credit checks on the borrowers. An environment like the early 2000s, where the mortgage industry was incentivized to make subprime loans to anyone, regardless of their ability to pay, and then bundled these poorly vetted loans together and sold them to others, should have raised common sense questioning of whether home prices and mortgage defaults might well exceed historical ranges. But this wasn't in the data and therefore was not incorporated into the risk models creating mortgage-backed investments.

The people you knew who were in the bottom of their high school and college classes academically and were suddenly making more money selling mortgages than other friends who were lawyers, doctors and business executives were the canaries in the coal mine for the impending financial disaster of 2007-2008. It didn't seem right, and in retrospect it wasn't. Just about any warm human body could be a candidate for a subprime mortgage in the mid-2000s, which would be issued with little information on the recipient's ability to pay. These were the NINJA loans— no income, job or asset verification. These dubious mortgages were then packaged up, given a high credit rating by compliant rating agencies, and sold to gullible buyers, oftentimes a European insurance company or bank.

The interest payments on the mortgage-backed securities depended on the payments of interest and principal from the underlying mortgages. When the subprime borrowers started defaulting, the market in mortgage-backed securities crashed, which took down the investment banks Lehman Brothers and Bear Stearns. This led to further deterioration of the global economy which led to further losses on the mortgage-backed securities and culminated in the worst depression since the 1930s.

Investment products created by the best and brightest in the financial world nearly took down the global economy in 2007-2008. The economic dislocation, loss of wealth and human pain resulting from the disaster were immense. Taxpayers are still paying the bill for the cleanup.

As a kid I liked to bake cookies with my mom. For a relatively modest

BAKING THE CAKE: INVESTMENT, TAX AND ESTATE PLANNING

effort there were big rewards—the bits of cookie dough scraped out of the mixing bowl, and the fresh cookies warm out of the oven. What a great thing coming from the chemical alchemy of combining sugar, butter, eggs, flour, baking soda, chocolate chips and heat. The whole was better than the sum of the parts.

Same goes for your financial life. You will have the best results by effectively combining financial planning, tax planning and estate planning into a coherent plan. Investing is just one piece of your lifetime financial plan.

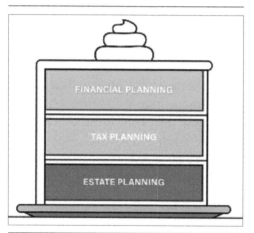

Working closely with your accountant or tax advisor can significantly enhance the management of your wealth. As noted, the money you keep after tax on your investments is what you actually have.

Additionally, working with an estate attorney to have well thought out and drafted estate documents will bring peace of mind, both to you and your heirs. As noted in Chapter 9, giving a power of attorney for investment matters to a trusted family member, friend or advisor should also be on your to-do list.

The better coordinated your investment, tax and estate planning, the better result you are likely to get from your life plan, just like the right combination of ingredients and baking makes for a spectacular chocolate chip cookie. You will also likely feel better knowing that as you enter the last phase of your life, you have done the best job possible to optimize your wealth, and that once you pass the transition will be smooth. Everyone likes a good ending, and to have one for your life with regard to your finances is doable with some thoughtful investment, tax and estate planning.

<hr>

ON YOUR OWN

In the US, the individual investor is increasingly forced to take responsibility for saving and planning for their retirement. It is not a very efficient or effective system. Few are educated in high school or college on how to manage their finances and plan and save for their retirement. Too many people don't get it right. They mismanage it themselves or pay high costs to have someone else do it for them, and are taken advantage of. Writes David Swensen,

> The shift in accountability from employer to employee caused a move from reasonably well-managed, low-cost investment programs to generally poorly managed, high-cost investment programs. The increase in employee-directed retirement programs threatens the retirement security of millions of Americans.[240]

As he notes, even a dedicated national educational effort is unlikely to produce a nation of effective investors immune from Wall Street's siren song or investors' own poor decision-making.[241] Swensen again: "Research shortcomings, rearview-mirror investing, and investor fickleness (in the face of both adversity and opportunity) cripple most investment programs. If the outside investment manager fails to diminish investor assets, then the investor steps in to administer self-inflicted pain."[242]

In 2003, 91 million individuals in 53 million households owned mutual funds, about ½ the households in the country.[243] In contrast, only 25 percent of households owned mutual funds in 1990, and only 6 percent in 1980.[244] See **Chart 7.5** on the change in ownership of the US stock market over time.

It's a convoluted and expensive system surrounding what should be a simple and inexpensive exercise for most people: some simple planning on how much money will be needed for retirement, and what indexed investment portfolio tapping the Base Case will likely produce the wealth needed to pay for it.

It will be interesting to see whether government goes beyond Social Security and becomes more involved in helping people finance their retirements. In the recent coronavirus crisis, the federal government has supplemented people's income with direct cash payments, and has subsidized investors with the broad provision of credit and outright buying of corporate bonds. In addition, 401(k) and other retirement programs are already regulated, and at the state level, a number of states are mandating that all employees have access to a retirement savings plan, and that they be put in default allocations that is some mix of stocks and bonds.

It is not too far to think that since most people would benefit from a low-cost, simple investment program for their retirement, that there may be a government plan that would give individuals the opportunity to elect this. It would in effect be a no-cost or low-cost government plan providing the Base Case returns on the amount the person invested. The investment industry would fight it, but there is some rationale for allowing professional investors to battle it out in the marketplace, while most people sit it out and passively participate in the wealth creation of the economy via indexed investments or an annuity-type return based on them. Many people would welcome the simplicity and the government guarantee.

Do you need thousands of advisors and fund companies to provide an indexed return of stocks and bonds? If the investment world, as Professor Kahneman notes, is built on the illusion of skill, then maybe many people in the industry should be doing something else, something that will better serve our collective well-being.[245]

THE ENERGY OF MONEY

Wealth creation in our universe began in a Big Bang some fourteen billion years ago when from nothingness the energy of the universe burst forth in an expansion of cosmic mass and light. (Yes, this is grandiose, but it's my book, and there is an investment-related point to it.) A tiny eddy of that energy coalesced to become our Milky Way galaxy, and a ripple of it produced our sun and its planets.

Some three and a half billion years ago the first lifeforms arose on Earth. A fortuitous mix of chemical elements was energized, perhaps in a tide pool by the rays of our sun. All life subsequent to this, from single-celled plankton to multi-celled humans, is based on the same premise—taking in energy from the environment and using it to grow and multiply. Phytoplankton take in energy from the sun's rays and via photosynthesis convert it into the energy needed to grow and propagate. Small fish eat the plankton. Bigger fish eat the smaller fish. And humans eat the bigger fish for the energy we need to live.

The basic process for life expanding across the Earth over the last few billions years, therefore, remains the same. Lifeforms take in energy from the environment, convert it and use it to survive, grow, and adapt to an ever-changing planet. Sixty-six million years ago, when a large asteroid hit the Earth, the sky went dark and little sunlight reached the Earth's surface for two years. The systems of life most dependent on the sun's energy collapsed, and three-quarters of all living things died along with the dinosaurs.

Energy, then, as a necessity of life, is highly valued by all of Earth's lifeforms. Likewise, money, a form of stored human energy, is highly valued in our world. Money can energize others to do things for you. Money can get a farmer to grow you sweetcorn, an autoworker to make you an electric car or a carpenter to build you a three-bedroom house. Your own energy and labor are converted into money—your salary or business income—and you exchange money with others for the things you want: the corn, the car and the house.

Surviving, growing and adapting money in the ever-changing economic and political environments created by humans is the goal of investing. Humans' complex and effervescent exchange of energy, with money being its fungible form, results in a complex web of shared benefits called our global economy. Just as the random combination of the sun's rays and chemical elements in the ancient tide pool created something new—life—

humans' purposeful combining of their mental and physical energy and the elements of the Earth creates the food, the goods and the services we need to live.

You can keep this "money-as-energy" analogy in mind when thinking about investing your wealth. It is a useful touchstone for the merits of any investment, for it grounds investing to something fundamental in the natural world. For our collective effort—our global economy—to survive, grow, and adapt to sustain us over time, money—in combination with physical labor and mental know-how—has to be used creatively and efficiently.

The Apple iPhone is a good example of this. Steve Jobs took his energy—his labor and ideas—and the energy of others—employees, investors, and know-how developed by other companies—and combined these elements to create something new that people valued. The iPhone facilitated communication globally, which helped others create businesses (apps, for example) and conduct their lives more efficiently and rewardingly. It produced wealth both in terms of money for Apple stockholders and well-being for a multitude by enabling people to more easily communicate with one another.

Does the Apple iPhone combine people's energy—capital, labor and ideas—in a way that promotes the survival, growth, and adaptation of ourselves and our global economy? Most would say, "Yes." Does an investment bank equity-linked structured product, which pays a very high dividend unless the price of a stock falls below a certain level, promote the survival, growth, and adaptation of human life? Not really. Do this shorthand exercise with each investment you own, and you will avoid the temptations of speculative nonsense, and instead focus on investments that have the highest potential to grow your wealth and the world's over time.

Investing in something that has the potential to produce more energy than it consumes is important both to your well-being and the world's. You may add onto this other priorities, such as environmental and social goals. The security of your financial wealth, and the economic and physical well-being of your human wealth—you, your children, grandchildren, friends, community, country and world—depends in the long term on the sustained growth of our global economy. A world of poor capital allocation and stagnant economies is a world of declining living standards and corrosive disparities of wealth between rich and poor. That is a world of instability, depredation, demagogues and war.

Investing in people and things with merit—again, those that are creating more energy (money) than they are consuming, and therefore promoting life on our planet—is in your best interests and everyone else's. So take the job of investing seriously. Next time you think about making an investment, think about whether this is a good use of the world's limited store of capital, and whether it promotes or diminishes the economic energy needed for our collective survival.

Conclusion

The great thing about investing is that you can do well at it with very little effort. In many ways, as discussed in this book, the less you do the better off you will be. Simple investments accessing the growth of the world's economy will nicely grow your wealth over time. Self-discipline to save and to stick with a long-term investment plan is mostly what is needed for success. I wish you good fortune on your money journey.

1.

John C. Bogle, *The Little Book of Common Sense Investing: The Only Way to Guarantee Your Fair Share of Stock Market Returns*, (New Jersey: John Wiley & Sons, Inc., 2007)

2.

Daniel Kahneman, *Thinking, Fast and Slow* (New York: Farrar, Straus and Giroux, 2011)

3.

Burton G. Malkiel, *A Random Walk Down Wall Street: The Time-Tested Strategy for Successful Investing* (New York: W.W. Norton & Company, 1973)

4.

David F. Swensen, *Unconventional Success: A Fundamental Approach to Personal Investment* (New York: Free Press, 2005)

5.

Jason Zweig, *Your Money & Your Brain* (New York: Simon & Schuster Paperbacks, 2007)

6.

Andrew L. Berkin and Larry E. Swedroe, *Your Complete Guide to Factor-Based Investing: The Way Smart Money Invests Today* (St. Louis, MO: BAM Alliance Press, 2016)

For additional insights into factor-based investing, see Dimensional Fund Advisors: https://us.dimensional.com/

[1] One of my favorite examples is that of Julius Rosenwald, who was one of the principals of Sears, Roebuck and Co. when Sears was in its heyday in the early 20th century. Rosenberg chose to distribute all of his fortune to charitable endeavors within ten years of his death. Via the Rosenwald Fund, he founded hundreds of libraries and schools for America's most disadvantaged citizens, particularly African Americans in poor parts of the rural South.

[2] Daniel Kahneman, *Thinking, Fast and Slow* (New York: Farrar, Straus and Giroux, 2011) 20-21.

[3] March 1, 1994, Letter to the Shareholders of Berkshire Hathaway Inc. from Chairman of the Board Warren E. Buffett, Topic: Summarizing 1993.

[4] February 28, 2006, Letter to the Shareholders of Berkshire Hathaway Inc. from Chairman of the Board Warren E. Buffett, 18.

[5] Abraham Okusanya, *Lessons from 118 years of asset class returns data* (March 28, 2018), finalytiq.co.uk.

[6] Peter Coy, "It's Been 40 Years Since Our Cover Story Declared 'The Death of Equities,'" *Bloomberg Businessweek*, August 13, 2019.

[7] Ibid.

[8] Ibid.

[9] David F. Swensen, *Unconventional Success: A Fundamental Approach to Personal Investment* (New York: Free Press, 2005), Preface.

[10] Burton G. Malkiel, *A Random Walk Down Wall Street: The Time-Tested Strategy for Successful Investing* (New York: W.W. Norton & Company, 1973), 312.

[11] John C. Bogle, "The Stock Market Universe—Stars, Comets, and the Sun" (remarks, Financial Analysts of Philadelphia, February 15, 2001).

[12] Ibid.

[13] Jason Zweig, "What You Can Learn from One of Warren Buffett's Smartest Investors," *The Wall Street Journal*, December 21, 2018.

[14] Malkiel, *Random Walk*, 403.

[15] Reinhold Niebuhr, "Serenity Prayer."

[16] Roger G. Ibbotson and Paul D. Kaplan, "Does Asset Allocation Policy Explain 40, 90, 100 Percent of Performance?" *Financial Analysts Journal* 56, no. 1 (2000): 32, cited in David F. Swensen, *Unconventional Success: A Fundamental Approach to Personal Investment* (New York: Free Press, 2005), 12.

[17] Swensen, *Unconventional Success*, 35.

[18] Duration measures a bond's sensitivity to a change in interest rates. It incorporates a bond's coupon payments and adjusts for the timing of cash flows.

[19] Swensen, *Unconventional Success*, 41.

[20] Kahneman, *Thinking*, 283-284.

[21] Malkiel, *Random Walk*, 304.

[22] Associated Press, "Hedge Funds Took A Serious Hit in 2008," January 12, 2009, https://www.cbsnews.com/news/hedge-funds-took-a-serious-hit-in-2008/.

[23] John Hechinger, "Harvard, Yale Are Big Losers in "The Game" of Investing," *The Wall Street Journal*, Sept. 11, 2009.

[24] Larry Swedroe, "Swedroe: Past Performance Deceives," ETF.com, November 10, 2017. https://www.etf.com/sections/index-investor-corner/swedroe-past-performance-deceives?nopaging=1.

[25] Swensen, *Unconventional Success*, 1.

[26] Dennis Hammond, "A Better Approach to Systematic Outperformance? 58 years of Endowment Performance," *The Journal of Investing* 29, no. 5 (August 2020); Richard M. Ennis, "Endowment Performance," *Richard M. Ennis*, December 1, 2020, https://richardmennis.com/blog/endowment-performance.

[27] Dennis Hammond, "A Better Approach to Systematic Outperformance? 58 years of Endowment Performance," *The Journal of Investing* 29, no. 5 (August 2020): 15.

[28] Richard M. Ennis, "Endowment Performance," *Richard M. Ennis*, December 1, 2020, https://richardmennis.com/blog/endowment-performance.

[29] Ennis, "Endowment Performance." Ennis estimates that the effective equity exposure of large endowment funds for the eleven years ended June 30, 2019 to be 72%.

[30] Swensen, *Unconventional Success*, 92.

[31] Ibid., 92-93.

[32] Ibid., 92.

[33] Ibid., 109.

[34] Berlinda Liu and Gaurav Sinha, "SPIVA US Scorecard," S&P Dow Jones Indices, March 11, 2021. 20. https://www.spglobal.com/spdji/en/documents/spiva/spiva-us-year-end-2020.pdf.

[35] Ibid., 23.

[36] Swensen, *Unconventional Success*, 114.

[37] Ibid., 118.

[38] Ibid., 125.

[39] Larry Swedroe, "Swedroe: Avoid Private Real Estate Assets," ETF.com, July 2, 2018. https://www.etf.com/sections/index-investor-corner/swedroe-avoid-private-real-estate-assets.

[40] Ibid. Swedroe adds that "While institutional investors obviously believe they are able to identify managers who will deliver outperformance, the evidence is clear that they have not done so. Like many other investors, it appears they are guilty of overconfidence."

[41] Swensen, *Unconventional Success*, 70.

[42] Ibid., 135.

[43] Ibid.

[44] Malkiel, *Unconventional Success*, 320.

[45] Jason Zweig, *Your Money & Your Brain* (New York: Simon & Schuster Paperbacks, 2007), 79.

[46] Malkiel, *Random Walk*, 253.

[47] Swensen, *Unconventional Success*, 138.

[48] Ibid.

[49] Ibid., 133.

[50] Cliff Asness, "The Illiquidity Discount?" *Perspective* (blog), AQR, December 19, 2019. https://www.aqr.com/Insights/Perspectives/The-Illiquidity-Discount.

[51] Swensen, *Unconventional Success*, 147.

[52] Ibid., 133.

[53] Ibid., 135.

[54] Ibid., 134.

[55] Ibid., 139.

[56] Ibid., 140.

[57] Ibid., 146.

[58] Ibid.

[59] Ibid., 144. Writes Swensen, "All of the top-tier venture capital partnerships limit assets under management, and none of the top-tier partnerships currently accepts new investors."

[60] Ibid., 146.

[61] Ibid., 139.

[62] Ibid., 126. Adds Swensen, "On average, investors lose by the amount of transactions costs incurred and management fees paid."

[63] Ibid., 129.

[64] Gregory Zuckerman, "Renaissance's $10 Billion Medallion Fund Gains 24% Year to Date in Tumultuous Market," *The Wall Street Journal*, April 17, 2020. https://www.wsj.com/articles/renaissance-s-10-billion-medallion-fund-gains-24-year-to-datein-tumultuous-market-11587152401.

[65] Swensen, *Unconventional Success*, 127.

[66] For a good read on this, see Roger Lowenstein, *When Genius Failed: The Rise and Fall of Long-Term Capital Management* (New York: Random House, 2000).

[67] Swensen, *Unconventional Success*, 127.

[68] Ibid., 131.

[69] Ibid., 126.

[70] Ibid., 130.

[71] Malkiel, *Random Walk*, 367. Says Malkiel, "With respect to the advice regarding annuities, I suspect that the percentage of misinformation is closer to 99 percent."

[72] Ibid., 369.

[73] Ibid., 370.

[74] Warwick Schneller, "Beyond the Label, ESG Funds May Miss Their Mark," *MyDimensional Weekly Digest*, August 12, 2021.

[75] David Stubbs, "Think ESG may become a bubble? We don't." *Investment Strategy*, J.P. Morgan Private Bank, August 18, 2021.

[76] Schneller, "Beyond the Label."

[77] Ibid.

[78] Kahneman, *Thinking*, 263.

[79] Nate Silver, *The Signal and the Noise: Why So Many Predictions Fail—but Some Don't* (New York: Penguin Press, 2012).

[80] Scott MacKillop, "Ignore the Gurus: Part II," Scott's Column (blog), The Summit: What We're Talking About, February 20, 2018. https://firstascentam.com/ignore-the-gurus-part-ii/

[81] Kahneman, *Thinking*, 215.

[82] Louis Menand, "Everybody's An Expert: Putting Predictions to the Test," *The New Yorker*, November 27, 2005. https://www.newyorker.com/magazine/2005/12/05/everybodys-an-expert.

[83] Jennifer Booton, "Jim Cramer doesn't beat the market," May 16, 2016, https://www.marketwatch.com/story/jim-cramer-doesnt-beat-the-market-2016-05-13.

[84] Kahneman, *Thinking*, 220. Writes Kahneman, "The first lesson is that errors of prediction are inevitable because the world is unpredictable. The second is that high subjective confidence is not to be trusted as an indicator of accuracy (low confidence could be more informative)."

[85] Ibid., 241.

[86] New World Encyclopedia, s.v. "Upton Sinclair," date of last revision April 21, 2009, https://www.newworldencyclopedia.org/p/index.php?title=Upton_Sinclair&oldid=1035849.

[87] Kahneman, *Thinking*, 212.

[88] Swensen, *Unconventional Success*, 153. Writes Swensen, "In an environment dominated by managers with skills insufficient to overcome the powerful forces of market efficiency, randomness plays a significant role in separating the winners from losers."

[89] Ibid., 267.

[90] February 24, 2018, Letter to the Shareholders of Berkshire Hathaway Inc. from Chairman of the Board Warren E. Buffett, 12.

[91] Swensen, *Unconventional Success*, 237.

[92] Ibid., 224.

[93] Anna Prior, "The Hidden Costs of Mutual Funds," *The Wall Street Journal*, March 1, 2010, https://www.wsj.com/articles/SB10001424052748703382904575059690954870722.

[94] Ibid.

[95] John C. Bogle, *The Little Book of Common Sense Investing: The Only Way to Guarantee Your Fair Share of Stock Market Returns*, (Hoboken, New Jersey: John Wiley & Sons, Inc., 2007), 33.

[96] Swensen, *Unconventional Success*, 342-343.

[97] Ibid., 266.

[98] Dimensional Fund Advisors, "Matrix Book 2021, March 2021, 94.

[99] Reuters, Business News, "Less than 18% of global stocks owned by index investors: BlackRock," October 3, 2017, https://www.reuters.com/article/us-funds-blackrock-passive/less-than-18-percent-of-global-stocks-owned-by-index-investors-blackrock-idUSKCN1C82TE. "The estimate on Tuesday showed that $11.9 trillion in stocks were owned by mutual funds, exchange-traded funds, institutional accounts and private investors that track an index. That accounts for 17.5% of the $67.9 trillion in global equity market capitalization, according to the data. Stocks in actively managed hedge funds, mutual funds and institutional accounts total $17.4 trillion, 25.6 percent of the global equity market cap, according to the report. The remaining 57% are assets held by governments, pension funds, insurers or corporations. Such holdings are not overseen by an asset manager and do not track an index."

[100] Larry Swedroe, "Wall Street's Foolish War on Passive Investing," *Advisor Perspectives*, ETF.com, July 9, 2018. Notes Swedroe, "The study "Conviction in Equity Investing" by Mike Sebastian and Sudhakar Attaluri, which appeared in the Summer 2014 issue of The Journal of Portfolio Management, found that the percentage of skilled managers was about 20% in 1993. By 2011, it had fallen to just 1.6%. This closely matches the result of the 2010 paper "Luck versus Skill in the Cross-Section of Mutual Fund Returns." The authors, Eugene Fama and Kenneth French, found only managers in the 98th and 99th percentiles showed evidence of statistically significant skill. On an after-tax basis, that 2% would be even lower."

[101] Malkiel, *Random Walk*, 55; Silvia Amaro, "Sell-offs could be down to machines that control 80% of the US stock market, fund manager says," CNBC, December 5, 2018. https://www.cnbc.com/2018/12/05/sell-offs-could-be-down-to-machines-that-control-80percent-of-us-stocks-fund-manager-says.html.

[102] "Index Investing Supports Vibrant Capital Markets," BlackRock ViewPoint, October 2017, 3, https://www.blackrock.com/corporate/literature/whitepaper/viewpoint-index-investing-supports-vibrant-capital-markets-oct-2017.pdf.

[103] Malkiel, *Random Walk*, 398.

[104] Kahneman, *Thinking*, 217.

[105] "Bear Down, Chicago Bears" (a song by Jerry Downs)

[106] Kahneman, *Thinking*, 215.

[107] Malkiel, *Random Walk*, 99. Malkiel also notes, "The efficient-market hypothesis does not imply, as some critics have proclaimed, that stock prices are always correct. In fact, stock prices are always wrong. What EMH implies is that no one knows for sure if stock prices are too high or too low. Nor does EMH state that stock prices move aimlessly and erratically and are insensitive to changes in fundamental information. On the contrary, the reason prices move randomly is just the opposite. The market is so efficient—prices move so quickly when information arises—that no one can buy or sell fast enough to benefit. And real news develops randomly, that is, unpredictably. It cannot be predicted by studying either past technical or fundamental information." 181

[108] Eugene F. Fama and Robert Litterman, "An Experienced View on Markets and Investing," *Financial Analysts Journal*, CFA Institute, 2012, Vol. 68, No. 6. 17.

[109] Swensen, *Unconventional Success*, 203.

[110] Fama and Litterman, "An Experienced View on Markets and Investing," 17.

[111] Hendrik Bessembinder, "Do Stocks Outperform Treasury Bills?" *Journal of Financial Economics* (JFE), *Forthcoming* (May 28, 2018).

[112] Ibid., 2.

[113] Ibid., 3-4. Bessembinder notes, "The largest amount of wealth creation attributable to any firm is $1.002 trillion, by Exxon Mobil. The second largest wealth creation is attributable to Apple, which created $745.7 billion in shareholder wealth, despite a CRSP life of only 433 months (compared to 1,086 months for Exxon Mobil and other firms that were present for the full sample.) Microsoft ($629.8 billion), General Electric ($608.1 billion), International Business Machines ($520.2 billion), Altria Group ($470.2 billion), Johnson and Johnson ($426.2 billion), GM ($425.3 billion), Chevron ($390.4 billion), and Walmart ($368.2 billion) comprise the rest of the top ten firms in terms of lifetime wealth creation." 31.

[114] Ibid., 3-4.

[115] Jane Wollman Rusoff, "Study Shows 96% of Stocks Don't Beat Treasuries in Long Term," *ThinkAdvisor*, August 21, 2017. https://www.thinkadvisor.com/2017/08/21/study-shows-96-of-stocks-dont-beat-treasuries-in-long-term/.

[116] Bessembinder, "Do Stocks Outperform Treasury Bills?", 33.

[117] Ibid., 24.

[118] Wollman Rusoff, "Study Shows."

[119] Larry Swedroe, "New Research on Performance Chasing," *Advisor Perspectives*, June 4, 2018. Swedroe cites the paper by Robert Ferguson, Anna Agapova, Dean Leistikow and Joel Rentzler titled "Chasing Performance and Identifying Talented Investment Managers" which appeared in the Spring 2018 issue of *The Journal of Investing*.

[120] Zweig, *Brain*, 60. Zweig cites Dartmouth College professor George Wolford: "There appears to be a module in the left hemisphere of the brain that drives humans to search for patterns and to see casual relationships," says Wolford, "even when none exist."

[121] Kahneman, *Thinking*, 116-117. Kahneman comments that the "hot hand" in basketball is a widespread cognitive illusion, and that "We are far too willing to reject the belief that much of what we see in life is random."

[122] Ibid., 117.

[123] Ibid., 175.

[124] Ibid., 175-176.

[125] Ibid., 214.

[126] Berlinda Liu and Gaurav Sinha, "U.S. Persistence Scorecard," S&P Dow Jones Indices, May 11, 2021, 4. https://www.spglobal.com/spdji/en/documents/spiva/persistence-scorecard-year-end-2020.pdf.

[127] Ibid., 10.

[128] Larry Swedroe, "The Persistence of Active Management Outperformance," *Advisor Perspectives*, September 15, 2018. https://www.advisorperspectives.com/articles/2018/09/15/the-persistence-of-active-management-outperformance.

[129] "2021 Investment Company FACT BOOK: A Review of Trends and Activities in the Investment Company Industry," Investment Company Institute, 57. www.icifactbook.org.

[130] Ibid.

[131] Swedroe, "Persistence."

[132] John Rekenthaler, "How Long Can a Good Fund Underperform Its Benchmark?) *Morningstar*, March 26, 2018, https://www.morningstar.com/articles/856831/how-long-can-a-good-fund-underperform-its-benchmark.

[133] Paul Kaplan and Maciej Kowara, "Are Relative Performance Measures Useless?" *The Journal of Investing*, June 2019, https://doi.org/10.3905/joi.2019.28.4.083.

[134] Swedroe, "Persistence."

[135] Robert Steyer, "Emory University agrees to pay $17 million to settle ERISA claims," *Pensions & Investments*, June 1, 2020. https://www.pionline.com/courts/emory-university-agrees-pay-17-million-settle-erisa-claims.

[136] Swedroe, "Persistence."

[137] Swensen, *Unconventional Success*, 179, 181.

[138] Ibid., 182.

[139] Bogle, "The Stock Market Universe."

[140] Fama and Litterman, "Experienced View," 17.

[141] Swensen, *Unconventional Success*, 214.

[142] Amit Goyal and Sunil Wahal, "The Selection and Termination of Investment Management Firms by Plan Sponsors," *Institutional Investor*, April 17, 2008.

[143] Swedroe, "Past Performance Deceives."

[144] Swensen, *Unconventional Success*, 150.

[145] Malkiel, *Random Walk*, 378.

[146] Kahneman, *Thinking*, 85. Kahneman talks about the shortcomings of analysis focused just on available data, what he calls WYSIATI (what you see is all there is).

[147] "The Illusion of Active Fixed Income Diversification," *AQR: Alternative Thinking*, 4Q 2017, 7.

[148] Bogle, *"Common Sense,"* xv.

[149] Jeff Sommer, "That Nagging Question of Mutual Fund Fees," *New York Times*, May 10, 2010.

[150] February 29, 1988, Letter to the Shareholders of Berkshire Hathaway Inc. from Chairman of the Board Warren E. Buffett.

[151] March 1, 1993, Letter to the Shareholders of Berkshire Hathaway Inc. from Chairman of the Board Warren E. Buffett.

[152] Mark Twain, *Following the Equator*.

[153] https://us.dimensional.com/

[154] Andrew L. Berkin and Larry E. Swedroe, *Your Complete Guide to Factor-Based Investing: The Way Smart Money Invests Today* (St. Louis, MO: BAM Alliance Press, 2016), 28-29.

[155] Malkiel, *Random Walk*, 266. Says Malkiel, "At least historically, the four factors considered above—value, size, momentum, and low beta—have produced good risk-adjusted returns. It would appear that tilting portfolios in these directions could be a smart investment strategy. But in practice it may not be possible for investors to capture the additional risk premiums that appear to be available."

[156] Berkin and Swedroe, *Factor-Based*, 35.

[157] Ibid.

[158] Ibid., 36.

[159] Ibid., 42.

[160] Ibid.

[161] Ibid., 44.

[162] Nicholas Barberis and Ming Huang, "Stocks as Lotteries: The Implications of Probability Weighting for Security Prices," *American Economic Review* 98, no. 5 (December 2008).

[163] Cliff Asness, Andrea Frazzini, Ronen Israel, Tobias J. Moskowitz, Lasse H. Pedersen, "Size Matters, If You Control Your Junk," *Journal of Financial Economics* (January 22, 2015).

[164] Berkin and Swedroe, *Factor-Based*, 62.

[165] Cliff Asness, Tobias J. Moskowitz, Lasse Pedersen, "Value and Momentum Everywhere" *AQR* (June 1, 2013).

[166] Larry Swedroe, "Swedroe: Value Premium Lives!" *ETF.com*, May 16, 2018. https://www.etf.com/sections/index-investor-corner/swedroe-value-premium-lives?nopaging=1.

[167] Malkiel, *Random Walk*, 260.

[168] Malkiel, *Random Walk*, 261. Says Malkiel, "Low P/E multiples and low price-to-book-value (P/BV) ratios can reflect risk factors that are priced into the market."

[169] Zweig, *Brain*, 170.

[170] Lu Zhang, "The Value Premium," *The Journal of Finance* (July 20, 2005).

[171] Berkin and Swedroe, *Factor-Based*, 71.

[172] Dimensional Fund Advisors: Dimensional US Large Cap Value Index and Dimensional US Large Cap Growth Index.

[173] Bogle, "The Stock Market Universe."

[174] Ibid.

[175] Ibid.

[176] February 28, 2001, Letter to the Shareholders of Berkshire Hathaway Inc. from Chairman of the Board Warren E. Buffett.

[177] Bogle, "The Stock Market Universe."

[178] Malkiel, *Random Walk*, 264.

[179] Narasimhan Jegadeesh and Sheridan Titman, "Returns to Buying Winners and Selling Losers: Implications for Stock Market Efficiency," *The Journal of Finance* 48, no. 1 (March 1993).

[180] Berkin and Swedroe, *Factor-Based*, 88-89.

[181] Cliff Asness, Andrea Frazzini, Ronen Israel, Tobias J. Moskowitz, "Fact, Fiction and Momentum Investing" *AQR* (September 23, 2014).

[182] Asness, Frazzini, Israel, Moskowitz, "Fact, Fiction."

[183] Berkin and Swedroe, *Factor-Based*, 105.

[184] Eugen F. Fama and Kenneth R. French, "Profitability, Investment and Average Returns" *Journal of Financial Economics* 82, no. 3 (December 2006). Robert Novy-Marx, "The Other Side of Value: The Gross Profitability Premium" *Journal of Financial Economics* 108, no. 1 (2013).

[185] Berkin and Swedroe, *Factor-Based*, 246.

[186] Ibid., 127.

[187] Ibid., 135.

[188] Ibid., 137.

[189] Ibid., 261.

[190] Ibid.

[191] Ibid., 263.

[192] Ibid.

[193] Ibid., 265. The authors cite the 1994 paper by Martin S. Fridson titled, "Do High-Yield Bonds Have an Equity Component?" They say that "In effect, a corporate bond is a combination of a pure interest rate instrument and a short position in a put on the issuer's equity. The put is triggered by a decline in the value of the issuer's assets to less than the value of its liabilities. A default, in other words, results in the stockholders putting the equity to the bondholders, who then become the company's owners."

[194] Ibid., 159.

[195] Ibid.

[196] Swedroe, "Value Premium Lives!"

[197] W. Harry Fortuna, "Read Albert Einstein's handwritten advice from 1922 on living a happy life," *Quartz*, October 24, 2017, https://qz.com/1109535/read-albert-einsteins-handwritten-advice-on-living-a-happy-life/.

[198] Michael S. Finke, John S. Howe, and Sandra J. Huston, "Old Age and the Decline in Financial Literacy," MIT Center for Finance & Policy, September 2015.

[199] Zweig, *Brain*, 193.

[200] Christine Benz, "100 Must-Know Statistics About 401(k) Plans," *Morningstar*, September 4, 2020. Article says 95% of large plans "offer some type of advice to participants (for example, online advice, in-house education, or managed accounts), 2019." https://www.morningstar.com/articles/1000743/100-must-know-statistics-about-401k-plans.

[201] Amy Fontinelle and reviewed by Ebony Howard, "How to Cut Financial Advisor Expenses" *Investopedia* (February 7, 20201). https://www.investopedia.com/articles/personal-finance/071415/how-cut-financial-advisor-expenses.asp.

[202] You can check a financial planner's background at the CFP Board website: https://www.cfp.net/verify-a-cfp-professional. You can check a broker or advisor's background at the FINRA website: https://brokercheck.finra.org/.

[203] Swensen, *Unconventional Success*, 178.

[204] Zweig, *Brain*, 61. Zweig notes that with regard to your brain's pattern recognition, it leaps to conclusions, is unconscious, is automatic and is uncontrollable. Zweig references Eric Johnson, a psychology professor at Columbia Business School, who says that "We like to think that we're 'thinking' when we estimate probabilities, but a surprisingly large portion of the process appears to occur automatically, below the level of consciousness." 75; Kahneman, *Thinking*, 20. Kahneman notes that the brain's System 1 "operates automatically and quickly, with little or no effort and no sense of voluntary control."

205 Kahneman, *Thinking*, 87-88.

206 Ibid., 225.

207 Malkiel, *Random Walk*, 231. Malkiel says, "Steve Forbes, the longtime publisher of Forbes magazine, liked to quote the advice he received at his grandfather's knee: 'It's far more profitable to sell advice than to take it.'"

208 Kahneman, *Thinking*, 40-42. Kahneman cites the research of Roy Baumeister. "Baumeister's group has repeatedly found that an effort of will or self-control is tiring; if you have had to force yourself to do something, you are less willing or less able to exert self-control when the next challenge comes around. This phenomenon has been named ego depletion."

209 Ibid., 44.

210 March 1, 1993, Letter to the Shareholders of Berkshire Hathaway Inc. from Chairman of the Board Warren E. Buffett.

211 Zweig, *Brain*, 26. Zweig cites Christopher Hsee, a psychologist at the University of Chicago. Says Hsee, "If this happened to someone else, and they asked for your advice, what would you tell them to do? I oftentimes try to make decisions that way, by putting myself in someone else's shoes."

212 Zweig, *Brain*, 147.

213 Kahneman, *Thinking*, 28.

214 Zweig, *Brain*, 28.

215 Jason Zweig, "If You Think Worst Is Over, Take Benjamin Graham's Advice," *Wall Street Journal*, May 26, 2009.

216 February 24, 2018, Letter to the Shareholders of Berkshire Hathaway Inc. from Chairman of the Board Warren E. Buffett.

217 Zweig, *Brain*, 84.

218 Ibid., 83-84.

219 February 28, 2006, Letter to the Shareholders of Berkshire Hathaway Inc. from Chairman of the Board Warren E. Buffett, 18.

220 Brad M. Barber and Terrance Odean, "Trading is Hazardous to Your Wealth: The Common Stock Investment Performance of Individual Investors," *The Journal of Finance* LV, no. 2 (April 2000).

221 Malkiel, *Random Walk*, 403. Says Malkiel, "To be sure, index investors are free riders. They do receive the benefits that result from active trading without bearing the costs."

222 Ibid., 229.

223 Zweig, *Brain*, 88.

224 Ibid., 88.

225 Ibid., 91.

226 K. Connie Chang, "Next Stop, the Pearly Gates," *Los Angeles Times*, October 24, 2003.

227 Zweig, *Brain*, 89.

228 Kahneman, *Thinking*, 9.

229 Swensen, *Unconventional Success*, 203.

230 Peter Bennett, "10 Warren Buffett Investment Tips to Build Your Wealth," *MyBankTracker.com*, March 12, 2021. https://www.mybanktracker.com/blog/investing/warren-Buffett-investment-strategy-161222

231 Tae Kim, "Buffett, quoting partner Munger, says there are three ways to go broke: 'liquor, ladies and leverage'," *CNBC*, February 26, 2018. https://www.cnbc.com/2018/02/26/Buffett-says-out-of-the-three-ways-to-go-broke-liquor-ladies-and-leverage-leverage-is-the-worst.html.

232 I worked for Paul Allen in the mid-2000s at his investment office, Vulcan Capital, where I helped oversee equity, fixed income, hedge fund and some private equity investments.

233 Allen's share has been estimated to have been worth about $30 billion in 1999-2000.

234 Allen left the company as head of research in 1983 after contracting Hodgkin's disease.

[235] John Talton, "Paul Allen, Charter and What Might Have Been," *The Seattle Times*, May 28, 2015. Deborah Yao, "Paul Allen's company, Charter Communications, drowning in debt," *The Seattle Times*, January 29, 2009.

[236] Yao, "drowning in debt."

[237] Ibid.

[238] Nathan Vardi, "Billionaire Paul Allen Is Finally Making A Little Money Off Of Charter Communications," *Forbes*, September 10, 2012.

[239] "The wired world of Paul Allen," *The Guardian*, Aug. 14, 1999.

[240] Swensen, *Unconventional Success*, 3.

[241] Ibid., 4.

[242] Ibid., 6.

[243] Ibid., 209.

[244] Ibid.

[245] Kahneman, *Thinking*, 212.

AQR Capital Management, LLC "The Illusion of Active Fixed Income Diversification," *Alternative Thinking, 2017*, 4th Quarter. (Accessed July 24, 2021 www.aqr.com).

Asness, Cliff "The Illiquidity Discount?" *Perspective* blog, AQR, December 19, 2019, (Accessed July, 2021 www.aqr.com/Insights/Perspectives/The-Illiquidity-Discount).

Asness, Frazzini, Israel, Moskowitz, and Pedersen, "Size Matters, If You Control Your Junk," *Journal of Financial Economics*, January 22, 2015.

Associated Press "Hedge Funds Took A Serious Hit in 2008," *CBS News* January 12, 2009, (Accessed July 28, 2021 www.cbsnews.com/news/hedge-funds-took-a-serious-hit-in-2008).

Barber, Brad M. and Odean, Terrance, "Trading is Hazardous to Your Wealth: The Common Stock Investment Performance of Individual Investors," *The Journal of Finance LV*, no. 2, April 2000.

Barberis, Nicholas and Huang, Ming, "Stocks as Lotteries: The Implications of Probability Weighting for Security Prices," *American Economic Review* 98, no. 5, December 2008.

Bennett, Peter, "10 Warren Buffett Investment Tips to Build Your Wealth," *MyBankTracker.com*, March 12, 2021. (Accessed July 21 2021 https://www.mybanktracker.com/blog/investing/warren-Buffett-investment-strategy-161222).

Benz, Christine, "100 Must-Know Statistics About 401(k) Plans," *Morningstar*, September 4, 2020. (Accessed July 25, 2021 https://www.morningstar.com/articles/1000743/100-must-know-statistics-about-401k-plans).

Berkin, Andrew L. & Larry E Swedroe, *Your Complete Guide to Factor-Based Investing*. St Louis, MO: BAM Alliance Press, 2016.

Bessembinder, Hendrick, "Do Stocks Outperform Treasury Bills?" *Journal of Financial Economics* (JFE), May 28, 2018.

Buffett, Warren L., "Chairman's Letter," Berkshire Hathaway Inc., March 1, 1993. (Accessed July 24, 2021 www.berkshirehathaway.com/letters/1992.html).

Bogle, John C., *The Little Book of Common Sense Investing: The Only Way to Guarantee Your Fair Share of Stock Market Returns*. Hoboken, NJ: John Wiley & Sons, Inc., 2007.

— — —. "The Stock Market Universe—Stars, Comets, and the Sun," *Financial Analysts of Philadelphia*, February 15, 2001.

Chang, Connie, K., "Next Stop, the Pearly Gates," *The Los Angeles Times*, October 24, 2003.

Coy, Peter "It's Been 40 Years Since Our Cover Story Declared 'The Death of Equities,'" *Bloomberg Businessweek*, August 13, 2019.

Downs, Jerry, "Bear Down, Chicago Bears," 1941, fight song, Chicago Bears NFL

Ennis, Richard M. "Endowment Performance," *Richard M Ennis* blog, December 1, 2020. (Accessed July 30, 2021 https://richardmennis.com/blog/endowment-performance).

Fama, Eugene F. & Robert Litterman. "An Experienced View on Markets and Investing," *Financial Analysts Journal*, Volume 68 no. 6 (2012).

Fontinelle, Amy, "How to Cut Financial Advisor Expenses," *Investopedia* February 7, 20201. (Accessed July 25, 2021 https://www.investopedia.com/articles/personal-finance/071415/how-cut-financial-advisor-expenses.asp).

Goyal, Amit and Wahal, Sunil, "The Selection and Termination of Investment Management Firms by Plan Sponsors," *Institutional Investor*, April 17, 2008.

Hammond, Dennis. "A Better Approach to Systematic Outperformance? 58 Years of Endowment Performance." *The Journal of Investing: Theory & Practice for Fund Managers*, no. 5, 2020. (Accessed July 24, 2021 www.JOI.PM-RESEARCH.com).

Hechinger, John "Harvard, Yale Are Big Losers in 'The Game' of Investing," *The Wall Street Journal* Sept. 11, 2009. (Accessed July 27, 2021 https://www.wsj.com/articles/SB125261209050800581).

Jegadeesh, Narasimhan and Titman, Sheridan, "Returns to Buying Winners and Selling Losers: Implications for Stock Market Efficiency," *The Journal of Finance* 48, no. 1, March, 1993.

Kaplan, Paul and Kowara, Maciej, "Are Relative Performance Measures Useless?" *The Journal of Investing*, June 2019. (Accessed July 25 2021, https://doi.org/10.3905/joi.2019.28.4.083).

Khaneman, Daniel, *Thinking Fast and Slow*. New York, NY: Farrar, Straus and Giroux, 2016.

Liu, Belinda and Sinha, Gaurov, "SPIVA US Scorecard," *S&P Dow Jones Indices*, March 11, 2021. (Accessed July 25, 2021 https://www.spglobal.com/spdji/en/documents/spiva/spiva-us-year-end-2020.pdf).

Lowenstein, Roger, *When Genius Failed: The Rise and Fall of Long-Term Capital Management*. New York, NY: Random House, 2000.

MacKillop, Scott, "Ignore the Gurus: Part II," *The Summit: What We're Talking About*, February 20, 2018. (Accessed July 30, 2021 https://firstascentam.com/ignore-the-gurus-part-ii/).

Malkiel, Burton G., *A Random Walk Down Wall Street: The Time-Tested Strategy for Successful Investing*. New York, NY: W.W. Norton & Company, 1973.

Menand, Louis, "Everybody's An Expert: Putting Predictions to the Test," *The New Yorker*, November 27, 2005. (Accessed July 30, 2021 https://www.newyorker.com/magazine/2005/12/05/everybodys-an-expert).

Niebuhr, Reinhold "The Serenity Prayer: Faith and Politics in Times of Peace and War." New York, NY: Norton, 2003.

Novy-Marx, Robert, "The Other Side of Value: The Gross Profitability Premium," *Journal of Financial Economics* 108, no. 1, 2013.

Okusanya, Abraham "Lessons From 118 Years Of Asset Class Returns Data," *Finalytiq*, March 28, 2017. (Accessed July 29, 2021 https://finalytiq.co.uk/lessons-118-years-capital-market-return-data).

Rekenthaler, John, "How Long Can a Good Fund Underperform Its Benchmark?" *Morningstar*, March 26, 2018. (Accessed July 27, 2021 https://www.morningstar.com/articles/856831/how-long-can-a-good-fund-underperform-its-benchmark).

Rusoff, Jane Wollman, "Study Shows 96% of Stocks Don't Beat Treasuries in Long Term," *ThinkAdvisor*, August 21, 2017. (Accessed July 25, 2021 https://www.thinkadvisor.com/2017/08/21/study-shows-96-of-stocks-dont-beat-treasuries-in-long-term).

Swansen, David, *Unconventional Success: A Fundamental Approach to Personal Investment*. New York, NY: Free Press, August 1, 2005.

Silver, Nate, *The Signal and the Noise: Why So Many Predictions Fail—but Some Don't*. New York, NY: Penguin Press, 2012.

Sommer, Jeff, "That Nagging Question of Mutual Fund Fees," *The New York Times*, May 10, 2010.

Steyer, Robert, "Emory University agrees to pay $17 million to settle ERISA claims," *Pensions & Investments*, June 1, 2020. (Accessed July 25, 2021 https://www.pionline.com/courts/emory-universty-agrees-pay-17-million-settle-erisa-claims).

Swedroe, Larry, "Swedroe: Avoid Private Real Estate Assets," *Exchange Traded Funds*, November 10, 2017. (Accessed July 27, 2021 https://www.etf.com/sections/index-investor-corner/swedroe-avoid-private-real-estate-assets).

— — —. "Wall Street's Foolish War on Passive Investing," *Advisor Perspectives*, June 4, 2018. (Accessed July 27, 2021 https://www.advisorperspectives.com/articles/2018/07/09/wall-streets-foolish-war-on-passive-investing.pdf).

— — —. "Swedroe: Value Premium Lives!" *Exchange Traded Funds*, July 2, 2018. (Accessed July 27, 2021 https://www.etf.com/sections/index-investor-corner/swedroe-value-premium-lives?nopaging=1).

— — —. "Swedroe: Past Performance Deceives," *Exchange Traded Funds*, July 9, 2018. (Accessed July 28 2021 https://www.etf.com/sections/index-investor-corner/swedroe-past-performance-deceives?nopaging=1).

— — —. "New Research on Performance Chasing," *ETF.com*, May 16, 2018.

— — —. "The Persistence of Active Management Outperformance," *Advisor Perspectives*, September 15, 2018. (Accessed July 27, 2021 https://www.advisorperspectives.com/articles/2018/09/15/the-persistence-of-active-management-outperformance).

Segal, Julie "Yale's Risk-Adjusted Returns Not So 'Superior' After All, " *Institutional Investor*, Trading Tech 40 April 16, 2018.

Tae, Kim, "Buffett, quoting partner Munger, says there are three ways to go broke: 'liquor, ladies and leverage'," *CNBC*, February 26, 2018. (Accessed July 25, 2021 https://www.cnbc.com/2018/02/26/Buffett-says-out-of-the-three-ways-to-go-broke-liquor-ladies-and-leverage-leverage-is-the-worst.html).

Talton, Jon, "Paul Allen, Charter and What Might Have Been," *The Seattle Times*, May 28, 2015.

Twain, Mark, Daniel Carter Beard, A. B. Frost, B. West Clinedinst, Frederick Dielman, Peter Newell, F. M. Senior, et al. 1897. *Following the Equator: a journey around the world.* Mark Twain.

Vardi, Nathan,"Billionaire Paul Allen Is Finally Making A Little Money Off Of Charter Communications," *Forbes*, September 10, 2012.

Yao, Deborah, "Paul Allen's company, Charter Communications, drowning in debt," *The Seattle Times*, January 29, 2009.

Zhang, Lu, "The Value Premium," *The Journal of Finance*, July 20, 2005.

Zuckerman, Gregory "Renaissance's $10 Billion Medallion Fund Gains 24% Year to Date in Tumultuous Market," *The Wall Street Journal*, April 17, 2020. (Accessed July 27, 2021 https://www.wsj.com/articles/renaissance-s-10-billion-medallion-fund-gains-24-year-to-datein-tumultuous-market-11587152401).

Zweig, Jason. *Your Money & Your Brain: How The New Science of Neuroeconomics Can Help Make You Rich.* New York, NY: Simon & Schuster Paperbacks, 2017.

— — —. "What You Can Learn from One of Warren Buffett's Smartest Investors," *The Wall Street Journal*, December 21, 2018.

A

"Absolute Return," 97, 101
Action Alerts Plus Portfolio, 114
active investing, risks of, 102, 121, 130,
        137, 142, 147–150, 198, 213
Aesop, 16
algorithmic trading, 123
Allen, Paul, 216–219
alpha, 71, 76, 93, 122, 125, 130, 136
alternative investments, 68, 72, 73, 76,
        85–88. *See also* diversification
Amaranth Advisors LLC, 149
Amazon, 163, 166
annuities, 102–103, 178, 181, 192, 221
ant vs. grasshopper, 16–19
Apple, 100, 107, 131, 166, 167, 168,
        223
AQR Capital Management, 165
Asian financial crisis, 215
Asness, Cliff, 165
asset allocation, 55, 59, 63–69, 70, 73,
        74, 190, 193, 195, 196
asset-backed securities, 77, 80–81,
        218–219. *See also* residential
        morgage-backed securities
asset classes, 56–57, 67
    bonds, 57–59, 70
    cash, 56–57
    non-core, 76, 110
    stocks, 59–60

B

"barbell" approach, 79
Barclays Aggregate Bond Index, 68, 150
Barclays US Corporate High Yield
    Index, 79
Base Case, 25–35, 50, 55, 110, 144,
        208, 220–221

active management and, 118, 125,
        128–129, 151, 209
advisors and, 189–190
alternative investments and, 85
beating, 111, 116
composition, 87, 206
vs. pension plans, 73
returns, 175
vs. Yale endowment model, 71
Bauhaus movement, 206
Bear Stearns, 218
beating the market, 121–125
beating the spread, 126–127
Berkin, Andrew, 155, 171
Bessembinder, Hendrik, 130–131, 148
Betterment, 195
bid-ask spread, 79–80, 117
Bitcoin. *See* cryptocurrencies
blockchain. *See* cryptocurrencies
Bogle, John, 13, 50, 51, 137, 151
bonds
    bid-ask spreads in, 79–80
    corporate, 25, 57–58, 59, 77,
        168–169, 221
    credit risk, 105
    foreign, 81
    junk, 77
    US Treasury, 25, 27
        historical return, 48, 67
        Long-Term government bonds,
            67
        one-month Treasury bills,
            48–49, 131, 158–159,
            167
    proportion of portfolio, 64
    risk, 79
    secondary market, 79
    tax-exempt, 79, 80

Buffett, Warren, 117, 151, 152, 164, 205, 214, 216
BusinessWeek, 48–49
buyouts, 76, 86–89, 91–92

C

Caesar, Julius, 111–112
callability, 77, 79
capital gains, 70, 79, 109, 118, 121, 144, 146, 166, 191
carry factor, 169–170
Center for Research in Security Prices (CRSP), 131
Charter Communications, 216–217
client reference risk, 45
Coinbase. *See* cryptocurrencies
collateral, 27, 170, 171. *See also* asset-backed securities
collateralized debt obligations (CDOs), 170. *See also* asset-backed securities
collectibles, 36
confidence bias, 211–212
consultants, 72–74, 93, 100, 136
Consumer Price Index, 103
coronavirus, 46, 67, 87, 113, 142, 209, 221
cost-of-living adjustments, 103
COVID. *See* coronavirus
Cramer, Jim, 114
credit risk, 77, 105, 148, 167, 168
cryptocurrencies, 108–109
currencies, 108, 124
currency, 57
    exposure, 81
    foreign, 81, 108, 170
    markets, 108
    for reporting, 170
    risk, 46

D

"The Death of Equities: How Inflation Is Destroying the Stock Market," 48
derivatives, 81–83, 124, 150
"deworsification," 69
Dimensional Fund Advisors, 155
direct indexing, 146–147
diversification, 46, 47, 53, 83, 87, 110, 148, 168, 171
    alternative investments, 73
    benefits, 67–69
    global, 42, 46
    hedge funds, 93, 102
    non-core assets, 75–76
    real estate, 83
dot.com bust, 178
Dow Jones, 84
    Indices, 45, 78–79
    Industrial Average, 45
downside protection, 78, 101–102, 120, 205
durable power of attorney, 183

E

Einstein, Albert, 178–179
Ellis, Charles, 136
Emory University, 136
endowment portfolio model, 71–74. *See also* Yale endowment model
Enron, 46, 48
equities. *See* stocks
ESG (environmental, social, and governance), 106–107
ETFs, 69, 85, 121, 146–147, 193, 196
Ether. *See* cryptocurrencies
exchange-traded funds. *See* ETFs

F

Facebook, 107, 163, 166
factor premiums, 158, 171–172
Fama, Eugene, 138
fat tail, 96–97, 98, 147, 153, 169
Federal Deposit Insurance Corporation (FDIC), 57
Federal Reserve. *See* US Federal Reserve
Federal Reserve Bank of New York, 215
fees
    assets under management (AUM) basis, 193
    ETF, 193
    12b-1, 117, 198
fiduciary standard, 198–200
financial literacy, 180, 220
financial information, security of, 183
529 plans, 195
FOMO (fear of missing out), 45–46
Fortress (hedge fund), 149
Fortune 500, 22
401(k), 70, 146, 183, 184, 221
403(b), 146
Fund of Funds (FOF) managers, 93–94

G

Gates, Bill, 216
General Electric, 131
goals
    intermediate-term, 19, 21, 64
    long-term, 19, 21, 22, 49, 64
    reviewing, 23
    setting, 15
    short-term, 19, 21, 64
Google, 107, 163
Graham, Benjamin, 30, 206–207
Gross Domestic Product (GDP), 41

Guggenheim Investment Advisory, 90

H

Haruspex, 112, 113
hedge funds, 68, 73
    as alternative strategy, 76
    Bridgewater Associates, 76, 106
    Pure Alpha II, 76
    returns, 95–96
    fees, 93–95
    See also Fortress; Long Term Capital Management (LTCM); Verition Fund Management LLC
Hobbes, Thomas, 131
home country bias, 44–47
Hunter, Brian, 150
hybrids, 81–83

I

IBM (International Business Machines), 131
illiquidity, 59, 76, 77, 84, 85, 89–90, 91, 97, 100, 161
index funds, 47, 50–52, 53, 55, 68, 71, 93, 123, 134, 194–195, 196
Individual Retirement Account, 70, 146, 183, 195
inflation, 25, 59, 62, 64, 106, 114
    annuity payments, 108
    cash, effect on, 56–57
    historical rate, 25, 178
    hyperinflation, 34, 57
    long-term, 60
    real estate as hedge against, 83
    returns, effect on, 57, 178, 179, 184
    risk, 103, 176, 177
    stocks as hedge against, 60
    vs. volatility, 178

initial public offerings. *See* IPOs

insurance. *See* life insurance; term
insurance

interest, 77, 98, 105, 142, 144, 217
bonds, 57–58, 60, 67, 79, 106,
168–169
cash, 171
Federal Reserve and, 170
insurance, 104
in IRA, 70
mortgage-backed securities, 80, 218

Internal Revenue Service. *See* IRS

International Business Machines. *See*
IBM (International Business
Machines)

investing
active vs. passive, 13. *See also*
active investing
factor-based, 155–174
risks
cognitive decline, 180–182
inflation, 176
longevity, 176–179
shortfall, 179
regret, 180
volatility, 175–176
value, 30

Investment Company Institute, 134

investment personality, 187–189

investment policy statement, 190

iPhone. *See* Apple

IPOs, 27, 88, 163

IRA. *See* Individual Retirement
Account

IRS, 108, 109, 144

J

Jefferson, Thomas, 205

Jobs, Steve, 223

K

Kahneman, Daniel, 13
on ego depletion, 205
on illusion of skill, 115, 116, 125,
134, 221
on influence of environment on
decisions, 204–205
on luck, 213
on passive investing, 207
on predictability, 115, 132–133
on uncertainty, 113–114, 126–127,
132

Keogh accounts, 146

kurtosis, 160, 169. *See also* fat tail

L

LBO (leveraged buyouts). *See* buyouts

Lehman Brothers, 46, 48, 218

"Less is more," 206–209

Lewis, Michael, 215

Liar's Poker (Lewis), 215

life insurance, 104–105

lifemap, 18, 55
components, 16
considerations, 17–23
definition, 20
sample, 21
sharing, 22
updating, 23

Long Term Capital Management
(LTCM) [hedge fund], 97, 215–216

M

Mad Money, 114

Madoff, Bernie, 100

Malkiel, Burton, 50, 52, 88, 103, 124,
125, 128, 142, 165, 211, 212

management, active
cost of , 118–121

vs. market, 132–139
Maounis, Nick, 149
Marcus Cable, 216
market beta, 158–159
Markowitz, Harry, 47, 63, 67
Meriwether, John, 215
Merton, Robert, 215
Microsoft, 27, 100, 107, 131, 216–217
Mies van der Rohe, Ludwig, 206
Money magazine, 207, 212
money-market funds, 57, 80
Morgan, J.P., 65
Morningstar, 134, 137
mortgage-backed securities. *See*
   residential mortgage-backed
   securities
Muggeridge, Malcolm, 113
Munger, Charlie, 152, 216
mutual funds, 69, 78, 93, 100, 116, 119,
      134, 135, 146–147, 198
   costs of, 118, 121, 151
   popularity of, 220
   vs. S&P 500, 212

N
NINJA, 218

P
P/E ratio, 29–30
pension funds, 73, 101, 136, 140, 179
portfolio
   balance, 70
   efficiency of, 67, 68
   tax status of, 69–70
   See also diversification; investing
power of attorney. *See* durable power of
   attorney
price-to-earnings ratio. *See* P/E ratio
priorities

of fund managers, 90
in investment strategy, 223
life, 20, 22
vs. desires, 16–18
private equity funds. *See* private equity
private equity, 55, 68, 71, 72, 73, 75, 76,
   85–92, 121, 176

R
A Random Walk Down Wall Street
   (Malkiel), 50
Reagan, Ronald, 199
real estate investment trusts (REITS),
   83–85, 87
registered investment advisors (RIAs),
   198–199
regression to the mean, 132–133
REITS. *See* real estate investment trusts
   (REITS)
Renaissance Technologies, 96
reporting bias, 96–100
residential mortgage-backed securities
   (RMBS), 46, 59, 80–81, 98, 102,
   147, 170, 218
retirement, 151, 152, 176–190, 194,
   196, 197, 215
   goals, 15, 22
   lifemap and, 15–17
   planning, 48, 220–221
   projections, 120, 176
   See also Individual Retirement
      Accounts (IRAs);Keogh
      accounts; 401(k); 403(b);
      Simplified Employee Pensions
      (SEP)
returns
   determining, 17
   risk-adjusted, 79
   stock market, historical, 25–27

stocks vs. bonds, 25–28, 37, 48
risk
  of active investing, 147–150
  adjustment, 61, 92
  company-specific, 47–48
  currency, 46
  default, 58
  factors, 60
  of investing, 51
  mitigation, 182–184.
  necessary, 65
  parity, 105–106
  premium, 59–60
  political, 46
  risk/return expectations, 55, 67.
    See also returns
  sequence of returns, 176
  term, 58
  tolerance, 59, 64–65
  See also currency risk; diversifi-
    cation; political risk.
    See also under investing
Robinhood Markets, Inc., 118
robo-advisors, 193, 195, 197
Russell 3000 Index, 107
Russian debt crisis, 215

S

Salomon Brothers, 215
S&P 500, 71, 76
  as benchmark, 45, 49, 172, 200, 212
  historic return, 46, 165, 178
Samuelson, Paul, 151
scenario analysis, 190
Scholes, Myron, 215
Securities and Exchange Commission
  (SEC), 109
Serenity Prayer, 52

sequence of returns risk, 176
Sharpe ratio, 61, 98–100, 158, 175
shortfall risk, 179
Simons, James, 96
Simplified Employee Pensions (SEP),
  146
Sinclair, Upton, 116
smoothed performance, 98–99
Social Security, 103, 178, 220–221
"soft dollars," 73–74
stale pricing, 84, 96–100
stocks
  emerging market, 45–46
  foreign, 60
  junk, 77, 147, 161, 167
  large vs. small cap, 159–161
  monitoring, 49
  P/E ratio, 30
  penny, 182
  pink sheet, 182
  return, 25, 32, 34, 37
  risk premium, 27
  volatility, 27
  See also asset allocation; index
    funds; S&P 500
subprime loans, 46, 59, 81, 98, 102,
  147, 170, 218
Swedroe, Larry, 84, 134, 136, 140–141,
  155, 171
Swensen, David
  on active management, 50, 102,
    121, 130, 137, 142, 198, 213
  on foreign bonds, 81
  on hedge funds, 95–97, 98, 101
  on junk bonds, 77
  on LBOs, 89
  on money-market funds, 80
  on mutual funds, 116

on non-core asset classes, 76, 91

on private equity investments, 86–87, 90, 91

on REITS, 85

on venture capital, 91–92

on Yale endowment model, 71

T

tail risk, 147

taxes

allocation of assets for, 191

for investors, 53, 144–147

reviewing, 191

tax-loss harvesting, 70

Treasury bond exemption, 79

See also capital gains; portfolio: tax status of

term insurance, 104

Thomson Reuters Lipper, 134

Treasury Inflation-Protected Securities (TIPS), 59

Tremont Capital Management, 97

trend-following

momentum, 171

strategies, 102

Twain, Mark, 153

U

Ulysses, 191–192

US Federal Reserve, 170, 215

V

Vanguard Group, 51, 117

500 Index Fund, 121

Personal Advisor Services, 195

Total World Stock ETF, 196

Total Bond Market Fund, 196

venture capital, 55, 71, 75, 76, 85, 87, 88, 92–93, 98, 110, 152, 216

Verition Fund Management LLC, (hedge fund), 149

volatility, 73, 74, 81, 82, 84, 90, 97, 176–179, 184, 215

of active investing, 147

"barbell" approach, 79

of bonds, 69

of cash, 56–57

of currency, 170

of foreign bonds, 81

investment, 175–176

market beta and, 158–159

in portfolio, 65, 73, 84, 179

of private equity, 90

and risk parity, 105–106

smoothed performance and, 98–99

of stocks, 27, 59–60, 76, 159, 167

tolerance for, 55, 64, 69, 82, 190

relative to return, 61, 200. *See also* Sharpe ratio

W

Walter, Mark, 90

Washington Mutual, 46, 48

Winfrey, Oprah, 180

WorldCom, 46, 48

Y

Yale endowment model, 68, 71

Your Complete Guide to Factor-Based Investing (Berkin and Swedroe), 155

Z

Zweig, Jason, 185, 206

Zweig, Martin, 212

Many hands helped make lighter the work of writing this book. I would like to thank Hannah Lamb-Vines for her editing assistance; Ashley Walker and Ryan Legaspi for their graphics and design work; Rachel Whiting for her book cover art; Vitaliy Gorobets for his illustrations; Jason Van Steenwyk for his editorial comments and Kathleen Carroll for the index. Special thanks to Dimensional Fund Advisors for use of their graphics and their return calculations.

While this publication is designed to provide accurate information related to the subject matter covered, no portion of the book content is or should be construed as a substitute for individual investment, financial planning, transaction and/or investment planning advice from any financial professional(s), including John Nicholas or other members of Chicago Partners Investment Group, LLC. If legal advice or other expert assistance is required, the services of a competent professional person should be sought.

Each individual's circumstances may be different. Also, investment management and financial planning activities pose some inherent risks. Individuals should seek legal, tax or other professional or expert advice or assistance, based upon their particular circumstances, from independent professionals.

Chicago Partners Investment Group and its affiliates, and their respective officers, directors and employees specifically disclaim any liability for any damages (whether direct or indirect, special, general or consequential) or loss (including loss of business and profits, or risk, personal or otherwise) which is incurred as a consequence, directly or indirectly, of the use or application of any of the contents of this publication, which contents are provided "as is". Neither the information nor any opinion expressed, constitutes a solicitation for the purchase or sale of a security or other investment. Mention of specific companies, organizations , or authorities in this book does not imply endorsement by the authors or the publisher.

Mr. Nicholas provides advisory services solely in his capacity as an investment adviser representative of Chicago Partners Investment Group, LLC, a registered investment advisor located in Chicago, Illinois.

The author makes liberal use of case studies and examples. Unless as otherwise noted, all identifying information has been changed so ANY resemblance to actual individuals, living or dead or companies is purely coincidental.

No reader should construe that any discussion in the book of actual client experiences serves as any indication or assurance that an existing or prospective client will experience a certain level of results if Chicago Partners Investment Group is engaged, or continues to be engaged, to provide investment advisory services. A copy of the Firm's current written disclosure statement discussing its advisory services and fees is available upon request. If you have ANY QUESTIONS regarding the disclaimers and limitations related to the information contained in this book, Chicago Partner's Chief Compliance Officer, James Hagedorn, is available to address them.

54785249R00143